Praise for David K. Shipler's

Freedom of Speech

"Shipler writes with crisp, concise earnestness. . . . This book is a pleasure to read both for Shipler's skill but also because he tells the stories of people bound up in these issues."
—*Providence Journal*

"[Shipler] gets it: The First Amendment is only a starting point. Free expression is a noble ideal that creates continual tension in our society. . . . Shipler's view of America's free speech landscape is nuanced and complex. Yes, people say awful things, and some-times seek to squelch expression with which they disagree. But in his book, good ideas and sentiments hold their own against bad and offensive ones."
—*The Progressive*

"Chilling. . . . For Shipler, it's essential that we find a middle ground where we can hear one another, where we can debate and disagree with respect. . . . We must participate in the conversa-tion about who we are and who we want to be. That it is unruly, disturbing, scary even, goes without saying; this is also why it's necessary."
—*Los Angeles Times*

"By providing intimate portraits of the lives of those who dare to speak against the odds, Shipler enables us to see the human element behind free expression. . . . Shipler pricks the conscience of readers who refrain from telling the truth, or whose selective listening has lead them to disrespect and delegitimize those with whom they disagree."
—*National Catholic Reporter*

"Good stories, great interviews, and a potent plea on behalf of vigilant listening."
—*Kirkus Reviews*

"A broad and deep look at free speech. . . . A fascinating look at one of our fundamental rights." —*Booklist*

"David Shipler reminds us in this important book that sometimes we have to listen to things we don't want to hear. But without freedom of speech, there can be no dialogue, and without dialogue, there can be no democracy. *Freedom of Speech* is a glorious celebration of its own subject!" —Barbara Ehrenreich, author of *Nickel and Dimed*

"At a time when the First Amendment is under siege as never before in our lifetimes, David Shipler, one of the nation's great journalists, reminds us what we are in danger of losing. His terrific, timely new book, *Freedom of Speech: Mightier Than the Sword*, takes us on a tour—sometimes shocking, often infuriating, always enlightening—of America's free-speech battlefields." —Philip Shenon, author of *A Cruel and Shocking Act: The Secret History of the Kennedy Assassination*

"Shipler tells real, often Orwellian stories of ordinary people— government workers, teachers, librarians, and playwrights—who risk everything to push the free-speech envelope, while challenging us to consider difficult cases when money buys speech and poverty promotes silence. At a time when many civil libertarians despair at the loss of freedom and privacy on so many fronts, *Freedom of Speech* reveals conflicts that must be understood if free speech is to prevail." —Barbara Jones, former director, American Library Association Office for Intellectual Freedom

"The freedom of speech enjoyed by American citizens is unique in all the world. In this brilliantly insightful and incisive book, David Shipler explores the many and varied facets of our nation's complex, extraordinary, and fascinating relationship with our most precious freedom." —Geoffrey R. Stone, author of *Perilous Times: Free Speech in Wartime*

David K. Shipler

Freedom of Speech

David K. Shipler reported for *The New York Times* from 1966 to 1988 in New York, Saigon, Moscow, Jerusalem, and Washington, D.C. He is the author of six previous books, including the bestsellers *Russia* and *The Working Poor*, as well as *Arab and Jew*, which won the Pulitzer Prize. He has been a guest scholar at the Brookings Institution and a senior associate at the Carnegie Endowment for International Peace, and has taught at Princeton, American University, and Dartmouth. He writes online at *The Shipler Report*.

shiplerreport.blogspot.com

Freedom of Speech

MIGHTIER THAN THE SWORD

David K. Shipler

VINTAGE BOOKS
A Division of Penguin Random House LLC
New York

FIRST VINTAGE BOOKS EDITION, APRIL 2016

Copyright © 2015, 2016 by David K. Shipler Living Trust

All rights reserved. Published in the United States by Vintage Books, a division of Penguin Random House LLC, New York, and distributed in Canada by Random House of Canada, a division of Penguin Random House Canada Limited, Toronto. Originally published in hardcover in the United States by Alfred A. Knopf, a division of Penguin Random House LLC, New York, in 2015.

Vintage and colophon are registered trademarks of Penguin Random House LLC.

Grateful acknowledgment is made to the following for permission to reprint previously published material:
Graham Swift: Excerpts from *Waterland*, copyright © 1983 by Graham Swift. Reprint by permission of Graham Swift.
Caryl Churchill: Excerpts from *Seven Jewish Children: A Play for Gaza*, copyright © 2009 by Caryl Churchill. Reprinted by permission of Caryl Churchill.
Ari Roth and Theater J: Excerpt from the program notes for *Andy and the Shadows*, 2013. Reprinted by permission of Ari Roth and Theater J.

The Library of Congress has cataloged the Knopf edition as follows:
Shipler, David K.
Freedom of speech : mightier than the sword / David K. Shipler.
pages cm
1. Freedom of speech—United States.   2. United States. Constitution.
1st Amendment.   I. Title.
KF4772.S55 2015   323.44'30973—DC23   2014032127

Vintage Books Trade Paperback ISBN: 978-0-307-94761-1
eBook ISBN: 978-1-101-87469-1

Author photograph © Deborah I. Shipler
Book design by Cassandra J. Pappas

www.vintagebooks.com

Printed in the United States of America
10   9   8   7   6   5   4   3   2

FOR THE THREE GENERATIONS:

Debby

Jonathan, Glynis, Laura, Matt, Michael, and Sweta

Madison, Ethan, Benjamin, Kalpana, Dylan, and Priya

Contents

PART V *Plays*

Freedom of Speech

Introduction

The listener is everything in telling a story.
—CHAYA ROTH

Freedom of speech implies the freedom to hear. Without willing listeners, brilliant thinkers cannot educate, brave orators cannot mobilize, daring leakers cannot reform. The unseen play, the unread book, the ignored appeal, fall silently away. The unheard lament flutters and fails.

So ideas do not have to be censored to die. Soviet dissidents used to say they were "writing for the drawer," where manuscripts were forced to lie in darkness. But in today's flagrantly open America, unwelcome facts and opinions disappear in other ways. They are concealed in the confusing clatter of argument. They are hidden by a lack of funding. They are confined to enclaves of narrow interests.

It may be that political debate in the United States has never been as boisterous, irreverent, and downright nasty as in the early twenty-first century. Yet speakers and audiences are not all listening seriously to one another. They assemble in a public square that is honeycombed with comfort zones where citizens cluster around the viewpoints that suit them, separated by soundproof barriers of disagreement. Many Americans do not want to consider what is being said beyond their walls.

Antonin Scalia, the conservative Supreme Court justice, made the point when he told a *New York* magazine interviewer that his preferred newspapers were the conservative *Washington Times* and *The Wall Street Journal*. He didn't read *The New York Times* and had canceled his subscription to *The Washington Post* because of "the treatment of almost any conservative issue," he said. "It was slanted and often nasty. And, you know, why should I get upset every morning? I don't think I'm the only one. I think they lost subscriptions partly because they became so shrilly, *shrilly* liberal."

The balkanization is facilitated by transformed demographics and moral values that leave some groups, especially white conservatives, with a novel sense of alienation from the mainstream. Those who want certain books out of classrooms feel marginalized and disempowered by school systems. Those who warn of subversion by Islam in America feel ridiculed and detested by big, hostile forces: the political class, the media, and even the Christian establishment. Divisions are deepened by the Internet and by radio and television broadcasters who have found that it's less profitable to give all sides of a story calmly than to shout and cheer on one side alone. Only a dwindling number of news organizations cling to the standards of thoroughness, which play to the curious against what seems to be a rising tide of the incurious.

The result is a peculiar landscape of fixed positions and fluid change, a turbulent coexistence of both unyielding certainty and constant questioning. No widely held attitude in American history has undergone such swift revision as the expanding acceptance of homosexuality and same-sex marriage. In no earlier period has the scope of speech been as broad. The kind of vilification hurled at President Barack Obama would have landed people in prison if directed against John Adams or Woodrow Wilson. The range of expression in the arts and media has opened to include sex and violence that would have scandalized the public decades ago. Traditional gatekeepers who accept or reject ideas for broad distribution—editors, publishers, producers, curators—are losing authority to the uncontrollable Internet. Small voices are amplified as never before, and scattered individuals of like mind can find one another and organize with an ease unprecedented in American history.

To measure the evolution, consider the criticism of President Adams for which Representative Matthew Lyon of Vermont was arrested, tried, and convicted in 1798, just seven years after the Bill of Rights had been ratified. Lyon wrote and published this:

As to the Executive, when I shall see the efforts of that power bent on the promotion of the comfort, the happiness, and accommodation of the people, that executive shall have my zealous and uniform support: but whenever I shall, on the part of the Executive, see every consideration of the public welfare swallowed up in a continual grasp for power, in an unbounded thirst for ridiculous pomp, foolish adulation, and selfish avarice; when I shall behold men of real merit daily turned out of office, for no other cause but independency of sentiment; when I shall see men of firmness, merit, years, abilities, and experience, discarded in their applications for office, for fear they possess that independence, and men of meanness preferred for the ease with which they take up and advocate opinions, the consequence of which they know but little of— when I shall see the sacred name of religion employed as a state engine to make mankind hate and persecute one another, I shall not be their humbled advocate.

We have traveled some distance. Those pungent lines, which stung in their time, seem quaint compared with today's slanderous bloviations. Rhetorical skills have declined. And even if a modern politician could skewer opponents that adroitly, no Sedition Act exists any longer with which to prosecute, and there would be no taste for it.

So, something remains unchanged after two centuries: grassroots indignation. Using prison to silence a congressman was not greeted enthusiastically then, and it would not be now. Sentenced to four months in jail, Lyon became an instant hero in his Vermont district, where he ran and won reelection from behind bars.

Freedom of speech is a central creed. A portion of the citizenry may tolerate coerced confessions, warrantless searches, and inadequate spending on lawyers for the poor, but Americans tend to take personally their right to speak. Rights preserved or violated in the criminal justice system look remote to upstanding citizens who cannot identify with accused murderers, thieves, and drug dealers. The right to speak, however, affects everyone who chooses to exercise it.

The people portrayed in these pages attest to the resilience of free speech used both to voice ideas and to try to suppress the ideas of others. So central is the liberty that even those who agitate against certain expression here and there—in libraries, onstage—insist that they are not against freedom of speech but opposed to only these words in this place at this time. They resent accusations that they are campaigning against the freedom itself, which is too sacred to deny. It is the wellspring of the great American idea, essential to an open society. Without the liberty of complaint and association, democracy fails. Without the space to argue and debate—and even to spread false "facts" and rumors—everyone's entitlement to hold and voice an opinion erodes, and into the vacuum flow hesitation and fear. No wonder that among all the noble rights protected in the Constitution, it is freedom of speech that ordinary Americans guard most jealously.

Yet speech has limits, both legal and cultural. From quiet discussion to coarse debate, from reasoned analysis to scurrilous propaganda, America's range of expression falls within certain parameters. Some are codified in the case law developed by courts over the more than two centuries since the ratification of the Bill of Rights, which restricts only what government can do, not what private employers and peers can do. The right to speech enshrined in the First Amendment does not define the cultural limits, whose blurry lines are drawn and redrawn by society's notions of the unacceptable, shifting from era to era as sensibilities evolve.

If you violate those cultural norms, you may suffer punishment. What could be said openly about African-Americans more than a generation ago would now torpedo a professional career. What a right-wing politician can say approvingly today about armed revolution cannot be spoken with impunity by a Muslim preacher. Different lines exist for different people, and crossing them can carry consequences.

Among the boldest restrictions on speech is incitement to violence, but the limit is hardly clear-cut. Political and legal definitions shift over time, moving the line that divides the exercise of liberty from the commission of a crime. In 1948, Eugene Dennis, general secretary of the tiny, marginal Communist Party of the United States, was prosecuted along with eleven colleagues for a vague conspiracy to advocate the violent overthrow of the government. The charges were based not on their actual words but simply on their membership in the party.

Sixty-two years later, the FBI did not even bother to investigate three Republican candidates for Congress endorsed by the Tea Party movement—Sharron Angle, Stephen Broden, and Rick Barber—who argued during the 2010 campaign that violent revolution should remain an option, that a tyrannical government could be met by the arms that the people were entitled to bear under the Second Amendment.

The difference lay both in the law and in the culture. The 1940 Smith Act, used to prosecute communists and socialists, remains on the books. But the Supreme Court narrowed its scope in 1957 by requiring that the advocacy of violence be linked to "concrete action," more than an abstract principle. By that interpretation, followers of neither the Communist Party nor the Tea Party could have been convicted.

The three Republicans suffered punishment short of prosecution, though. In part because of their extremist statements, they were abandoned by parts of the Republican establishment. Angle lost her Senate race in Nevada, Broden lost to the Democrat in Texas, and Barber lost the Republican primary in a runoff in Alabama.

While right-wing Republicans didn't alarm law enforcement after 9/11, radical Muslims did. In 2005, a Muslim cancer researcher named Ali al-Timimi was tried, convicted, and sentenced to life for his words alone—for "inducing others to conspire" to provide material support for terrorism. In a dinner talk, he had told a small group of young Muslims that they could serve Islam by becoming holy fighters in Kashmir, Chechnya, or Afghanistan. Four of them then went to Pakistan for training to do just that.

In the realm of psychology, there is no clear formula to determine whether certain statements induce violence. Was it dangerous for Bill O'Reilly to joke on his Fox News television show about beheading Dana Milbank of *The Washington Post*? Milbank thought so. He replied with an acerbic attack, sparking an unapologetic retort by O'Reilly, who accused the reporter of having no sense of humor. Fox took no action against O'Reilly.

Yet there has been a rash of antigovernment violence by perpetrators who describe their motives in the language of Fox and the talk-show propagandist Rush Limbaugh: An unemployed carpenter, Byron Williams, shot at police because, his mother said, he was angry at "the way Congress was railroading through all these left-wing agenda items." After the Arizona shootings that killed six and critically wounded the Democratic representative Gabrielle Giffords, the left accused the right of setting the stage with toxic rhetoric and campaign images, including Sarah Palin's map putting a rifle's crosshairs on Giffords's congressional district. Palin and other conservatives angrily rejected blame, but Roger Ailes ordered his Fox News anchors to "shut up, tone it down, make your argument intellectually." A House Democrat proposed criminalizing such speech.

Most Americans never bump up against limits on their expression. They stay on safe ground, traveling through the middle of a landscape of ideas so vast and varied that taboos are barely visible in the distance.

Like any territory, however, this one is defined by its borders. It can be mapped by surveying its frontiers. Different Americans have different ideas about where the cultural limits of acceptable speech should be, and the skirmishes along those boundaries tell significant stories. Whether individuals test the taboos deliberately or trip across them unwittingly, they reveal a land wide open to unorthodoxy and pockmarked with intolerance. We are a country exhilarated and troubled by the raucous nature of the arguments.

Government attempts to impose limitations on speech are usually dangerous to liberty. Cultural restrictions are more complicated. Some are viewed as justified by the standards of civil discourse, others as stifling impositions of conformity. Civil society's diffuse inhibitions on racist speech, for example, look enlightened and morally sound to some, oppressive to others. This landscape has few absolutes.

Even among established democracies, the United States stands out for its expansive permissiveness, enshrined in a First Amendment whose value lies not in protecting the broad consensus—which doesn't need protection—but in insulating the unpopular, the extreme, and the hateful from government censorship and prosecution. The right to preach bigotry in America is atypical of open societies.

Canada's Human Rights Commission can levy hefty fines for communicating, by telephone or Internet, "any matter that is likely to expose a person or persons to hatred or contempt." That worries Valerie Price, a Montreal resident who identifies herself on her business card as a "free speech warrior" but is better known for her activism against what she believes are the Muslim Brotherhood's plans to take over North America. She is concerned about being bankrupted by a fine for what she says. By contrast, her like-minded colleagues in the United States worry chiefly about being sued for libel, which is only a slight inhibition, since it is hard to prove defamation in American courts.

Australia's Racial Hatred Act punishes expression and actions based on "the race, colour, or national or ethnic origin of a person or group" that are "reasonably likely . . . to offend, insult, humiliate, or intimidate." A man who shouted racial epithets from his veranda at his Aboriginal neighbor was ordered to pay the neighbor $1,500 plus legal costs; a fine of $1,000 was imposed on another resident, attending a local council meeting, who suggested shooting Aboriginal people.

South Africa's constitution includes, in its article on freedom of expression, the caveat that the right "does not extend to . . . advocacy of hatred that is based on race, ethnicity, gender, or religion, and that constitutes incitement to cause harm." American courts have also punished incitement, but case law requires the danger to be imminent or the purpose directly threatening. The U.S. Supreme Court has ruled, for example, that burning a cross in an empty field as a symbol of the Ku Klux Klan cannot constitutionally be prohibited, but doing the same thing on a black family's front yard can be criminalized.

Germany, the first country to ban Holocaust denial (in 1985), punishes with up to five years in prison anyone who "incites hatred against segments of the population . . . or assaults the human dignity of others by insulting, maliciously maligning, or defaming segments of the population." In 2007, the neo-Nazi Ernst Zündel got the five years for repeatedly writing and publishing assertions that the Holocaust did not occur.

Holocaust denial, anti-Semitism, and/or displaying Nazi symbols are crimes also in Austria, Belgium, the Czech Republic, France, Hungary, Israel, Italy, Lithuania, Luxembourg, Poland, Romania, Slovakia, Spain, Sweden, and Switzerland. The Czech Republic prohibits the denial of communist crimes as well.

No such law has prevented the alarming rise of virulent, right-wing groups in Europe, however, just as the Soviet prohibitions against ethnic hostility failed to prevent bigotry expressed around people's kitchen tables and could not stop the ultimate breakup of the country along ethnic lines. In the United States, the Anti-Defamation League (ADL), which is quick to sound the alarm over anti-Semitism, opposes such laws and prefers education; that is, fight it in the classrooms, not the courts.

Americans who speak and write from the margins are especially sensitive to their free-speech rights. When I first contacted Robert Spencer, who makes a career of warning about the Muslim Brotherhood's purported designs on America, he wouldn't answer my questions until he knew more about my book research. I e-mailed, "The book will be a look at the broad landscape of speech in the U.S.—and its limits."

Spencer replied, "Ah, I see. So I take it you will be characterizing me as an 'extremist' and calling for limits on my freedom of speech?"

"I hope you're joking," I answered, and assured him that as a journalist I was "naturally adamant in advocating and protecting freedom of speech—yours and everyone's across the broadest political spectrum . . . So I'm planning to describe limits that exist, not endorse them."

"Pardon me for jumping to conclusions," Spencer then apologized, but "it was a reasonable surmise," he said, since virtually all inquiries from journalists were "from hostile people who want to impugn my work." He noted that he and others who write similarly "have been smeared, mocked, and vilified."

Given Spencer's assumption about me, I suppose I have to be clear that I am as close to being an absolutist on the First Amendment as possible without quite being one. I can accept the Supreme Court's differentiation between cross burning as symbolic speech in an empty field and cross burning as intimidation on a family's lawn, although defining intimidating or threatening behavior is like treading into a swamp. Lines are murky, and it's always risky to use vague characterizations to give authorities the power to shut down speech whose *content* (rather than method) displeases them.

Similarly, while I would like to see protections for journalists whose confidential sources are sought by prosecutors, there are rare and exceptional situations where such privilege should be overcome: a deadly crime being planned, for example, or an ongoing threat, such as sex trafficking or child pornography, that could be halted by a reporter's testimony. Here, too, however, prosecutors are good at leveraging small caveats into large loopholes; if they force reporters to choose between exposing their sources and going to jail—as some have—we citizens will learn less about the misdeeds of government and the scourges of society.

When it comes to either legal limits or cultural limits, the real answer to offensive speech is more speech, not retribution. Truth is the best response to propaganda. Hatred festers in places where speech is suppressed, where unwelcome ideas are consigned to darkness. Sunlight is the first step in the cure—necessary but not always sufficient. Without it, countries disintegrate along ethnic lines, the powerless lose their voices, victims remain victims, and no remedies can be found. In the glare of honesty, an open society can activate its mechanisms of self-correction, provided people listen and take steps. Denial of the right to speak silences the speaker and also deafens the audience, impoverishing everyone.

American citizens stand everywhere across the spectrum. Some take their right to speech for granted; others fight for it. Some are intimidated too easily at workplaces, in schools, and online, and others stand up undaunted. Some agitate to remove certain books from libraries and classrooms, and others demand that the books remain. Some prosecute and persecute government officials who leak information, and others risk their liberty to leak and report. In sum, some push for silence, and others will not be silenced. All will say that they fully support the right to freedom of speech, as articulated in the First Amendment and woven into the culture of the United States.

Some of their stories in these pages map the frontiers of expression and describe the contours made by the weight of words. Parents in Michigan rally to teachers who are vilified for the novels they have their students read. Playwrights, actors, and donors in the nation's capital rally to a theater assailed over its edgy political plays. Conservative ministers risk their churches' tax-exempt status to preach politics from the pulpit. History teachers in Texas quietly navigate around the conservative curriculum to give students pieces of unapproved truth.

At their peril, government officials disclose wrongdoing to national security correspondents in Washington, who adopt stealthy techniques more common in dictatorships. Subtly and explicitly, purveyors of racial images deftly use the Internet and broadcasting to sound dog whistles about the first black president. Some lose their jobs as a result. In politics, the wealthy are heard, and the poor are muted, unable to buy their way into the debates where money equals speech, and poverty equals silence.

The Landscape

Zones of Silence, Zones of Speech

The V.A. isn't a place where you speak out.
—DR. JANET STOUT, formerly of the Veterans Administration

We Americans, while imbued with the legal and cultural right to speak our minds, are forever choosing our words, depending on time and place and circumstance. On my navy destroyer in 1964, we fifteen or so officers, living together in close quarters, never talked about the high-stakes, emotional presidential campaign then raging between Lyndon B. Johnson and Barry Goldwater. It wasn't officially forbidden; we just didn't feel comfortable doing it.

Today, I have a friend in a small New England town who doesn't discuss politics with her neighbors, sensing that such conversation would be unwelcome and probably unpleasant. Even some politically divided families under the same roof avoid contentious topics. And most employees know to keep complaints about wrongdoing on their jobs inside their workplace, out of the public eye.

The Internet, by contrast, has become a place of liberation, especially for the anonymous who are impatient with common courtesy. For those willing to stand by their words responsibly, American territory is complicated. They travel from restriction to freedom and back again, staking out space in which they can say what they want to say but respecting the limits as they cross into situations where restraint is advisable.

When Jill Abramson was summarily fired in 2014 as executive editor of *The New York Times,* writers elsewhere swarmed to the paper's staff for insights, quotes, and juicy morsels of explanation. She had been the first woman to lead the *Times,* and her dismissal amid descriptions of her brusque management style raised the question of whether a man displaying the same behavior would have been sacked. The answer was probably yes, given her reportedly fraught relationship with the publisher, Arthur Sulzberger Jr.; her purported dissembling about a top editor she'd arranged to hire without informing her No. 2; her strained relations with her senior staff; and her dispatch of a lawyer to inquire at the top about her salary, which she claimed was less than her male predecessor's. The publisher denied any pay disparity, but the gender issue and the brutal suddenness of the dismissal made it a story full of intriguing semi-facts.

The funny thing about all these reports, allegations, and revelations couched in the passive voice—whether in *The New Yorker, The Washington Post, Politico,* or a dozen other outlets—was their anonymity. No reporter or editor at the *Times* was ever quoted on the record being critical, as far as I could determine. Not a single employee dared to do what reporters every day try to get their sources to do: speak for attribution, with their names attached to the opinions they express, the allegations they make, and the truths they disclose.

There was nothing new in this. The *Times,* like other private institutions, never countenanced public comments on internal difficulties. It was one thing to complain inside the family, as I did frequently, and quite another to do so outside, which I did not. Reporters and editors knew this instinctively, and if they didn't, they had only to look at how close Thomas L. Friedman came to being fired in 1982.

Covering Israel's war in Lebanon, Friedman saw a shift one day in the pattern of Israeli attacks on Beirut and led a story by describing the bombardment as "indiscriminate." When the foreign desk told him it had deleted "indiscriminate," he fired back that he was a careful reporter who did not exaggerate. "You knew I was correct and that the word was backed up by what I had reported. But you did not have the courage—

guts—to print it in *The New York Times*. You were afraid to tell our readers and those who might complain to you that the Israelis are capable of indiscriminately shelling an entire city . . . I am filled with profound sadness by what I have learned in the past afternoon about my newspaper."

That might have been the end of it except for some bruised feelings at both ends. But his message was leaked and published in *The Village Voice,* and the *Times*'s executive editor, Abe Rosenthal, incensed, summoned Friedman to New York.

Abe did not easily relinquish the moral high ground in journalism. He was tough on sources, almost always backed his reporters, and took no prisoners when influential people or governments tried to throw their weight around to get favorable coverage. He also ruthlessly kept reporters' opinions out of the news columns, and the editors thought the word "indiscriminate" was just that—editorial opinion. I thought it was defective in another way, as I later told Tom: It was a mind-reading term, implying that Israeli commanders had a certain intention, which Friedman could not possibly know. The word took the story a step beyond the reporting, which should have stopped at what he could verify—that the bombing and shelling *appeared* indiscriminate because of the widespread variety of the destruction or the targets' lack of evident military value.

By the time Friedman arrived in New York, Rosenthal had been calmed down by other editors. The two had a stern talk and Friedman kept his job, reported brilliantly from Beirut and then Jerusalem, became a *Times* columnist, and won three Pulitzers. His success since has made him practically invincible to retribution for speaking up, which he says he feels free to do, although he usually prefers the in-house route to avoid giving ammunition to *Times* bashers. (An exception came when he argued publicly, as well as internally, against the paper's "paywall" that charged online viewers to look at his and others' columns. The wall separating columnists was soon removed, later replaced with restrictions on free access to the entire paper.)

I took the same approach during the years I worked there. Only outsiders who tediously placed the *Times* under a microscope would have been interested in most of the minor flaws of misjudgment that reporters encountered. Editing decisions that carried the faint whiff of political motivation were extremely rare, and I dealt with them inside the paper. I didn't have to be told that making a public stink would neither improve editors' behavior nor endear me to my bosses. Was this cowardly? No, it was pragmatic. How I would have handled a major violation of journalistic ethics I can only guess. We can all imagine that we'd sacrifice ourselves for a greater good, but we find out only when we get to the crossroads.

And that's the point as we survey the landscape of free speech. Most of us who have worked for bureaucracies, whether private or governmental, sense the limits and internalize the restraint. It takes a great deal for us to break the bond of loyalty to the institution and toss self-preservation aside. That's why whistleblowers stand out. That's why those who quietly carve out zones of independence are admirable and inspiring, most of all when they take risks to disclose information essential to the people's self-rule.

Sometimes they miscalculate. They don't see the hidden taboos that lurk like trip wires, set to trigger unexpected retaliation.

Morris Davis, a retired air force colonel and chief prosecutor at Guantá-namo, wrote and spoke liberally in criticism of the military commissions set up to try terrorism suspects. For that, which the Library of Congress thought undermined his neutrality and credibility, he was fired from his job at the Congressional Research Service providing members of the House and the Senate with information on matters of national security. He sued in federal court for reinstatement and lost.

A rash of employees for the Veterans Administration lost their jobs or had their performance ratings downgraded after complaining about wrongdoing. Dr. Jacqueline Brecht, a urologist in Alaska, objected strongly to the widespread practice of making waiting times appear shorter by listing phantom appointments, then marking patients as no-shows. In response to Brecht's complaint, an administrator placed her on administrative leave and ordered her escorted out of the building by security officers.

Dr. Janet Stout and a colleague, Dr. Victor Yu, were forced out after complaining about budgets and salaries. The lab where they were working on deadly Legionnaires' disease was closed, and their specimens were destroyed, which they claimed "contributed to a 2011 outbreak of

Legionnaires' at the Pittsburgh hospital that killed six people," *The New York Times* reported.

Anne Mitchell, a nurse in the small town of Kermit, Texas, was criminally tried for "misuse of official information" after she gave to the state medical board files demonstrating unsafe practices by a doctor at her hospital. The sheriff who investigated the case was a friend and patient of the doctor's, and the prosecutor was the doctor's lawyer. He accused Mitchell of waging a vendetta against the physician, but she mustered other nurses to confirm her accusations, and the jury quickly acquitted her. If convicted, she could have been sentenced to up to ten years.

Descending from the sublime, employees have been dismissed for all manner of expression.

Debbie Almontaser was forced to resign as principal of New York City's first Arabic-language public school after she was asked by the *New York Post* for her reaction to a T-shirt reading "Intifada NYC," being sold by an Arab women's group. "Intifada" is the term Palestinians have used to label their violent uprisings against Israel, which she acknowledged, but she also explained that the word "intifada" meant "shaking off" in Arabic and did not necessarily connote violence. She doubted that the T-shirt represented violent intentions. Rather, "I think it's pretty much an opportunity for girls to express that they are part of New York City society . . . and shaking off oppression."

Her mastery of Arabic notwithstanding, the vocabulary lesson infuriated pro-Israel, anti-Muslim constituencies in New York, and she had to leave her job to save the school. A federal judge dismissed her lawsuit on the ground that she made the statement not as a private individual protected by the First Amendment but as an administrator whose words were subject to oversight by her employer. That is a basic distinction for government employees.

It's what protected New York City's head prison chaplain, a convert to Islam named Umar Abdul-Jalil, from anything more than a two-week suspension after he made inflammatory remarks in Tucson. He said in a speech that "the greatest terrorists in the world occupy the White House" and that American Muslims should not allow "the Zionists of the media to dictate what Islam is to us." His lawyer insisted that he was speaking not as a city representative but as an individual, which put his words under the shield of the First Amendment. He hadn't made that disclaimer in his address, but it would have been a strong defense had he been dismissed.

Edward R. Lane, fired by a public community college in Alabama, won vindication on that point in 2014 from a unanimous Supreme Court, which ruled that a public employee has a First Amendment right to testify about corruption as a citizen, outside the parameters of his job, "even when the testimony relates to his public employment or concerns information learned during that employment."

Lane, director of a youth program, had been subpoenaed to testify in the trial of Suzanne Schmitz, a state legislator who was paid $177,000 a year, he discovered, even though she never showed up at work. She was convicted, fined, and sentenced to thirty months in prison. Then Lane was dismissed, but the Court awarded him only the legal victory, not his job—which no longer existed—and no damages from the college, because the constitutional question had not been clearly established at the time. The standard now seems firm enough that if it happens again, a government worker would have a case for compensation and reinstatement.

The navy captain Owen Honors, however, had no such shield when a four-year-old video surfaced, which he had made in uniform, aboard ship, as a lame attempt at comedy by using obscene gestures, profanity, slurs against gays, and staged scenes of women showering together. He was relieved as commanding officer of the aircraft carrier USS *Enterprise*.

Private institutions have considerable latitude to punish speech, as a congressional candidate with Tea Party support learned to his misfortune. Running in the 2014 Republican primary in Ohio against John Boehner, Speaker of the House, J. D. Winteregg put up an ad to treat "electile dysfunction," which a voice-over explained "could be a question of blood flow. Sometimes when a politician has been in D.C. too long, it goes to his head and he just can't seem to get the job done." As Boehner shakes hands with Obama, the narrator remarks, "If you have a Boehner lasting more than twenty-three years, seek immediate medical attention." Then, in a quick clip from some archive, Boehner is shown saying, "It's boner."

Winteregg was counting on voters to guffaw, or at least snicker, at his adolescent parody of television ads for Viagra and other treatments for erectile dysfunction. Nobody who watched TV could miss those commercials. But the electorate failed to be amused sufficiently to propel his share of the primary vote above 15 percent. Further, if the administrators at Cedarville University guffawed or snickered, they did so in private. It's a Baptist college. Winteregg taught French there part-time, as an adjunct professor. He was fired.

There are many ways to run afoul of your boss. For John Stone, a car salesman in the middle of Chicago Bears country, it was his display of affection for the Green Bay Packers. Stone's late grandmother had been a huge Packers fan, just as he was. So in her memory, the day after they beat the Bears in the play-offs to win a spot in the 2011 Super Bowl, he wore a Packers tie to work at Webb Chevrolet in Oak Lawn, a Chicago suburb.

As he should have known, car lots are off-limits to sentimentality of any kind—even for grandmothers and especially for opposing football teams. Webb Chevrolet advertised during radio broadcasts of Bears games. Webb's business was at stake. If a Packers tie were allowed to adorn the showroom, Stone's manager feared, hordes of Chicago fans, who were customers, would turn on their heels and flee. He asked Stone five times to take off the tie. Five times, Stone refused. Sorry, man, no First Amendment there. Private companies aren't covered. So, naturally, he was fired, and then just as logically was immediately hired at a competing Chevy dealership in another town, which valued stubborn persistence in a salesman. At his new job, Stone sold so many cars that he was named salesman of the month in four of his first eight months.

There is one category of speech for which private employees have legal protection against dismissal: when they blow the whistle on fraud against shareholders. Then they come under the Sarbanes-Oxley Act, passed in the wake of malfeasance in the investment business. The law covers employees of publicly traded companies, and—as the Supreme Court has interpreted it—also private companies that do business with publicly traded firms. No such company "may discharge, demote, suspend, threaten, harass, or in any other manner discriminate against an employee in the terms and conditions of employment because of any lawful act done by the employee" to provide information about fraud or other violations of securities laws. You can even get a reward for providing evidence.

Americans respond variously to the web of inhibitions imposed by their workplaces. Some quietly acquiesce; others quietly resist. Teachers fall into both groups.

In Texas, whose state board of education has politicized some of the curriculum, the classroom of Helen Bradley seems like a refuge of integrity. Since 1976 she has taught at Nimitz High School in Irving, and I happened to observe a lesson of hers that struck a sensible balance on the sensitive issue of capitalism or, as the board prefers that teachers call it, "the free enterprise system."

It's hard to imagine conservatives on the state board applauding Bradley's approach, but she seems devoted to a red-blooded American principle of liberty: to speak honestly. She does this in a difficult context. The board conducts rolling authorizations of textbooks and revisions of standardized tests from decade to decade, from subject to subject. In 2010 its conservative majority made a few sensational changes in social studies, which includes economics, sociology, psychology, geography, and history.

It removed Thomas Jefferson from the list of those who inspired revolutions of the eighteenth and nineteenth centuries, because of his leadership in advocating the separation of church and state. (He appears frequently elsewhere in the curriculum.) It added religious figures John Calvin and Thomas Aquinas. It voted down a provision, introduced by a Democratic board member, explaining that "the founding fathers protected religious freedom in America by barring the government from promoting or disfavoring any particular religion above all others."

The board passed changes to justify McCarthyism's suspicions that communists infiltrated the government; to note the Black Panthers' rhetoric of violence alongside Martin Luther King Jr.'s nonviolence; and to emphasize "the conservative resurgence of the 1980s and 1990s, including Phyllis Schlafly, the Contract With America, the Heritage Foundation, the Moral Majority, and the National Rifle Association." Students should study "the unintended consequences" of affirmative action and Great Society programs, the board decided.

Teachers sitting around a table at Gaston Middle School in Dallas grumbled anonymously about some of this: a tilt toward the Confederacy, for example, exemplified by the requirement that eighth graders read the inaugural address of Jefferson Davis as well as Lincoln's. The curriculum is also "completely skewed toward states' rights, pro–free enterprise, pro-capitalism," one teacher observed. The term "capitalism" is to be avoided, given the pejorative connotation that it's acquired in some quarters.

It is clear by reading the approved standards that the free-market economy is to be heralded. Students are to study communism, socialism, and fascism and "formulate generalizations on how economic freedom improved the human condition, based on students' knowledge of the benefits of free enterprise," particularly in comparison with communist command economies. The topic of free enterprise is integrated into practically every course, including U.S. history, world history, world geography, U.S. government, and sociology. In high school economics, the requirements are titled "Texas Essential Knowledge and Skills for Economics with Emphasis on the Free Enterprise System and Its Benefits."

Benefits, yes, but in Helen Bradley's classroom, where she is teaching the rise of the Populist movement of farmers in the face of industrial and financial monopolies, there is less than reverence for the "free enterprise system." She and her eighteen students are role-playing; the students are the farmers, and she is the railroad owner, then the banker, then the middleman and wholesaler.

The students have been given a xeroxed chapter, copied from an earlier textbook, on the rise of Populism in the Midwest in the late nineteenth century. For the moment, Bradley owns a railroad. "I have helped build this country," she boasts with a sly, warm smile, trying to needle her students a little.

Playing their role as farmers, the teenagers complain that the railroad has taken land and charges high fees. "I'd think farmers would like the railroad," says Bradley. "How are you gonna get your goods to market? If you don't like it, use somebody else's railroad."

"You have a monopoly," counters one of the boys. "You can charge us whatever you want."

Bradley smiles a delicious smile of regard for the boy's insight, then puts down the farmers. "Don't you all understand economics? Oh, that's right. You all haven't had much schooling. You spend all your time in the fields."

"Ooooooh!" groan the students/farmers. Bradley the industrialist doesn't let up. She is a sharp debater who keeps the kids thinking.

"On average, how many harvests do you have a year?" she asks.

"A couple," says a boy.

"A couple," the industrialist repeats. "OK, so the rest of the year you're not using my railroad, are you?"

"No."

"You think my railroad exists only to support your farm and transport your goods. So yes, I'm going to charge you higher prices. And yes, I have other customers. The big industries that use my railroad year-round, shouldn't they get lower prices because they're more loyal customers? . . . You also brought up the fact that you don't have many other choices. Therefore, you're kind of stuck with whatever I'm going to charge you, right?"

A girl: "But it's unfair, because we only make a certain amount of money." We farmers need to buy supplies and equipment, she explains.

Bradley leads them through a simple supply-and-demand scenario. Aren't farm implements "helping you generate more crops? And if you're generating more crops, aren't you generating more money?"

A boy explains: "You're creating more so the price goes down."

"So you buy the new equipment, and you're making more crops, but you're telling me that you're making less money."

"Mmmm hmmmm," the class hums in agreement.

"I think I'm going to suddenly change into a banker," Bradley announces. And there she is, in tense dialogue with the students who say they need to borrow to buy equipment, that they don't make enough profit to pay cash, that they'd like to purchase more land but can't get loans from the bank.

"You know," says Bradley, "banks are basically not going to be out in the rural area. We're going to be where the money is, and the big money right now is going to be over on the East Coast. We have these wonderful industrialists that are building these huge new companies. When they come to us for a loan, we're happy to lend it to them, because we know we're gonna get our money back. But I'll be frank here: Loaning money to you folks is no fun. You are so bad about paying back your loans. Why is that?"

Now she's got the students worked up. A girl complains that their money is going to the railroads.

"I keep hearing that it's all somebody else's fault here," Bradley scolds.

"Sometimes the harvest isn't good," another girl pleads.

"What happened? You must not be a very good farmer," the banker says.

"The weather," says the farmer.

"You have a lot of variables that come into the situation when you're growing," offers another girl. "Crop infestation." Another adds, "Overworked land."

Bradley the banker is unsympathetic. "But all these sound once again like they're your problems that you're trying to put on somebody else. You have overworked land. Why don't you do something about it? Why don't you get new land? Now, I understand there's not much I can offer you about dealing with the weather. But it seems like these are just excuses. Are these why you're not paying back your mortgages?"

The students challenge their teacher/banker to take risks and make investments so that farmers can produce and then pay back original loans.

"Perhaps you're going to understand the position that I'm in," Bradley responds. "I don't really want to loan you money, but I understand the argument that you just made. So the thing is, I'm sure you'll understand when I charge you higher interest rates. I'm going to have to charge you higher interest rates simply because you're a higher risk."

"If you charge us higher interest rates the chances are even bigger that you're not gonna get paid back," says a boy, "because we'll have to pay back more."

"Well then, don't borrow from me next time. Find another bank."

"What other bank?"

"Oh, so now we're saying it's like the railroads. You don't have a selection of choices?" Bradley mocks them: "Any other complaints? So far, I'm not seeing that you have much of a case against our industrialists or our bankers. Who else are you upset with?"

The question leads naturally to the wholesaler who buys their crops low and sells high. Bradley magically becomes a middleman.

"So you're saying that you do all the work and I make all the money? Now, how many of you all think that?" Every hand goes up. "OK. But you have to understand my role as the middleman. Are you all gonna take your crops to the cities and sell them? Are you going to mill or process or can all the food that you take off your farm? . . . So yes, when I buy up your crops, I'm going to buy them at the lowest price that I can possibly get that crop from you. And if you're out there trying to make more crops because you have to pay off your mortgage, and you have bills to pay to the railroads to transport the goods to my warehouse, well, that sounds like it's your problem, not mine. I'm in business, too."

Students challenge her profiteering. She retorts that if they don't want to sell to her, she can "find some other desperate, hungry farmers" who will. "I think you rely on me. I don't think there are that many middlemen out there, and you have to bring your goods to me because I'm the only one in the area that you can sell to."

"Again, that's monopolizing," says a boy.

"Not my problem," Bradley replies. "I love monopoly. Monopoly is the perfect form of business in my opinion, because I hold all the cards."

By the end of the hour, the students as farmers are organizing. They are pooling their resources, setting up the Grange to advocate for themselves, and developing a platform to press the government, which "is only helping out the industrialists and doesn't care about the farmers," as one girl puts it. They are, in conclusion, creating the Populist movement.

I'll bet these kids will never forget this class. Bradley has taken the school board's advocacy of free enterprise and taught it with all the nuance and contradiction of reality—the interdependence of competing interests, the evils of monopoly and exploitation, the clash of classes, and the virtues of organizing into political and economic groups.

The spirit of free inquiry is like one of those trick candles that keeps bursting back into flame after you try to blow it out. It can't even be extinguished by the Texas Board of Education.

The board's curriculum preferences have influenced textbooks nationwide. It's a big state, and the adopted textbooks once had to be used in every public school. Since 2006, however, individual districts have been authorized to select and buy their own books, while bearing in mind that students still have to pass standardized tests containing particulars dictated by the state board. This limited autonomy gives teachers some wiggle room, but only within the confining parameters of time. The more specifics on which the state commands that students be tested, the fewer hours available for improvisation by creative teachers.

In only ten days to cover the American Revolution, the state mandates that about twenty-five historical figures be taught, "which is ridiculous," says Stephen Smith, an African-American teacher and basketball coach at Nimitz. He finds the history curriculum at once Eurocentric and symbolically diverse. Unfamiliar and relatively insignificant people have been added to enhance the representation of women, Hispanics, and African-Americans in history, he says. Yet he believes that Native Americans receive too little attention. "If you talk to the students, they're under the impression that when Columbus arrived, and the English and so forth later on, there was nobody there. They just arrived in the woods, and they just started moving in."

Therefore, Smith does what he calls "teaching a little outside the curriculum, because there are things I want them to know that they're not necessarily going to be tested on, but there are things they'll come in contact with in the real test, away from school."

That's why nobody can know what actually happens in the classroom by reading the textbooks, exams, and study guides. Consider the additional material on World War II included by a young teacher named Jennifer Swegler, a honey blonde who wears a cross on a chain around her neck. She is propelled by family stories of residual wartime prejudice directed at her grandmother, who moved from Germany, after the Allied victory, to a small community in Ohio. There, she was shunned by townspeople. Clerks in the grocery store refused to wait on her.

So Swegler is attuned to the ethnic retributions that are bred by war. As a result, the Japanese internment camps get extra attention in her classes. "That's something I do on my initiative, because I don't like the fact that it's so often glossed over," she explains. "They have to research the internment camp and write a letter as a boy or a girl who was inside."

Here is the candle that cannot be extinguished. Here is the inventive teacher who resists orthodoxy, and here are her students who, it is hoped, learn to listen, take the knowledge, and use it well. "We're kind of renegade" in the classroom, explains a woman who teaches American history at Gaston Middle School in Dallas. "It's the Wild West around here. The very act of teaching itself is a bit of a rebellion," like "Prometheus, the first teacher [who] gave the knowledge of fire to the mortals, right? I'm gonna teach about fire, and the upper gods aren't gonna be real happy about this. This is the nature of teaching. Here's a bit of knowledge."

Here's a bit of knowledge. Are we listening?

PART I

Books

1

Trouble in River City

We need censors, because they generate reading.
—ANNIE BUSCH, former director,
Springfield–Greene County Library District, Missouri

On a December Monday shortly before Christmas vacation, Gretchen Miller had some startling news for the twenty-one students in her advanced placement English class. Because of a parent's complaint, she told them, the celebrated novel they had been reading, *Waterland* by the British author Graham Swift, was being withdrawn from the course immediately. They should return their copies to the school's book room.

Few did. The book, ponderous and soporific to some, was suddenly intriguing. The local bookstore was soon sold out, and the public library had to order more. Parents who had never noticed what their children were reading picked it up. Unprecedented discussions of literature blossomed around dinner tables. Certain parents revealed themselves to their children as never before, making connections at new levels of honesty about hidden family history, a theme of the book. It was as if the hammer of censorship had struck stone, sending showers of sparks that ignited patches of indignation throughout the district, a Detroit suburb of diverse classes, ethnicities, religions, and politics.

In some American towns, banning a book from a high school course—or even from a school library—is greeted with accolades from protective parents. Here in Plymouth and Canton, Michigan, however, flares of outrage burned through the landscape, bisecting the community into passionate camps, each with its righteous agenda.

The larger movement defended the teachers with high appeals to academic integrity and intellectual freedom. Mothers and fathers proclaimed respect for their teenagers' maturity and right to explore difficult subjects through fine literature. From the other side came anguished, angry calls for public schools to guard youngsters from sexually explicit, obscene, profane, and immoral material, no matter what prestigious prizes the works might have won. Neither group made much effort to listen to the other.

The dispute began the day a high school senior in Miller's class showed her mother two paragraphs from *Waterland* describing a fifteen-year-old boy and girl fingering "what we called then simply 'holes' and 'things,'" as Swift's protagonist remarks: "I put the tip of my index finger into the mouth of Mary's hole, and was surprised to discover what an inadequate word was 'hole' for what I encountered. For Mary's hole had folds and protuberances, and, so it seemed to me, its false and its genuine entrances, and—as I found the true entrance—it revealed the power of changing its configuration and texture at my touch . . . And yet the chief and most wondrous power of Mary's hole was its capacity to send waves of sensation not only all over Mary's body, but all over mine."

The passage is the only one in the book that comes close to being erotic, and not very close at that, but it is explicit enough to have propelled the student's father, Matt Dame, into the superintendent's office, armed with a photocopy of the pages. He objected to *Waterland*'s being taught, and to the next book to be read in the course as well, the Pulitzer Prize–winning *Beloved* by the Nobel laureate Toni Morrison.

His complaint began to open a view into some of the great divides of current American culture—not just about the written word, but about something else: the expanding sense of alienation from public schools for being too liberal, too secular, too sexual, too morally loose as seen by a segment of parents who press for charter schools, homeschooling, and state-funded vouchers they can use in private and religious education. For many it's a final grasp for some measure of control as their kids get older in an Internet-saturated world, as public schools seem less and less responsive to families with conservative values. Some parents reach for influence by running for the local school board, which Matt Dame did unsuccessfully on a slate of four Tea Party candidates, two of whom won.

He rarely smiled when he was on this topic, but he had a dry laugh when he came up with a cutting line of sarcasm. "I'm fifty years old now. Now, how did I ever go through life not having read those books?" he asked, then teased me: "You're a Pulitzer Prize winner, and you did it without ever reading *Beloved*?" I did read *Beloved* when it came out in 1987, I told him, but not *Waterland*—not until this controversy. "Oh, really? And you still won a Pulitzer Prize? Incredible!"

Dame was tall and neat, with a goatee and a mustache cropped short. His voice boomed seriously, as if he were always speaking at a school board hearing, which he and his wife, Barb, did with unyielding clarity. Their worries about books came in a larger context of concerns about sex education and troubling tales they'd heard about overt sexual behavior at school.

It's not easy to separate fact from rumor, but some students say that, yes, they've heard about oral sex in restrooms; they've seen simulated sex called "grinding" at school dances (one student called it intercourse with clothes on); and there's so much explicit fondling in school corridors that it's earned its own abbreviated euphemism: PDA, for "public displays of affection." Further, Dame said, his younger daughter, aged twelve, came home with an acute stomachache after a sex-ed teacher talked about oral and anal sex—a subject that had been absent from the curriculum sent to parents in advance.

The distress over those issues had reached a crescendo when the book challenge arose. "A parent group formed to restore decency to our schools, and they have a website," Superintendent Jeremy Hughes explained anxiously. "In the midst of all this, here comes Mr. Dame, and I said to myself, Oh, my God, this is the last thing we need right now. I've got to nip this in the bud. Mr. Dame didn't threaten me but said, 'I bet if I went to a school board meeting and read this out loud, they'd shut me up before I finished.' I thought, Oh, that's not what I wanted. I didn't want this to blow up given what else was going on."

What neither he nor Dame knew, because neither had read all of *Waterland,* was that it portrayed premarital sex as a tantalizing venture of great risk and teenage pregnancy as a terrible result. They had not read the terrifying scene of Mary's violent abortion, done crudely by an old crone who uses a hollow reed to suck out the embryo. They had not witnessed how that trauma leads to Mary's infertility, departure from reality, and eventual madness. Judging by comments from some girls who read the whole novel, it did more to scare them away from abortion than Operation Rescue ever could.

Having seen only the pages Dame handed him, Superintendent Hughes got a double surprise. First, he was "pretty upset and shocked" by the photocopied passage about "holes" and "things." Then he was stunned by other parents' negative reactions when he ordered the book withdrawn. He decided essentially alone, after consulting with three or four of his top administrators but not with the high school principal, who objected aggressively and was then excluded from further deliberations.

"I saw myself acting not for one person but for a whole bunch of people who would also be upset," Hughes said. "I was kind of surprised that in the midst of this whole debate, I can count on two or three fingers the number of people who came forward with support for me based on the content of the book."

He did not come across as a dictatorial sort. New to the district, in the job only six months at the time, he was a congenial man not yet in tune with the community. He admitted with pleasant candor that he had slipped in seeking neither consensus nor due process. "I made a mistake here," he said later to anyone listening, and months afterward went to the school to apologize to the teachers—although not for his negative judgment of the book, only for failing to consult widely through some procedural mechanism. He retired the following year.

The mistake had immediate consequences for the three AP English teachers, who were given the edict in phone calls at home over the weekend. "My immediate reaction was, what am I going to do?" Miller recalled. She had no ready substitute. *Waterland* had been selected a decade before by her colleague Brian Read as an accessible introduction to a literary form known as postmodern nonlinear structure, in which a story wanders back and forth through time and, when told by the most skillful practitioners, weaves history into the present almost seamlessly. *Waterland* has been accepted as a classic example of the technique.

Beloved is the real and surreal, the meandering and mystical story of an escaped slave who, about to be recaptured, kills her infant daughter

(Beloved) to spare her a life in bondage. After slavery ends and freedom is bestowed, the ghost of Beloved inhabits her mother's house, then haunts her mother's life as the girl at the age she would have been. The spirit and the mother share a needy affection, wrapped in the daughter's despairing resentment and the mother's defensive guilt. So do the reverberations of slavery continue their drumbeat of sorrow and yearning.

That is Morrison's novel reduced to a miniature, a caricature. All of what she achieves can be witnessed only by immersion in her writing, which stays faithfully in the vernacular—and sings. (Some opponents, seeking to puncture what they deride as an inflated admiration for the novel, criticize it for using seventh-grade vocabulary. Perhaps so, but exquisitely.) No brief summary can capture the musically calibrated rhythm, the eloquent journey through layers of hardship. Some have called it a modern masterpiece on slavery and its legacy.

It can make for difficult reading, though, especially by high schoolers, even bright kids who get into AP courses, and especially without an easier book of the same genre beforehand. So Brian Read adopted *Waterland* and *Beloved* simultaneously, placing *Waterland* first in the syllabus. "It occurred to me how well the two would work together," he said. In *Waterland*, "as a history teacher is narrating and talking to his class, he would actually talk about history and how to process it, how to explain the idea of history, how to deconstruct the past and deal with the present. Once we had that, we could transfer to *Beloved*," which carries readers into an understanding of "the legacy of trauma and how that lasts not only within a lifetime but is passed on to other generations," as Read explained.

Dame was having none of it. He had no intention of reading *Beloved*, but that didn't stop him, because conservative websites posted sensational quotations out of context, listing infanticide, incest, rape, and the casual mention of "fucking cows" among the objectionable citations. These were read aloud at a school board meeting by one of his friends, Sharon Lollio, the grandmother of a seven-year-old. Lollio declared, "I will not be made to feel like I am some kind of closed-minded fanatic because I have a problem with understanding how the passage of a book stating, 'All in their twenties, minus women, fucking cows, dreaming of rape, thrashing on pallets, rubbing their thighs and waiting for the new girl,' promotes writing, reading, and arithmetic."

Lollio was interrupted by the chairwoman, who scolded, "Would you please respect us and not use that language?" The hall erupted in guffaws. The words could be read in a high school class but not in a board meeting, apparently. But of course in class they are embedded in the flow of a study of the literary work, and besides, school board meetings are streamed live; any kid of any age can watch them.

In fact, *Beloved* does not go as far as to depict bestiality, nor does it offer actual scenes of rape—although it contains an oblique episode of slaves forced to perform sodomy on their white male overseers. Lollio was unrepentant.

"I guess to be honest with you, I wasn't really going in there trying to listen to the other side," Lollio told me a month later. "I was in there to say, OK, you keep referring to page numbers in a book, why don't you exactly read out loud to people so they understand what these parents are objecting about?" Did she have any regrets for doing that? "Absolutely not," Lollio replied. She was not one for compromise in such matters; she had helped found the local chapter of the Tea Party, called Rattle with Us (as in the rattlesnake on the American Revolutionary flag, "Don't Tread on Me"). "No, I'm not sorry about it at all," she repeated, although the chair's reaction had startled her. "When she gaveled me down, I thought to myself, Are you not even aware of what's in this book?"

This standard practice of quoting out of context bugged Debbie Piotrowski, the mother of an AP English student, who put an acerbic post on a local news site. She declared it "a shame most people opposing the book have only read the controversial sentences. I hope you don't ever take your almost-adult child to a Holocaust museum or to an art museum if there are Michelangelo paintings there."

To which Tina Waldrep, the mother of a sophomore, replied, "A student should have the opportunity to take this class based on academic ability, not based on their moral comfort level."

Parents had, in fact, been sent the course's book list in advance, but the Dames hadn't devoted the time to look into it. Barb Dame insisted in an online post that their argument "is not about censoring books, it is about informing parents about the full content of reading assignments prior to a book being covered in class. The handouts received by parents over the summer did not state that the Swift novel contained explicit imagery of female genitalia and graphic descriptions of underage sex." They now demanded more information about the readings, and they got it the following year.

"Topics such as violence, slavery, and sexuality are addressed in some of the literature and will be discussed in class," says the updated application, which requires a parent's signature and links to plot descriptions and content alerts for about a dozen works to be studied: *Waterland* contains "one-half page of detailed description about teenage sexual exploration, abortion, incest," parents and students are informed. *Beloved* contains "sexual scenes, infanticide, rape, racism, slavery."

So does a lot of great literature. "You need look no farther than the classics of Greek and Roman literature to find texts that contain exactly the same material," wrote Kristina Chew, who teaches classics at St. Peter's, a Jesuit university in Jersey City, New Jersey. Greek tragedy is full of "horrifying depictions of violence," she noted. *Medea,* by Euripides, is "also about a mother in desperate straits who kills her children." *Oedipus Rex* and *Hippolytus,* by Sophocles and Euripides, respectively, contain episodes of incest. "Scatological and bodily humor" abound in the comedies of Aristophanes, along with bawdy language. "If we're going to ban *Beloved,*" she concluded, "we'd really have to ban *Medea,* and all [those] classical literary works."

How opponents and proponents of controversial books absorb them is an intriguing issue in these disputes. If you imagine activists on both sides poring over the texts with rapt attention to every allusion and allegory, you'll be disillusioned to learn that a good many people with passionate opinions are less passionate about actually reading the works they deride. In an era of 140-character tweets and three-second sound bites, a number of hurried parents want books to be rated, like films, so precious time need not be spent in reading and due consideration. It's more efficient to glance at isolated words and phrases, get fired up by like-minded websites, and demand suppression.

"No, I didn't read the whole thing," Lollio admitted when I first asked about *Beloved,* then added an amendment a few minutes later: "I did read through the book very quickly just trying to think, OK, can I get a grasp of it?" Whether anyone could succeed by just skimming such a complex, multilayered work was a question. Lollio reads fiction—she favors romantic novels, her husband disclosed with a grin—and during the book controversy was in the middle of a thriller, she said, *The Secret Cardinal* by Tom Grace.

Dame's wife, Barb, read *Beloved* and concluded that its reputation exceeded its merits. "Like the emperor's new clothes," he said she'd told him, "where everyone's saying how wonderfully dressed he is, and then this one child says, 'Wait, he's naked,' and everyone goes, 'Well, yeah, he's naked.'"

This made it sound as if the book's admirers were elitists who deserved to be resented, mocked, and dismissed. "Well, Pulitzer Prize winner, this, that, and the other thing," Dame sneered. "It's like you hear that and you just got to accept it. The herd mentality . . . How dare you say that you don't like it. My golly. What are you? You're one of those— how do I put it? You're a simpleton because you don't see the literary value in this."

Barb dealt with words professionally, Matt with visual images. He designed websites and produced videos. She taught English as a second language and did English assessment testing at a university that he did not want named for fear that her employer, a hotbed of liberalism, would exact some retribution. He called Barb "an avid reader," but he, by contrast, was not a fan of made-up stories, so the rhapsodies about *Waterland* and *Beloved* left him unmoved.

"We're talking about two works of fiction," he declared, "two works of fiction no more historically accurate than any other piece of fiction. You know what I find of value? If you're going to talk about the horrors of slavery in American history, let's look at factual statements, factual things that happened, on both sides of the story."

Asked what he meant by both sides of the story, he went off the record for a few sentences, then came back for quotation: "I think as a country we have to dwell on our successes and not just our failures. Don't we have an African-American who's president [illustrating] that we've come a long way from that era? Absolutely. So let's not just dwell on our failures. Can't we throw in some of our successes as a nation too as we go about this? There's that whole apologetic—we as a nation, we've got to apologize to the world for some of the things that we do wrong, when we helped save the world in the two world wars, for crying out sideways. Does that mean nothing?"

Later, over dinner at the Ironwood Grill in Plymouth, he added this: "I think some of these people are taking works of fiction way too seriously. You hear someone say this book changed their lives. Come on. It would be a different thing if these were real people being quoted as saying real things."

Here was a literal thinker who did not abide the metaphor, the allegory, the surreal as avenues into human understanding. Alongside politics and religion, this revealed another divide, which separated those who saw literature as poetically illuminating from those who did not.

2

The Discerning Audience

Children, be curious. Nothing is worse (I know it)
than when curiosity stops.
—TOM CRICK, history teacher in *Waterland*

If you drive quickly along Joy Road, Salem High School could be mistaken for a modern factory. Its walls, mostly of brick, have few windows. Nearby stand a couple of other big structures, Plymouth High School and Canton High School, which are clustered in an unusual "educational park," the centerpiece of Michigan's third-largest school district. Throughout the day about 6,000 students flow among the three buildings for various classes and activities. Salem's indoor corridors are so wide that after school on a winter afternoon, athletes in training can jog several abreast.

"The park," as residents call the complex, has scope not only physically but in its cornucopia of course offerings, in English and other subjects. Juniors and seniors and their parents who object to readings in the four AP Literature sections have plenty of other choices. An AP English Language course, also designed with a college-level curriculum to prepare students for AP College Board exams, uses an anthology of essays. In advanced and honors classes, students can study Shakespeare and Dante, Homer and Virgil, *The Epic of Gilgamesh*, *The Turn of the Screw* by Henry James, Christopher Marlowe's *Doctor Faustus*, Jean-Paul Sartre's *No Exit*, Gustave Flaubert's *Madame Bovary*, *A Portrait of the Artist as a Young Man* by James Joyce, and his *Dubliners,* among other works. Miller and Read have both taught an advanced science fiction course that includes *Frankenstein* by Mary Shelley; *I, Robot* by Isaac Asimov; and *Childhood's End* by Arthur C. Clarke. Miller also teaches a grammar course and advanced composition.

Above the door into her room, number 2210, is a sign bearing a hopeful admonition:

THE VOICE OF REASON
BEYOND THIS POINT

Inside, Miller has tempered the institutional coldness with decorations. Some twenty cloth hangings are suspended from the ceiling, rectangles of thin fabric in blue, black, and translucent lavender that soften the fluorescent light. High in each of the four corners she has put collages of pictures and quotations on backgrounds of blue cloth: "The Realists," with portraits of Mark Twain, John Steinbeck, Langston Hughes, Harper Lee, and others; "The Romantics"; "Modernism"; and "Postmodernism." The walls are covered with posters and sayings. You could spend a good while just contemplating the surroundings.

On the floor tiles of blue, gray, and white, black lines are drawn to indicate the proper places for the metal chairs attached to desks; she likes them arranged facing inward so students can see one another for the class discussions that she favors.

Miller is short, with curly brown hair, glasses, and an open and welcoming manner. In jeans and an olive sweater pulled over a flowery blouse, she is neither dressy nor sloppy, just down-to-earth and ready to work. She is interesting and demanding, according to some of her students, and she shows them warm respect. In other words, she is the English teacher we all wish we'd had—perhaps the English teacher she also wished she'd had.

She recalls her own high school, in the Nebraska town of Kearney, as a place to leave. Her senior English was "very standard twelfth grade," she said: "*Hamlet,* sections from *Beowulf,* a couple of stories from *Canterbury Tales.*" The school had no advanced placement classes, and she had "a limited number of people I could talk to." She remembered this not with self-importance but with frustration.

Intellectual restlessness provoked her to construct an independent study regimen. "I read a book a month with a teacher, and then I'd write a paper about each book," she recalled, such works as *Moby-Dick, Crime and Punishment,* and *King Lear.* When she graduated and went to the University of Chicago, "I felt as if I'd been set free. And I wanted to give students that experience."

After teaching elsewhere and editing standardized tests for a decade, she arrived at the Plymouth-Canton district, stepping into an exciting English department whose AP curriculum had been shaped ten years earlier by Brian Read. "I wanted to get a little bit more minority voices in the course," Read said. He also wanted to teach critical theory, which had not been done there before, so he arranged novels in a sequence that he thought would help students learn how to analyze literature using New Historicism, a method developed in the 1980s.

It is a challenging technique. "A new historical reading is very interested in power and authority," explained Tita Chico, an English professor at the University of Maryland. "The emphasis is on looking for ways that works of art confirm dominant ideologies" of their times and, simultaneously, "looks for fissures or breaks" in that prevailing dogma, for "marginal voices or rebellions against that hegemonic voice." Those marginal voices may be no more than whispers in the work, or may be silenced altogether, but if a piece of literature is viewed "in conversation" with other disciplines and discourses of its era—religion, medicine, history—New Historicism "can give us a lens into how power reproduces itself and how there are subversions of power," she said. "I'm very surprised it would be introduced in high school . . . You have to know a huge amount."

Brian Read introduced the method of interpretation with *Waterland,* set in the marshy fens of eastern England, then followed with *Beloved,* the harder novel to read, immersing students in the early years of Reconstruction in a black household not distant enough from slavery to have forgotten, not healed enough to be rid of the ghosts of suffering. Finally, Read led the students on to *Maus,* the graphic novel based on the cartoonist Art Spiegelman's interviews with his father, a Holocaust survivor.

In *Waterland,* the history teacher, Tom Crick, wanders in and out of the approved study of the French Revolution, giving his teenage students a truer history of his family and other locals whose deeds and misdeeds ebb and flow through time. Crick tells his class irreverently of power relationships, of revolutions and supposedly heroic wars, as if to examine history by means of New Historicism itself. "Why is it that every so often history demands a bloodbath, a holocaust, an Armageddon?" he asks his students. "And why is it that every time the time before has taught us nothing?" Crick loses his job.

Graham Swift, having read about the challenge to *Waterland,* wondered later in an e-mail to his publisher whether anyone in Plymouth-Canton had noted "that a class of teenage students actually plays a protagonistic role in the novel and that the book's as much about education and the ethos of the classroom as anything. The whole narrative—heavily ironic in the Michigan context—is triggered by the sacking of a teacher for transgressing his formal curriculum." Curiously, the intersection of fiction and reality did not become a centerpiece of argument in Michigan, perhaps because the novel's plot is too complicated to reduce to a debating point.

Swift knew of no opposition to the book in the United Kingdom. "*Waterland* has been in print here for over thirty years," he wrote, "and has been extensively used on school syllabuses and exam courses—much more so, I imagine, than in the US—but I'm not aware of any case in the UK like the Michigan one or of any objection to the novel's being a set book for teenage students. A difference between us and the States? I don't know."

Matt Dame's complaint about the scene in *Waterland* was not the first that Brian Read had received. Eight years earlier, a Catholic boy's parents had objected, which seemed ironic to Read because they'd let the young man go multiple times to see the gory depictions of flagellation in the film *The Passion of the Christ.* As in the nation at large, those seeking to protect their children found sex more troubling than bloody violence, even the raw flesh of Jesus.

The parents went only to Read himself, not to higher authorities, so he handled it quietly by sticking white address labels over the offending paragraphs in all copies of *Waterland.*

"Before it was covered up," he said, "I would tell the kids that it's there. I'd always say, Look, pages 51 and 52, there's this passage, it's relatively detailed, it deals with two teenagers and their sexual encounter with one another, and if that makes you uncomfortable, skip it. You're not going to miss the point of the novel."

Through the following years, most of the labels stayed stuck, although kids learned how to hold the pages up to the light to read through them. When thirty or forty additional books were ordered in 2011 to accommodate larger classes, Read forgot to cover the passage. The Dames' daughter got one of the new volumes.

At a glance, Read might pass as a biker who mounts a Harley on weekends; he accentuates his baldness by keeping his remaining hair and graying beard cropped short. But he's no tough guy, and it doesn't take long to notice that he is a gentler sort, calmly focused and deliberate, a man with a quick wit and a knack for listening. He graduated from this school, so he is still at home, and he gives his students a comfortable setting more like a dorm's common room than a classroom: art posters of Kandinsky, Dada, Picasso; two couches in a corner, a couple of floor lamps in the middle. He banters easily with the kids as he challenges them.

Most students in Read's two classes, and the few I interviewed in Miller's, were outraged, insulted, or sardonically amused that the book had been withdrawn, even kids who weren't wildly enthusiastic about the part of it they'd read. They circulated a petition that drew about 100 signatures from practically all the AP students, plus some outside the classes. Jessi Longe made a four-minute video in which a fellow student, Erin Bensinger, quotes a janitor as telling her, "Don't ever let them take books away from you, because otherwise you're gonna end up like me, working with your hands and your back . . . So you need to read all the books you can. You need to work with your brain; you need to get a job that uses your intellect."

At school board meetings, recent graduates came home from college to hail Read and Miller as exemplary teachers whose AP classes had given them a running start into university courses, putting them ahead of their peers. "Great literature doesn't exist to make us feel good. That's for the major media and the real pornography industry," said Julie Rowe, who took Read's class before going to the University of Michigan. "Life is complicated and humanity is flawed, and the point of great literature, the point of great education, is to prepare us for this reality and allow us to confront it. Reading *Waterland* and *Beloved* as emerging adults was transformative because it provided us with an intellectual understanding of how to process the worst parts of our society."

That term "emerging adults" was not embraced by the books' opponents, who were trying to hold back the tide of adulthood before it inundated innocence. They gave their movement the name Parents & Community Advocates for Plymouth-Canton Community Schools and put up a website.

Some of them smeared teachers as a category, based on the misdeeds of a few abusers elsewhere in the country. "You've heard it on the other side: We've got to trust our teachers," said Matt Dame. "Well, Google 'teachers' and Google 'sex' and you find there are a lot of teachers out there we can't trust. Yeah, the majority are good, but it's the same stigma now as the Catholic priests, for example. Yes, the majority are good, but you have to have your guard up."

This generalized apprehension seems a driving force in book challenges. Sharon Lollio mentioned recent news stories about "teachers having sex with their students" and restraining kids with duct tape. "I think it was in California." (The incidents were more widespread than she remembered: In Louisiana, a teacher taped a special-needs child to a chair; another youngster was taped to a chair in the Bronx; a Missouri child was taped to a desk; and duct tape was plastered across pupils' mouths in Louisiana and California.)

"When you have children," Lollio explained, "and you send your children and you teach your children to respect authority, there's a confusing message there . . . We've always taught our kids, Respect your teachers." So when a "dirty" book is assigned by a teacher, it is given the imprimatur of the school. That infuriates parents who listen to the hard right's frequent broad denunciations these days of schoolteachers—especially those in labor unions—as lazy, incompetent, and uncaring. You'll hear this line if you tune in to local talk shows.

But those parents were in the minority as the controversy roiled the Plymouth-Canton district. The majority, the parents who rallied for the teachers and the curriculum, displayed less fear. They seemed to revel in their children's standing at the threshold of adulthood. As they organized, these parents found neighbors with common values, made new friendships that have continued, forged an alliance to lobby the school board, also created a website, and jammed the small room where the board held hearings. Some wore black T-shirts labeled "Supporters of Academic Integrity" in front, and in back emblazoned in white letters with a quotation from the history teacher in *Waterland:* "Children, be curious. Nothing is worse . . . than when curiosity stops. Nothing is more repressive than the repression of curiosity."

The AP English teachers were happily stunned. "I don't think we realized how much the community supported what we were doing until this came up and people started speaking out," Gretchen Miller said. "I have learned to trust my parents . . . I think there's a new understanding of what this community is like, a new understanding of what the kids are like, how sophisticated they are."

Faced with the grassroots uprising, Superintendent Hughes shifted ground. He convened two review committees comprising teachers and administrators to consider *Waterland* first, then *Beloved.* After reading the novels and listening to a cacophony of voices, the members held secret ballots in which both panels decided to retain the books in AP English.

It was too late in the course to do *Waterland,* so the kids had to read *Beloved* without the benefit of that easier introduction to postmodern nonlinear structure and New Historicism. Most of them struggled. "They couldn't deal with it," said Miller. "In fact when they got to their papers at the end of the year, they just weren't able to do that New Historicism criticism."

A student agreed. Without *Waterland,* she found *Beloved* close to impenetrable. "Not understanding every concept that was thrown at me kind of probably made it difficult transitioning into *Beloved,*" she said. "I finally kind of get it, whereas I feel if we had had [*Waterland*] before, we wouldn't have had to have so much time explaining what on earth would be happening in random chapters of *Beloved.*"

The Dames' daughter did not have to go through this. Because of her parents' objections, Miller gave her an alternate book, *As I Lay Dying* by William Faulkner, which she went off to read in the library as the class discussed *Beloved.* It wasn't the ideal learning process, but she did get a kind of tutorial with Miller, who worked individually with her on the Faulkner. And Miller encouraged the other students in the class to reach out to her, treat her respectfully, and honor her preferences, which by all accounts they did considerately. But there's no doubt that they all missed something in the absence of *Waterland*.

The following year, with *Waterland* back, Miller saw her students engage *Beloved* with greater depth, a difference between "night and day," she noted. "I think it's absolutely necessary to the progression. They think *Beloved* is a masterpiece. The word they use is 'amazing.'"

In 2012, the year without *Waterland*, students spent two class periods and some after-school time talking with me about the sudden withdrawal of the book. They were promised anonymity, so their names are changed.

"I was absolutely furious that they would treat us like we couldn't handle what was in there," said Martha. "I mean, honestly, most of us are more mature even than other high schoolers, just based on the fact that we're willing to take the challenge of taking a course like AP English. It's a college class."

Was the sexual scene embarrassing? "It didn't bother me," Barbara remarked. Then she added, "I thought it was lovely," and blushed.

"You hear more in the hallways than in these books," Beverly declared. "What are you gonna do when your kid's in college? You can't go through life and not read something that's uncomfortable. At seventeen or eighteen, a lot of kids have already—this is gonna sound bad—*experienced*."

The claims of maturity failed to impress Matt Dame, who scoffed when I told him what students were saying. "What sixteen- or seventeen-year-old kid doesn't think they're more mature than they are? We've all been there."

He had a point, but parents sometimes forget that many teachers are also parents, and they bring their parenting perspectives to the classroom as they try to take the measure of youngsters' emotional and intellectual abilities. "I've never been sure about how to handle that passage," said Miller, who had a daughter in college. "It's hard to get that sweet spot where you're pushing them to do things they can do, but beyond what they're doing."

"Initially, I didn't push them hard enough," Read admitted. "Then I pressed them harder and harder, but I didn't know where that line was. It took me three years to build up to that." Studying *Beloved*, "we spend time reading through the first chapter in class [aloud] which has a reference to fucking cows. They're juniors and seniors and they're AP kids. Would I do that in a tenth-grade class? No, I'd make a different call. I wouldn't teach these books in a tenth-grade class. I think they understand there's a difference between words that appear in a literary work for a purpose and words that are used in a casual conversation in a hallway."

"I understand that the parents see themselves as protecting their child," Miller acknowledged, but she was now witnessing a fundamental divide over "the way we see teenagers. Seventeen-year-olds, I see them on the verge of adulthood." She continued, "I raised my daughter differently. I sent her out and trusted that the world would take decent care of her and that she would learn to take care of herself."

Several students who knew the Dames' daughter said that she seemed sheltered and innocent. Matt Dame might not object to those adjectives. (Her first name was never reported in the local press and is omitted here at her father's request.)

"We've been careful all along as to what our kids watch, I mean from cartoons on down," he explained. "When they were younger and they saw something inappropriate, they changed the channel themselves. I don't believe in being a conformist where, Hey, it's all around us, so just accept it. Baloney. What that tells me is that the parents don't want to take the effort to do their job and protect the kids' innocence as long as possible. They've got the rest of their lives to be adults and be subject to all the smut and vulgarities of the world. What my wife and I wanted to do was build a foundation to help them make better decisions as adults, because that is one of the primary jobs of parenting."

Yes, building a foundation. So I tossed him an idea I'd heard from some of the AP students: that if they're going to read these books, better to do so under the guidance of a seasoned educator who can lead them through the material as literature, giving them a foundation, rather than reading without a framework for discussion and processing.

Dame's reply was telling. "Why is there such a hurry to give these books to minors, anyway?" he asked. "They've got the rest of their lives to read those books. What is the hurry? It's fiction, for crying out sideways . . . There's such a short period of a person's lifetime where there's some innocence. Why are we in such a hurry to take that away from these kids?"

Several kids had answers, which they would surely have given if they and Dame had been in the same room. "Some of the topics in the book are adult topics," said Mary. "Wouldn't you rather talk about them, have a discussion of them in class rather than just going out into the world not really knowing everything, not having that group of peers to talk about things? They're trying to make it a taboo, but it's not. It's life. Honestly, in freshman year I don't know that I would have been comfortable reading that in class." But as a senior, she said, "as long as we talk about it and we talk about why it's important and the meaning behind it and . . . have a mature conversation about it . . . it, like, helps us be able to deal with things that we wouldn't want to just go off and deal with ourselves."

Charlie seconded the argument. Books in this course have so many layers, he noted, "and Mr. Read does such a good job explaining them to us, teaching us all these ideas . . . If I just would have read *Waterland* or *Beloved* on my own, a bunch of the things in the books I wouldn't have been able to get."

Besides, sex is an easier topic in class than at home. "Mr. Read is our teacher," said Margaret. "He's not going to be interrogating us about our boyfriends or what we're doing. With your parents, you're a little bit less inclined to talk about things, because they're like, No, you're our baby. I don't want you doing this and this and this. You're too young. And here Mr. Read, he's having a conversation with us, and he's not going to be giving us the moral lesson of life . . . I know my parents, they're not very comfortable talking about these things, and the conversations that we do have always end awkwardly. My dad especially . . . he doesn't want me growing up, 'cause I'm the oldest. I'm his first child, so it's a little hard for him."

Then came the issue of "control," a word the students applied with resentment to the Dames for trying to dictate to others, to usurp other parents' preferences in child rearing. "I felt very offended, because I felt they're not my parents, so how can they decide what I can read?" asked Alicia. "They're not the ones who raised me, and they're not the morals and the values that I was taught. Have they read the whole book? . . . Do you even know what the book is about? Do you know that this is an AP class, which means that you're gonna learn college content? Which means it's not always gonna be innocent, like flowers and roses and daisies and sunshine? We're not gonna be sitting here reading *Pippi Long-stocking* in AP English class. Get real."

Bob had a lighter reaction. "I was actually kind of amused," he said. "I thought it was kind of funny. We all kind of knew which part was the questionable part. I had already read through that passage; I didn't think it was that bad. I thought it was kind of funny that somebody else's parent would try to control me more than my own mother would."

Dame's response: "We're not telling people how to parent their kids either. We just don't want anybody telling us how to parent ours." And after a school board meeting in which he was strongly criticized: "When you feel you're doing something right, you get through it. And I'm protecting many more kids than my daughter."

By the time I got to the AP classes, a couple of students were all talked out and wanted to move on. "The fact that we're taking time out of school to vent about people taking the book away is really taking away from our learning in school," said Richard. "If you want to learn from the book, go read it on your own."

That's what Molly and many others said they'd do, once they had a break from their relentless homework. "If I'd picked it up in the library on my own, I probably would have returned it, because it's really slow, and I couldn't really get into it," she admitted. "But now that somebody's told me that I can't read it, I'm planning on finishing it." This got a burst of sympathetic laughter from the class. "So the plan to save me from the horrible book didn't work."

Others were not done talking about their concerns, because they saw serious implications in the episode. They echoed worries heard at home about a long-term conservative political agenda. When "parents think it's OK to come and intervene in the school curriculum like this," said a student, Sarah, "I suppose a lot of us are wondering, if this is the first step, what next? What's the next thing the parents are going to want banned? And where is this quote unquote movement going to be heading? Is it heading to a place that's going to be beneficial or detrimental to us? And I don't really see that as wasting our time, because, if not immediately impacting our lives, it will become very impactful in the near future, because this is the world that we're growing up in and these are the people we have to deal with."

That anxiety about the conservative book-challenging movement infected the group of parents supporting the curriculum, some twenty of whom gathered with Read and Miller in a bar after a board meeting. They pulled tables together to make a large rectangle and talked strategy.

They saw their opponents—"the people we have to deal with," as one put it—as bent on mobilizing to infiltrate and undermine the public school system. "I don't think the issue has much to do with books," said Steve Sneideman, who had lost his school board seat in a close election. "It's a Tea Party attempt to discredit public schools across the country."

A few parents worried about Matt Dame's computer skills. Somebody might hack their Facebook page and website, several said, and suggested that the pages be taken down, then reconstituted more securely so the group could discuss plans without fear of surveillance. To an outsider, it all seemed slightly paranoid.

"We have lots of conspiracy theorists in the group," Jeff Longe told me later, laughing.

He and his daughter Jessi, who created the video quoting the janitor, made a virtue of the experience. They talked with each other about books as never before.

Jessi described herself as "really confused and angry" when the withdrawal of *Waterland* was announced in class. But she obediently turned in her copy, remembered the page number where she'd stopped reading, and over Christmas vacation walked to the library near her house, checked out the novel, and finished it in a week. She asked her parents' opinion about the offending scene. They thought it couldn't be judged out of context.

"She asked me to read the book, too," said her father, Jeff. So he picked up the library copy when she was finished. "I came to the conclusion that in context I really didn't have a problem with it," he said. "I could see that some parents were a little less comfortable with it, but I didn't really see that it needed to be pulled out of the curriculum."

Jessi and her dad then embarked on a family seminar of sorts. They had read books together before—Harry Potter, the Twilight series—and sex was not a brand-new topic. After a film on reproduction three years earlier, back in eighth-grade health class, "Jessi and I were taking our dog for a walk," Jeff remembered, when she started asking questions. "It wasn't like we could cut the walk short. We were forty-five minutes away from the car. I had no way out. We had the Talk," he said. "She was, 'Dad, they explained where the sperm comes from, and they explained where the egg comes from, but they didn't explain how they get together.' So they're leaving it for the parents to continue it. So I told her, and she said, 'Oh, that is so gross!' Then it was quiet; we were walking along. 'Oh, my God! That means you and Mom did that *twice*!' There are two kids in the family."

The controversy over the challenged books took them into more searching conversations. "He's a lawyer," Jessi noted, "and my parents always instilled in me that if I don't like something and I think there's a reason that I shouldn't like it, then I should fix it. He saw how torn up I was." So they discussed *Waterland,* read *Beloved,* and talked and talked.

"My dad's adopted," she said, and the sprawling family histories in each novel moved him to reflect on his lack of clear, known ancestry. "I guess he didn't feel like he was necessarily missing out," she said, "but it was interesting; it was a different look for him, seeing someone with this long line of family history, and him not having that . . . and how he kind of wished he had that."

There were more insights. Before the *Waterland* episode, Jessi's class had read *One Flew Over the Cuckoo's Nest,* Ken Kesey's novel set in a mental institution where emasculated patients, entangled in their own pasts, struggle for power and survival—and are driven to suicide. Jessi and her sister had always wondered why Jeff's adoptive father, their grandfather, was "very buttoned-up emotionally," Jeff said. The book prompted him to tell her "the story of my dad's older brother who committed suicide and who had been hospitalized at the same time as the character in *One Flew Over the Cuckoo's Nest* . . . He'd undergone electrotherapy, it was thought that he'd recovered, he was released. He was found dead by his two young sons . . . We used *Cuckoo's Nest* and *Waterland* to explore the lingering effect of a family's past—and my dad won't talk about it to this day."

Once Jeff and Jessi had read *Beloved,* they tackled the subject of slavery in America, the "whitewashed history," as he called it, "where this country has not always lived up to its ideals, 'all men are created equal' in 1776, but that is if you're a white man—no women—of the propertied class. Those men were created equal." Father and daughter talked about the westward expansion, the massacres of Native Americans, the Japanese internment during World War II, "not from a complaining or a whining standpoint," he said, "but from a balanced approach to history." This "balanced approach" sounded exactly like what Matt Dame and other conservatives found objectionable.

On a personal level when he read *Beloved*, "my own cultural sensitivity was enhanced," Jeff said, and so was Jessi's. He was able to see that just as his father's scars remained, so did those from slavery, even across generations. "People say that was 150 years ago, just get over it. Some people do, and some people don't and hang on to those things a lot longer . . . It was enlightening."

He and Jessi talked with remarkable maturity about the sexual themes and images in *Beloved*, how the word "f—ing," as he put it, was used to describe bestiality but not to portray loving relations between man and woman. "We talked about how different words were used to describe sexual acts of different types." Jeff and his wife, both raised Catholic and now "semi-practicing Catholics," talked openly with Jessi about the undesirability of "premarital sex before you're a certain age, before a certain amount of emotional connection." He called the entire episode "a teachable moment in our house."

It's hard to measure the extent of teaching that went on in homes, but judging by comments from AP students and parents, it seemed significant. Those already inclined to talk and listen to one another did so more intensely, and some who rarely discussed schoolwork began to talk. A lot of the teenagers seemed hungry for these conversations with parents and delighted by them. "I feel like I've learned a lot," said Jessi. "It's cool to know that all three of us agree on this and it's something that we can all do together. It's cool to have that. My parents have always supported me in everything I do, but this is showing how much they're committed also."

The connections were a silver lining for a number of families. Parents and their "emerging adults" were venturing across boundaries into a new territory where grown-ups resided in nearly egalitarian relationships. They had been on the verge of this frontier anyway, on the cusp of the children's imminent departure for college. But the transition, accelerated by the book challenges, now had momentum.

Most of the AP students were girls, and girls made up nearly all those who spoke perceptively about their shifting interactions at home. Their fragmentary comments were like rough family vignettes, hastily drawn sketches.

Melissa's father, confronting her indignation, laughed and said he was sure it was a practical joke designed "to teach you about censorship: You're probably going to write something about it." Alissa's mother "was really annoyed that some other parent had more influence on what I read than she did." Amanda's mother "said that it's kind of like them trying to cover up what they don't want their kids to know about history and how they don't want their kids to know about the things that are hurtful in the world."

Katrina said this: "I'm really passionate about literature and the books that I read. It's something that I really enjoy, and I don't often talk to my family specifically about what's going on in the books, but once these books were banned, *Waterland* and *Beloved,* my parents were actually kind of intrigued: Oh, so what are you actually learning in these books? What are these books about? What are the main messages? I kind of want to know now. What do you think is important about it?"

(It is worth noting that the word "banned," tossed around too freely, applies to neither book: *Waterland* was withdrawn from the course, not banned from the school or its library, and *Beloved* was only threatened, never deleted from the curriculum.)

"I was telling my mom what *Beloved* was about," Katrina continued. "I got really excited. I was telling her, these are the themes, this is why it's really important. That was really important to me, that I could talk to my mom about this and she was listening to me about something I thought was really important . . . She doesn't read many books, but it was cool to have that kind of connection with my mother." As they talked about the books, "I found out a lot about her, because she was able to relate to some of the things and tell me some stories about her childhood."

They discussed ethics, as they had previously, but now "I was more equal with her," Katrina said, "rather than [getting] a lecture on what's right and what's wrong from her." Had they ever talked before about a book she'd read? "Not in this depth. We'd talked about the superficial aspects of books before. But to talk about the layers and the theme and the messages and the morals of the book was something a little bit newer."

For Kaylie Lobb and her mother, Debbie Piotrowski, the attempt to pull the two books from the curriculum created a confluence of literature and politics. "I don't really talk to my mom about school," Kaylie said. "Like, I come home and she's, 'How was your day?' And I'm like, 'Good.' And she's like, 'What'd you learn?' And I'm like, 'Oh, nothing really.'

"But when the book got banned, or withdrawn, whatever you want to call it, I came home really mad, and that sparked a conversation about why the book got banned and how I felt about the material, how she felt about the material, and we had a discussion about the actual literature. And we were able to discuss our different opinions on things and come to our own conclusions, and even if my opinions don't agree with her on this literature, she respects that I have my own opinion and I respect that she has her own opinion. And I think, especially in this class where we have so many good discussions with so many opinions, it makes us so much more open to listening to what other people have to say and respecting what other people have to say. And now my mom is one of the head parents at all the school board meetings, and she's planning on reading the book and she's just been really involved, and I feel that it's brought us closer together, because she's now more involved in what I'm reading and in my life also. So I think it's been a really good experience for our relationship."

If Kaylie and other students were opened to listening and respecting, that was not the case for everyone, especially adults. Jessi Longe told the school board that after one meeting, "as everybody was mingling outside, I heard the word 'enemies' and how people here are enemies. And I think that's really wrong. I would hope no one would find me an enemy or would find anyone in this room an enemy just because we share different opinions. I think we need to respect each other's opinions regardless of what they are."

She held up a copy of *Waterland* and opened it. "In these books, inside of them, are just words, and we shouldn't be afraid of words."

3

Fear of Reading

And a word carries far—very far—
deals destruction through time.
—JOSEPH CONRAD

If you listen closely, a note of anguish can be heard among parents who organize against certain books. Beneath the hard din of certainty and indignation runs a softer worry about their kids emerging too soon from childhood into an abusive, tempting world.

Yet mothers and fathers have trouble answering concretely what direct consequences they imagine from these readings. "What is this parent so afraid of?" a student in Brian Read's English class wondered. "Do they think their child is now going to go perform sexual acts? Do they think that just reading this one passage, their kid is going to be forever warped and twisted and go out to destroy the world? I don't understand where the whole fear in their kid's reading the book came from."

Sardonically, an adult resident of the Michigan district proposed a research project to see if teen pregnancy is more prevalent among AP English students who read *Waterland* and *Beloved* than among the less achieving who study tamer literature in lower-level courses.

Book challengers often use a word that is also heard frequently from parents in general: "desensitize." There is broad concern, cutting across political and religious lines, that children, at too early a stage of maturity, can be desensitized emotionally by graphic accounts or images of sex and violence—especially sex, which generates the most intense objections. Copies of *Merriam-Webster's Collegiate Dictionary* were removed, briefly, from fourth- and fifth-grade classrooms in Menifee, California, for defining "oral sex." An unabridged edition of *The Diary of a Young Girl* by Anne Frank was opposed by the mother of a seventh grader in Northville, Michigan, just north of Plymouth, not for its depiction of a frightened Jewish family hiding during the Holocaust, but because it includes Anne's rather clinical description, edited out of the original, of her labia and clitoris.

But why books? Music is practically impossible for parents to manage and control. Films can be selected by their industry ratings, although theaters rarely check the ages of their patrons. Television may be susceptible to strict rules at home—but only in your own home, not necessarily at your children's friends'. The same with violent video games, which the Supreme Court has ruled cannot be prohibited from purchase by minors. Computer software may filter out pornography and—to the satisfaction of antigay parents—block websites sympathetic to homosexuality. But the Internet generally remains a wild place. Those who can't resist their teenagers' pleas for smart phones are giving them access to social media with all of its wonders and dangers, including online bullying and "sexting." Digital files housed and transmitted electronically cannot be locked away or thrown into a fire.

But actual books can be, so the objectors do what seems possible. Even as the book goes electronic, it also remains in tangible form. The bound volume can still be held in a hand; the words can still be printed on a page. The novel, the story, the poem, are still subjected to a paradox with a long history: Fighting the written word acknowledges its power. A perverse tribute is paid literature that has the authority to inspire awe and contempt, as in Drake, North Dakota, in 1973. The board of education ordered that the school janitor burn, in the basement furnace, all copies of *Slaughterhouse-Five,* Kurt Vonnegut's vividly profane antiwar novel salted with anti-Christian allusions. Students' lockers were searched to ferret out unreturned copies. Did the educators object to the firebombing of Dresden, on which the story turns, or to the brutal portrayal of war? The board president cited obscene language as the reason. It is a fearsome book that must be banned or burned.

What parents have never scrambled to keep unwelcome facts and ideas away from their children? Who has not turned off the news or censored his own conversations? Questions constantly present themselves: What facts, which ideas, are unsuitable at what ages? Tender minds are malleable, and a child's edge of seeing is a complicated region for all parents, including the passionate defenders of the freedom to read and to know. The younger the child, the more wrenching it is for a parent to watch the encounters with the unwholesome world.

My daughter, Laura, felt the sharpness of it when her son Ben, just five and a half, heard a well-meaning person warn her family about pickpockets as they walked in the area of St. Paul's Cathedral in London, where they lived. Laura remembered her exchange with Ben this way:

"'Are pickpockets *real*?' Oh yes, my dear sweet boy, they are.

"And another question: 'Are bad guys real?' My answer: Yes, there are people in the world who do bad things, but even most of those people have something good in them.

"Follow-up question: 'How many bad guys are there? Like five?'

"'Oh, my boy, there are more than that.'"

Ben's questions map the boundaries of innocence, which are less clearly marked among older children, those in middle and high school, who are the concern of virtually all of the 400 to 500 known book challenges annually in the United States. What is age appropriate? What shards of reality should be allowed to penetrate the protected universe of childhood?

The portrayal of violence rarely provokes parental complaints. It is ubiquitous and therefore unremarkable. The main triggers are sex, profanity, aspersions on Christianity, and the defiance of authority in stories that wink and chuckle at kids who resist adults' commands. That's one reason why J. D. Salinger's recalcitrant Holden Caulfield of *The Catcher in the Rye* is a perennial candidate for parental distaste—and teenage delight.

A special annoyance to conservatives these days is homosexuality. In an era of emerging tolerance for same-sex relationships, conservative parents have mounted vigorous campaigns against the plethora of books being written for "young adults" to induce compassion for adolescent gays and lesbians. These leading characters are shown discovering their homosexual orientation and then going through the trials of denying and concealing, being brought under suspicion and ostracized, and finally coming out to friends and family. Making a gay or lesbian liaison look acceptable makes the behavior more likely, some parents fear. They see homosexuality not as genetically determined but as a choice or a mental defect, so they often urge libraries to stock "ex-gay" books to tell stories of gays and lesbians "cured" and returned to "normal."

The controversies often leave the objecting parents feeling like victims. That may seem odd, since they quickly find comfort in like-minded circles of fundamentalist Christians, far-right Republicans, or dogmatic combatants in the culture wars. They tap into the online communities hosted by Phyllis Schlafly's Eagle Forum, Glenn Beck's 9/12 Project, and a one-man website with the impressive name SafeLibraries.

These are not movements devoted to pluralism. They assert a monopoly on truth. Therefore, parents who adopt their style often look self-righteous and imperious in their quests to impose orthodoxy. They may ridicule their opponents and their public schools as morally loose and uncaring, as "part of a whole agenda of indoctrination from . . . the secular humanists," in the words of a father named Aldo DeVivo, who lives in a town north of Manhattan.

But listening to DeVivo, a friendly guy with a rich New York accent, you can also hear the note of helplessness against the very institutions to which he entrusts his children. Classrooms and libraries are supposed to be repositories of decency, sanctuaries of legitimate learning and inquiry. DeVivo's definitions of decency are more confining than the schools', "being we're a pretty fundamentalist family." So he feels marginalized and ignored. He and others like him see their values being dismissed and despised by the educational establishment. They are gnawed by disquiet as they send their kids to school each day, until an offending book breaks their growing resentment into the open.

That happened when his daughter, Jessica, a junior at Clarkstown High School North in New City, New York, brought home *The Perks of Being a Wallflower*. Much challenged around the country, the coming-of-age story by Stephen Chbosky features a kid named Charlie, who deals with the suicide of a friend; witnesses forced sex at a party; sees his pal Patrick kissing the high school quarterback; later kisses Patrick himself; has a bad LSD trip; smokes surreptitiously; is not understood by his parents; dates a girl who wants to explore lesbianism; learns that his aunt was abused; and accompanies his sister when she has an abortion. He is Holden Caulfield Lite, confused but not bitter, lost but not angry. A teacher calls him "one of the most gifted people I've ever known" in a moving scene with the one adult who admires him. He gets straight As the entire year and thinks that on his birthday he should get his mother a present, "since she was there, too."

"My wife came down and read me an excerpt," DeVivo remembered, "and I said, You gotta be kiddin' me. How can they send a book that's this explicitly profane and sexually inappropriate and every type of thing you can imagine—how can they send this home without any consultation with the parent?" On the question of whether the book belonged just in the library, instead of the classroom, his wife, Patti, issued this verdict: "Personally, I believe it doesn't belong anywhere. It belongs in the garbage can."

A range of issues troubled Patti, who worked as an administrative assistant at a Christian school, which their children had attended through the eighth grade. "Violence, language, and sexual content" were at the top of her list, plus politics, and not only in books. "These kids have grown up with these games, Xbox," she said. "These kids have become desensitized. They don't know right from wrong." Moreover, she said, the public high school used such "liberally slanted" books as Howard Zinn's *People's History of the United States,* a revisionist take on the country from the viewpoint of Native Americans, blacks, women, and workers. She contended that it characterizes "Christopher Columbus as a rapist and the Pilgrims as evil people."

Among Aldo's grievances was what he misunderstood to be a smear on Jesus in Barbara Ehrenreich's *Nickel and Dimed,* her account of posing as a low-wage laborer. She writes cynically of a tent meeting: "Jesus makes his appearance here only as a corpse; the living man, the wine-guzzling vagrant and precocious socialist, is never once mentioned, nor anything he ever had to say." (She was actually deploring the preacher's failure to pay attention to Jesus's teachings about the poor and began the passage by writing, "It would be nice if someone would read this sad-eyed crowd the Sermon on the Mount, accompanied by a rousing commentary on income inequality.") DeVivo finished half the book and concluded, "This author, she's got issues."

The DeVivos' efforts to get *The Perks of Being a Wallflower* removed from their daughter's course reinforced their sense of the school as alien territory. First, he went to the teacher, who asked him what book he would prefer for his child. "I'm in the moving and storage industry," DeVivo said, "and here's an English teacher asking me if I know anything that would be more appropriate for the kids to read?" He then went through the process of filing a complaint, but "being that we're in a fairly high-populated liberal area, we knew we were up against it. And I personally felt we would not get a fair shake at it because somewhere along the line a committee would be filled with people who were in favor of anything." Sure enough. "They voted five to nothing to keep the book in."

And what harm would it do? DeVivo imagines: "When you're a kid and you read this, you say, Wow, the school is giving me this to read; maybe this stuff isn't all that bad. How do we know this book might not become the beginning of him becoming a pedophile, a sex offender, or whatever? These kids are at a fragile state of trying to know what niche they're going into."

An answer to this anxiety came from halfway across the country. "Reading about a gay character does not make them gay; reading about drinking and driving does not make them want to drink and drive," Kristin Pekoll declared. She had gone through an ugly fight as the young adult/reference librarian in the public library of West Bend, Wisconsin, a town of about 30,000. "For some kids," she explained, "reading about things makes them not feel alone—coming from an abusive family, being gay, knowing that someone else survived—it can be very helpful."

Furthermore, as teachers are urged to explain to concerned parents, requiring a reading does not necessarily mean accepting all the ideas or behaviors it contains. If the conflict becomes "a melodrama of The Upright People vs. The Evil Corruptors of Our Children," writes Bruce McMenomy, a teacher of Latin and Greek, "we're going to lose." Instead, he suggests that teachers adopt a collaborative tone in making clear "that neither the students nor the parents nor the teachers have to approve of or condone everything that emerges in a text just because it's assigned. Often establishing that fact is half the battle. Many parents haven't actually thought about it: some consider that assigning a text for a class is synonymous with endorsing it *in toto*. That's wrong, of course, but sometimes we need to say as much." A goal is for students to "develop their own critical acumen . . . [T]hey don't have to buy it just because it's been delivered in a book."

Permitting skepticism may be a line of argument appealing to some complaining parents, but others simply do not want their kids exposed to certain ideas, such as positive portrayals of homosexuality. In West Bend, it was the public library, not the school, that became the target.

The activist there, Ginny Maziarka, sprang to alert "after my daughter [aged sixteen] brought home, and promptly returned, *The Perks of Being a Wallflower.*" Maziarka went to the public library's website to look at the young adult selections and happened upon a list headed "Out of the Closet," a problematic title, she thought, that "lends a positive connotation to the subject of homosexuality." After reading the synopsis of each book and noticing no book offering "an opposing viewpoint," she asked the library to reclassify thirty-eight books by moving them to the adult section.

It would not have made much difference. The library is shaped like a square donut, Pekoll explained, with the children's section on one side, the adult section on the other, and the young adult area in the back of the building, around a corner. Anyone with a library card can check out any book from any section, she noted, and any minor can get a card with a parent's authorization. No further parental permission is required to check out anything except R-rated movies.

Public libraries are the most protected by court rulings on such matters, and it is nearly impossible to get books that are already on the shelves removed entirely without violating the First Amendment. Courts have decided that schools have the right to exclude books from course curricula, as in Plymouth-Canton, Michigan. But once government-employed librarians in a public school or a public library order a title for circulation, its subsequent withdrawal tends to run afoul of the Constitution unless it can be shown to be obscene.

The law is not the only force in a small community, however, and West Bend was torn by the controversy, which drove wedges even within families and brought hostility through the Internet from locations unknown. Library employees were spurned in public, at the grocery store and the gas station, by people who would normally greet them. "We had a lot of people come into the library [saying], 'Where are those bad books, where are those dirty books?'" Pekoll recalled. "I had a patron who refused to let me help him at the information desk one day. I had tons of e-mail and voice mail: 'You're going to hell.' 'How dare you?' 'How can you do this to our children?' 'What kind of mother are you? I feel sorry for your children.' At the time I was pregnant."

She received no physical threats but endured "a lot of stress, a lot of emotional turmoil. I would dread checking my voice mail or e-mails. I was afraid of what I would find. It was hard on my family, my husband, and my parents who would read things about me."

An alderman called the library a porn shop and said that it should be closed down because it was within 1,000 feet of a school. He didn't have a library card, according to the director at the time, Stephen Michael Tyree, and refused an offer of a tour. "It got to the point where I couldn't go get gasoline without people recognizing me and making comments," Tyree said. "I work with women who heard in their churches about the library. They couldn't get their hair done, couldn't get gasoline, couldn't go to the grocery store, couldn't go to churches, without hearing that we were slimebags."

Maziarka's group "kept increasing the amount of books they were challenging," he said. "They went from specificity to generalities. They didn't want anything to do with sex, especially same-gender relations. They wanted us to put labels on the books, like a dot. When I was a kid, that would have labeled it forbidden fruit, and I would have wanted to taste it. They wanted a special library card saying what they could read. We didn't have staff to do that, and it would be censorship. I told them there are no über-parents."

Maziarka also suffered. "I was raised Catholic," she said, "but have since become a born-again Christ follower. I attend a nondenominational Bible-believing church. I am an army veteran. Two years of college. Nobody special, as you can see." She dabbles in conservative politics. She's against abortion, gay marriage, and Obama, and she supports Scott Walker, the conservative governor of Wisconsin who shut down collective bargaining by teachers' and other government employees' unions.

Unaware of how ravaging online brutality could be, Maziarka made a basic mistake in her campaign, she later conceded, by opposing books' homosexual themes rather than broader sexual content. "I wish I had done a more thorough job of researching young adult books and collecting my thoughts instead of knee-jerk reacting to the 'Out of the Closet' website," she said. "The overall issue was one of sexually explicit books—period. Unfortunately, I can't redo the time clock. This made the focus a 'gay' issue instead of a local community issue wherein the library could have served parents in a much more effective manner."

At the height of the battle, she reported, someone hacked into her Facebook account, changed her password, took over two Facebook pages registered in her name, "and used them to publish gay 'hate' messages, making it appear as though I was the one who was publishing hurtful and cruel messages." These were picked up by her opponents in West Bend and circulated by Internet, part of what she called "a tool to silence us." It didn't work, but it was intimidating.

In the end, the library's board voted to keep the books where they were, in the young adult section, while making one concession: It changed its web page title from "Out of the Closet" to "Over the Rainbow."

The city council then voted not to renew four of the board members' terms. Eventually, conservatives were brought in to fill the vacancies, and they turned out to be more interested in allowing guns than excluding books. In response to signs saying that no weapons were permitted, Pekoll reported, several townspeople wrote letters complaining that they wouldn't bring their families to a place where they were denied their Second Amendment right to protect them with firearms. So the conservative majority on the board voted to allow guns in the library.

"The staff was not happy," Pekoll said. When she was interviewed for the job of director, a board member "sat through my interview with a gun on his hip. Talk about intimidating! Obviously, I wasn't given the promotion."

The risk of controversy can make librarians hesitate to order certain books in the first place. "In the beginning I was a little gun-shy," Pekoll admitted—no pun intended. She gave any book with gay characters close scrutiny, ordering it only if it got a glowing review in the *School Library Journal, Kirkus Reviews, Booklist,* or *Voice of Youth Advocates.* As time passed after weathering the Maziarka challenge, she regained trust in her own judgment. "I don't find myself analyzing how the community is going to react to a book as I once did. I'm not sitting here chewing my fingernails thinking, What are they going to think if I order the book?" If she needs to consult, a Listserv of the Young Adult Library Services Association provides a forum where "librarians discuss openly if there are things to be cautious about, especially in school libraries," which are more careful than public libraries.

Indeed, the West Bend West High School librarian, Jason John Penterman, said he watched his step after parents' protests over the *Gossip Girl* series of novels, popular among young teenagers for the characters' romantic intrigues, flirtations with drugs, and sexual liaisons. Using highlighters, the parents flagged vulgarity and other offensive passages, and despite backing for the library by the superintendent, Penterman said, "We decided we would take the books off the shelves."

Since then, he's done a balancing act. On the one hand, he ordered many of the books that Maziarka had targeted in the town's public library, so the high school library "would have them to fill in the gaps." On the other hand, he ordered one "ex-gay" volume that Maziarka had recommended, *A Parent's Guide to Preventing Homosexuality*. "The book was stolen from my library," Penterman said. "About a month prior to its disappearance a student had approached me and said, 'I find this book offensive. If I was gay, it would make me want to kill myself.'" Penterman didn't replace the copy.

"I'm very careful" when ordering adult fiction, he said. "If I think there is something controversial, I'll dig into two or more book reviews rather than one book review. I'm much more careful about screening books by first-time authors." Yet books designated for young adults don't worry him very much, "because America's Puritan mind-set drives the plot lines," he observed. For characters who engage in "libertarian sex, libertarian drug and alcohol use, a libertarian approach to life in general," he noticed, "their fate is quite negative. It's not a happy ending."

Some parents don't see the moral of the story, though. They are captivated by the profanity and sex and—to a lesser extent—the violence, and they trust others who are agitating online for an uprising of opposition.

"It's kind of an open secret within the profession that there's a lot of self-censorship that takes place, especially in school libraries," said Deborah Caldwell-Stone, deputy director of the Office for Intellectual Freedom at the American Library Association (ALA). "You can understand it. A lot of these people are working in small communities. They don't have the ability if they lose their jobs to pick up and move to another place."

Furthermore, the ALA or the American Civil Liberties Union cannot always find aggrieved parents daring enough to stand up and file lawsuits challenging book removals from libraries, even when the constitutional violation is clear and a court victory is practically inevitable. There is too much risk of ostracism and retaliation along the way to winning.

So it seemed as school libraries got hammered in two small Missouri towns. After complaints, the Stockton board of education voted unanimously to remove *The Absolutely True Diary of a Part-Time Indian,* by Sherman Alexie, a Native American writer whose first-person story follows a boy commuting from his reservation life with an alcoholic father to a white school and placing himself in a no-man's-land—ridiculed at the school initially, rejected at the reservation as a traitor. As he negotiates his way between the two cultures, he copes with poverty, identity confusion, racism, self-hatred, and the deaths of several people close to him. We are left to believe that he will find his way in a mostly white world.

American Indians might legitimately resent the book for stereotyping them as constant drunkards. Whites may think it portrays them as perpetually bigoted. But the book has been challenged mainly because of its occasional profanity—"shit," but usually "fricking," not "fucking"—and especially its half page of ecstasy about masturbating. That didn't go over well in Stockton, a rural Ozark town where local officials are church elders and an influential pastor got hold of the cause, preaching against the book from the pulpit.

The other town, Republic, outside Springfield, settled things somewhat differently, but not to students' advantage. Vonnegut's *Slaughterhouse-Five* was taken from the school library, along with a teenage novel, *Twenty Boy Summer,* which gets its title from a girl's dating goal. It's a sassy tearjerker about boy-obsessed adolescent girls, secret loves, sexual opportunism that's neither graphic nor erotic, clueless parents who are easy to deceive, and touching insights into kids' dealing with death. It's a book steeped in morality, in the end, but not enough for vocal adults in Republic.

In an inventive response, high school students in Republic were offered free volumes of *Slaughterhouse-Five* by the Kurt Vonnegut Memorial Library in Indianapolis, thanks to an anonymous donor who paid for 150 copies. The library announced on its website, "We're not telling you to like the book . . . We just want you to read it and decide for yourself. We will not share your request or any of your personal information with anyone else." A total of seventy-eight kids accepted the gift, according to the director, Julia Whitehead. "Anytime a book is banned, it raises interest in the book," she said. "I've received many e-mails from teachers around the country saying this has renewed my interest in teaching Vonnegut in the classroom." The publisher reported increased book sales, especially to libraries, where librarians might have been ordering it as a preemptive strike against future objections.

In the end, the Republic school board, peppered with letters from various national organizations, put the two books back in the high school library, but with the restriction that only parents could check them out. Caldwell-Stone called this "a classic unconstitutional action," citing a similar case in Arkansas (*Counts v. Cedarville School District*), where a federal court overruled a decision to place Harry Potter books on a locked shelf accessible with parental permission only. But nobody in Republic with standing—that is, a student or a parent—came forward to mount a legal challenge.

The Republic board also drew up a set of standards for books at various grade levels. In elementary school, for example, "minimal profanity will be present," "depictions of mild violence are minimal," and "no sexual content exists."

For middle schoolers, "some crude humor may be present," "some depictions of violence may be present," but "no promotion or sensationalism of violence." "Minimal sexual content may be present in realistic situations" but "no promotion or sensationalism of sexual promiscuity," and "references to drugs/alcohol/tobacco may be presented in realistic situations," but the use of those substances may not be promoted.

Readings for high school students may contain "minimal use of mature humor and suggestive themes" and "some depictions of intense violence." Sex is more restricted: "References to sexual themes presented in realistic situations are minimal," and "no promotion or sensationalism of sexual promiscuity exists." Realistic references to drugs, alcohol, and tobacco use are OK, but not their "promotion or sensationalism."

Caldwell-Stone called the policy on standards "fully subjective and probably wouldn't survive court scrutiny, if it got to court. But school boards have considerable discretion in identifying materials they don't want to purchase in the first place."

"This freedom of speech, it drives me crazy," said Patti DeVivo, the mother in New York who objected to *The Perks of Being a Wallflower*. "We have to have some standards. It really has to be good for our children. What's the next thing, you have freedom of speech, are they going to be allowed to swear in the class?"

Maybe she was being unusually frank. Most book challengers profess a reverence for the First Amendment's guarantee of free speech, and they are stung by the vocabulary used to caricature their efforts: "banning," "censorship." "I am not in favor of censorship; I am not in favor of book banning," Sharon Lollio declared as she opened her testimony to the Plymouth-Canton school board. "I will not be made to feel like I am some kind of closed-minded fanatic because I have a problem with understanding how the passage of a book stating—" and then she read aloud the fragments of obscenities from *Beloved*.

Similarly, Ginny Maziarka in West Bend, Wisconsin, dissociated herself from a small group of supporters calling themselves the Christian Civil Liberties Union, which urged that the offending books be taken from the library and burned. She didn't know the members but thought they were outsiders who "made unreasonable demands in a most unethical and unfortunate manner. This group did more harm than good . . . Book burning is nothing more than an expression of one's position under First Amendment rights . . . I would not personally do this simply because I choose not to. If someone purchases a book and burns it to make a statement, that's their business, I suppose. Taking a book from the library and burning it, however, is stealing."

Professing a reverence for the First Amendment and an abhorrence of censorship is part of book challengers' standard spiel, an effort to preempt accusations that they are undermining the country's constitutional liberty. It's mostly sincere, too, because they typically want the books taken out of the hands of children, not taken out of print. The American Library Association marks Banned Books Week every fall, but there is a semantic argument about whether "banning" or "censorship" accurately describes the goal of removing a book from a course, a school library, or the young adult section of a public library while leaving it available online, in bookstores, and in the library's adult section. It would be more precise to say that the challengers want the books restricted or curtailed, made inaccessible to minors.

Some religious advocates do suspend their affection for the First Amendment—its bar on government establishing religion—in wishing that the Bible could be taught as a religious text in public schools. It is studied as literature in Plymouth-Canton courses, which skate on the constitutional side of the line, but book challengers often see an irony in "pornography" being allowed and the Bible being excluded.

Tony Lollio, Sharon's adult son, made the argument in an open letter. "Literature with questionable, often offensive material is included in curriculum because of its cultural relevance or historical value; while the Bible, arguably the most culturally relevant work in Western civilization, is off the table as a teaching tool," he wrote. "If this issue was about an AP English teacher assigning readings from the New Testament, would everyone file into the same side of the boardroom as they did on Monday night? Would the ACLU and the usual list of bloggers still talk about censorship and book burning?"

Of course the Bible itself has tales of violence, rape, incest, and other forms of debauchery, which those who want the challenged books retained cannot resist mentioning to those who want it taught in schools. As a rule, neither side gets anywhere with the other on this plane of religious dispute. One speaker in West Bend stood up to warn that the book supporters would face their day in judgment before God. The ultimate threat did not appear to change minds.

The great national defender of freedom in literature is the American Library Association, which is vilified from the extreme right for its efforts. The ALA advises librarians across the country on how to handle complaints, its staff helps arrange for "banned" authors to make appearances at libraries in the middle of disputes, and it assists with legal action when appropriate, often working with the American Civil Liberties Union.

The ALA is frequently pictured by book challengers as an elite, leftist, alien organization with no legitimate interest and no right to interfere in a town's affairs. The caricature is encouraged by Dan Kleinman, a New Jersey lawyer who populates his SafeLibraries website with posts such as this: "It appears some librarians support the 'Occupy' effort to overthrow the American government through violent means." Other posts carry the headlines "ALA Controls a Third of Libraries," "ALA Is Leading Porn Facilitator," "George Soros Controls ALA," "ALA Pushes Porn on Children." Beneath these titles is a set of icons with credit card logos and a button labeled "Donate."

Kleinman sounds less shrill in conversation. He is concerned about retribution, which is why he has no listed landline and uses a private mailbox as his address in Chatham, New Jersey, where he says he does not live. He's been hacked and impersonated online and, he complained, excluded from posting on Wikipedia for publishing the "truth" about the ALA. But he also urges book challengers to stick to the law in pursuing their objectives. He criticized Ginny Maziarka for raising the issue of homosexuality and urged her to calm down.

"There are plenty of people out there who are opposed to homosexuality and are opposed to reading about how the world is older than 6,000 years, or there's witchcraft," he said. "That is completely apart from the First Amendment. If you're going to bring a challenge, you've got to bring a challenge based on the law. As far as I know there is no law that says if it's about homosexuality, you've got to get it out of the library. The fact is, people with weird beliefs are never going to win, because there's not anything to back them up."

But some of them do win, not because the law is on their side, but because the local culture supports them, as in Republic and Stockton, Missouri, two cases in a long list kept by the ALA's Office for Intellectual Freedom. These victories over the freedom to read may be temporary and geographically limited, however. For every book that is challenged or removed, a new impulse of resistance is generated. A new part of the latest generation is mobilized by resentment, and a new group of young people is shaped by the denial.

That is what happened to the director of the ALA's Office for Intellectual Freedom, Barbara Jones, when she was going to high school in Sterling, Illinois, during the 1960s. Her history teacher, a Mr. James, a veteran of World War II, gave his students *The Ugly American* to read, "because he wanted us to understand how America was perceived overseas," she remembered. When Mr. James had a heart attack and was replaced for three weeks by a substitute named Dolly Fauth, the class got a cold dose of conspiratorial conservatism.

"She told us that anybody who would assign that book is not a real American," Jones said. "She handed out John Birch Society stuff." She called James a communist.

Students were outraged. "We went to the principal, and my parents did, too. When [Mr. James] came back, he stood in front of the class, and I remember tears going down his face, because it was very scary to see him like that. He said, 'I'm really glad to be back. I just want you all to know I'm a patriotic American. I love my country. I served my country. But part of my job as a teacher is to make you aware of my country's role in history.'"

Provoked by the substitute, Jones wanted "the right to read what the John Birch Society was so upset about," so she went looking for *Das Kapital* at the public library, where the librarians "wouldn't let me into the adult section." Her mother, a Republican in the bygone days of moderates, went in screaming at the librarians—a vivid memory for her daughter, who got the dense tome. "I never got through it!" she confessed.

How has the country changed since then? "Things are worse in a way," said Jones. "When I was growing up, there was a certain amount of understanding that people did not want the government messing with what they read. When my mother went into the public library and said, I want my daughter to go into the adult section, they kind of caved. Keep the government out. That's what being Republican meant.

"Now there's a moral overlay. There's more of an effort to help the parents protect the kids." She heard of a college freshman's parents who wanted to see what was on the reading list at his university. "Parents now think that keeping kids away from bad stuff will keep them safe."

The opposite may be the case. "The people in prison are not the people who read," observed Annie Busch, who ran Missouri's Springfield–Greene County Library District, which includes the branch in Republic. "Kids who read are exceptional. They understand things."

PART II

Secrets

4

The Loneliness of Thomas Tamm

We need to control the truth.

—LES RICHARDS, former NSA contractor,
quoting a counterintelligence agent

Thomas Tamm caught the first whiff of smoke, in a way. What he read as he sifted through secret communications in an office at the Central Intelligence Agency was a telltale sign of the conflagration that would eventually consume the moral standing of his country. He told no one. He said nothing to his colleague in the office, and his colleague—who had surely read the same things—said nothing to him. They went methodically about their business, keeping their silence.

"Whistleblower," a term made popular by Ralph Nader, the consumer safety crusader, is an imperfect simile. The insider who exposes wrong-doing is not exactly like the referee who whistles down a foul. It takes more than a split second to decide to risk speaking out. Only gradually, if at all, does the heat of indignation burn through the instinct for self-preservation. Only by increments does the yearning for integrity lead a man like Tamm step-by-step into the lonely reaches of his conscience.

He was a bespectacled lawyer from the Justice Department's Capital Case Unit, detailed to CIA headquarters in Langley, Virginia, to search for any exculpatory evidence that would have to be disclosed to Zacarias Moussaoui, who had been charged with involvement in the attacks of September 11, 2001. The Constitution, as interpreted by the courts, requires that prosecutors provide criminal defendants with information that supports their claims of innocence. And Tamm, a veteran prosecutor, loved the Constitution. He loved the law. So he was fulfilling a high obligation as he read classified CIA files in 2002 to see whether any prisoners anywhere had told interrogators "that Moussaoui was not part of anything and was just a clown," Tamm explained. "I think there were some cables that indicated that he wasn't a major player."

But what stunned Tamm had nothing to do with Moussaoui. It was his discovery of "extraordinary rendition," a then-secret program to torture by proxy. "It was clear reading some of the cables that we were rendering people that had been picked up on the fields of Afghanistan or in other areas," he said, "that we were rendering people to countries that conducted torture, and we knew that they conducted torture. And yet publicly the administration said that we were not doing that. So that really troubled me . . . A light went off and said, Wow, the government, they're just lying to the people."

Yet he kept it to himself.

"Yeah, I did," he answered softly. Looking back, he couldn't even think of an avenue of complaint within government, so closed was the secret system. He never went to the press about it. Only years later did others reveal, to *The Washington Post,* the practice of seizing people clandestinely and the existence of CIA "black sites" for holding them in foreign countries.

Initially, the government's duplicity bothered Tamm more than the practice of sending prisoners off to be tortured. In the CIA messages, he noticed, "we were kind of chuckling about it. My first reaction, quite frankly, is, They deserve it. Good. They deserve it. But then, you know, after you saw it again and again and again and you heard politicians saying that we don't torture people and we don't render people, it started to kind of just rub me the wrong way, really." He recalled thinking, "What we're doing, and whether that's the right or wrong policy, that's one thing. But whether we should be telling the American people that we're doing one thing and we're actually doing the exact opposite, that to me is just kind of more troublesome." It was not the last of his "troublesome" discoveries, and the next one put him in jeopardy.

Tamm did not speak in hyperbole. He was not pretentious. Unlike some leakers and whistleblowers, he did not boastfully claim to be saving democracy. His posture seemed one of simple legal rectitude, "to uphold the rule of law," as he described his devotion. He seemed partial to facts, meticulously stated. He was not flamboyant, and no stage director would have cast him as what he had been—a tough-minded courtroom prosecutor. He could play a professor or an ambassador with an exacting charm. He wore his gray hair perfectly trimmed, a white shirt and yellow tie, and a smile that rippled across his whole round face. He could laugh sardonically at his own undoing, albeit with a trace of wistfulness. In short, he was a pleasant and interesting man to be with, the kind of even-tempered moderate that reporters favor over the dogmatic whistleblowers they often meet when ferreting out important truths.

Nobody sheds his upbringing entirely, especially an official who courts retribution by exposing government transgressions. Crossing that line is an intimate journey, often begun invisibly in more youthful times. Looking back, Tamm seemed able to trace, in a feathery way, some of the origins.

Years after being driven out of the Justice Department, he still spoke with nostalgia about his childhood days in the massive building, among its somber corridors. He had been there often, for his father and uncle had risen to senior levels in the FBI. His father, Quinn, served as assistant director overseeing the FBI laboratory in Quantico, Virginia. His uncle, Edward, a ranking FBI agent who gave domestic intelligence briefings to President Franklin D. Roosevelt, later became a federal appeals court judge. Both had died well before Tamm exposed a deep government secret, so he could only speculate on how they would have reacted to what he'd done. He guessed that his father, if not his uncle, would have understood.

At home in suburban Maryland, Thomas kept a photograph of himself playing as a toddler under the desk of the FBI director, J. Edgar Hoover. Born in 1952, the boy watched John F. Kennedy's inaugural parade in 1961 from the balcony outside Hoover's office. "I remember growing up obviously being very proud of my father," Thomas said, "and enjoyed going to picnics down at Quantico and seeing rifles fired and target practice and FBI agents jumping out of helicopters. Those were very fond memories, memories of walking the halls of the Department of Justice."

Decades later, as an official, he was swept with the old sense of familiarity. "What was really kind of neat was when I went back to the Department of Justice, it looked pretty much the same. They had the same kind of opaque glass on each side of the doors of the offices."

It may seem surprising that a man who grew up embedded in a law enforcement family would eventually break the institutional code. But there was a higher code. Hoover wielded excessive authority, and when the FBI was found by the congressional Church Committee in the 1970s to have spied illegally and played demented tricks on antiwar and civil rights leaders, including Martin Luther King Jr., "my father was really upset about that," said Thomas, who was then finishing at Georgetown Law School. "He thought that it had tarnished the reputation of the bureau. He would always tell me that he thought that J. Edgar Hoover had built a really fine institution, but I knew that he was really disappointed that they had done that."

Thomas briefly considered joining the FBI, as his brother did, but was drawn instead to the courtroom, where he spent nineteen years prosecuting "murders, rapes, crimes of violence, kidnapping," in Montgomery County, Maryland. "I probably had a hundred jury trials," he said. "I consider myself first and foremost a trial lawyer."

Still, his father's legacy played on him, and he kept gazing upward, from the local level to the federal. "My goal was always to go to the U.S. Department of Justice," he explained, so when Attorney General Janet Reno created a unit to consider each capital case and recommend whether to seek the death penalty, he applied. That's how he got into the Moussaoui investigation and the CIA communications.

Reno's goal was to bring some semblance of uniformity to the Justice Department's pursuit of capital punishment, which varied geographically: If you were charged with murder in one district, the federal prosecutor there might be more inclined to seek execution than his counterpart elsewhere. In this, Tamm played an unusual role.

"I was the only attorney in the unit—there [were] eight of us—who was philosophically opposed to the death penalty," he recalled. "I remember when I was interviewed for the job and they said, If you were a legislator which way would you vote? And I said I would hope that I would have the political courage to vote against it. I know it's popular, but I don't think it's effective, I don't think it's a good deterrent. And they said, you know, that's Attorney General Reno's view. And first I said, Oh, that's good. But then the second reaction was, You know, I should have known that before I interviewed!"

At first he was very happy in his work. "It was my dream job, and I loved it," Tamm said. "I loved walking the halls and remembering that I'd done that with my father. They have a beautiful library and something that's called the Great Hall in the old Department of Justice that was built during the Depression years. And I helped try the first federal death penalty case in the Southern District of Alabama, in Mobile. We tried the case in August, and I understood why people had seersucker suits." He won commendations.

The work began to sour after George W. Bush was elected in 2000 and his new attorney general, John Ashcroft, pressed federal prosecutors to seek the death penalty routinely. Reno's rigorous skepticism was replaced by Ashcroft's enthusiasm for the ultimate punishment. That left little room for genuine discussion and challenge among Tamm and other government lawyers.

By 2003, two years after terrorists had flown planes into the World Trade Center and the Pentagon, Tamm felt moved to do more than prosecute "major drug dealers killing other major drug dealers," which typified federal death penalty cases, "and I just thought, you know, as a patriot, I thought it would be patriotic to be involved in trying to go after bin Laden and other people that were trying to harm the country."

So he applied, and was accepted, to a highly sensitive unit, the Office of Intelligence Policy and Review (OIPR), which prepared secret warrant applications under the Foreign Intelligence Surveillance Act (FISA) for clandestine monitoring of people not necessarily suspected of crimes but deemed agents of foreign states or terrorist organizations. "In retrospect, it was a horrible career move," he quipped, and he allowed himself a wry smile.

The job demanded a security clearance even more restrictive than top secret, which he obtained after a thorough background investigation. To enter the office, which was designated a SCIF, a Sensitive Compartmented Information Facility, members of the unit had to place their hands in a scanner that checked their fingerprints. "The room has been debugged; any phones in there are encrypted," he explained. "They had safes lined up and down the hallways where the documents were kept, and only certain people had the combinations. And I walked into there and the atmosphere was just really, remarkably tense." He admitted that he had never before understood the line "The only thing we have to fear is fear itself," Roosevelt's famous warning during World War II.

"The fear was just really palpable," Tamm said. The office pulsed with the "thought that any day a bomb was going to be exploded and a building was going to get blown up. In a lot of ways it was really a miserable, miserable place to work."

Tamm had been led to believe that he would be collaborating directly with FBI agents, which had appealed to him. "What I thought that meant was that I'd work with agents the way I'd worked with homicide detectives in terms of trying to put together a case, making suggestions as to what leads might be followed, you know, trying to determine when it would make sense to try to obtain a FISA warrant to try to conduct electronic surveillance."

But the decisions on monitoring had already been made by the time they reached him, and he was assigned to fill out forms and prepare files for the secret court. "There was very little discretion—and I valued the discretion I'd had as a prosecutor greatly—and there was very little investigation. It was basically almost an assembly line," he said. "There wasn't a quota system, I don't think, in the FBI, but it was viewed as an accomplishment if you obtained a FISA warrant. You got a check in your personnel file, similar to making an arrest. And so the goal was to go up on as many people and as many, what they call, facilities, which is Internet addresses and that sort of thing, as many facilities as possible."

It might sound exciting, but Tamm found it tedious. "As it progressed, I kind of learned that really what attorneys did in that unit was word processing," he said. "I actually had carpal tunnel syndrome. That's how much typing I did—that's how much typing I did!" A big laugh embraced him. "I frequently joked with people that we should get T-shirts that said, 'We Were Typists in the War on Terror.'"

The FISA system was designed for privacy protection. Enacted in 1978, after the disclosures of the FBI's domestic spying, the law restricted intelligence gathering inside the United States by requiring agencies to get approval from federal judges who sat as the Foreign Intelligence Surveillance Court in closed sessions in the Justice Department, on the same floor as the OIPR, where Tamm worked. The process was supposed to prevent the executive branch from investigating crime by evading the

Fourth Amendment, which requires officials who want search warrants and wiretap orders to swear an oath to a judge that they have probable cause to believe that specific criminal evidence will be found at a particular place.

No such probable cause or particularity is required by FISA, because "the purpose" of a FISA warrant, the law said initially, was intelligence collection, not criminal investigation. The Patriot Act after 9/11 changed "the purpose" to "a significant purpose," allowing the secret warrants for gathering criminal evidence as well as foreign intelligence, and thereby diluting the strictures of the Fourth Amendment.

But even that flexibility was not enough for the Bush administration. What Tamm did not know, as he worked diligently on FISA warrant applications, was that a shadow practice was under way to monitor communications without any warrants at all. While sending some requests to the court, the administration was also evading the secret FISA judges in ordering the National Security Agency to do surveillance on certain targets inside the United States. "The program," as it was vaguely called in Tamm's office, was held in deep secrecy, unseen to most of those who worked there. Only gradually were Tamm's suspicions aroused.

During training for his position in OIPR, Tamm had been reminded of his father's distress over the FBI's illegal surveillance three decades earlier. "Part of the training is that you learn that the [FISA] statute was formed by the Church Committee in response to overreach by law enforcement and specifically by the FBI," Tamm recalled, "so it really was sunk into me that if you're going to conduct surveillance, wiretapping, it really had to be done according to the law and not overreach." Those were the formal, official instructions—echoes of his father's principles.

But then Tamm entered a cascading sequence of discovery. "We were told that whenever you got a request for an application for a warrant, even if you are renewing one that had been in place for ninety days, you had to contact this one person in the office who would then let you know whether the phone number, we'll call it, was 'in the program.' So you would give the number. And it turns out that that was the person who was in direct contact with the NSA, and people kind of quickly learned that, or figured it out, that his connection was with the NSA, and he was checking with the NSA to see if that number was 'in the program.'"

If word came back that the number or the e-mail address or other identifying information was, indeed, "in the program," the warrant application had to be signed by the attorney general—no others who were normally authorized, not the deputy attorney general, not the CIA director, not his deputy. Furthermore, it had to be presented to the chief judge of the FISA court, not to any of the ten other judges, who served on a rotating basis.

"I was curious," Tamm said. "I tried to figure out what was different about those two tracks of cases." So he compared applications put through the normal procedure and those receiving the special treatment. "I couldn't see that there was any difference" in the documents themselves. He began to think that the difference lay in the targets, the people being monitored. In the case of at least a couple of targets, "at first it wasn't in the program, and then after ninety days when you got ready to keep it for another ninety days, all of a sudden it was in the program."

Tamm started to wonder whether some warrant applications for certain targets, considered so sensitive that they could be approved by only the attorney general and the chief judge, had been preceded by illegal surveillance that formed the basis for the applications. It was a question generated from "growing up in the house that I did," he said. His father had strongly disapproved of the FBI's "black-bag jobs," he recalled. "It came out that on occasion the FBI would break into somebody's house, get information, and then based on that information would go back and get a search warrant, and act like nothing had ever happened." His father, who had retired by the time the public learned about this violation, made no secret to his son about how he felt. "They were breaking the law to break in and get the information," Tamm said. "He was very proud of the FBI and didn't like to see them fall into disrepute.

"So that was going on in my mind, and I remember one time when I had to walk down a case that was quote 'in the program,' and I was in the judge's chambers, and the judge literally looked at this document for two hours. I mean it was an unbelievably meticulous review." Tamm let out a big sigh, as if reliving the boredom of sitting there while the chief judge at the time, Colleen Kollar-Kotelly, scrutinized the sheaf of forms in silence. "There was something about that that led me to conclude or to think or to posit that she's checking to make sure that there's nothing in there that was illegally seized," he said. She signed the order in the end.

"I did think that there was the equivalent of black-bag jobs," that the government was conducting warrantless surveillance, then bringing the result to the FISA court to get warrants, "cleaning it up," as Tamm put it. "I don't think we know the extent. My own guess is that five years down the road, ten years down the road, we're gonna learn that there were enemies lists. I'm not a conspiracy theorist . . . But I do think there's a chance, that it would not surprise me, that some of the people that [Vice President Dick] Cheney did not particularly care for in the administration were actually captured in 'the program' and reviewed."

An uneasy Tamm started asking "discreet questions." He approached one of his supervisors, Lisa Farabee, "and I said, 'Do you have any understanding of what "the program" is?' And she said no." He then quoted her as telling him, "I just assume that they're doing something illegal." Tamm got the message: Don't ask questions. "That bothered me, 'cause I thought I was there to enforce the law."

Word soon came that "the program" was "down," that "you weren't to be presenting to the court any cases that we were informed were in the program." Mark Bradley, one of the deputies in the office, who'd been a CIA officer, told Tamm he'd heard that Judge Kollar-Kotelly had discovered, in a warrant application, information collected illegally under the program, which—Tamm remembered Bradley saying—could lead to the indictment of the attorney general. (Royce Lamberth, the former chief of the FISA court, confirmed to *Newsweek* that Kollar-Kotelly believed that intelligence agencies were gathering information on American citizens without warrants, then laundering it through her court.)

All this fed Tamm's gathering indignation, but he had only a worm's-eye view: limited clues from his narrow perspective but no big picture of what later became known, that the NSA's "program" continued without FISA court approval, that the executive branch picked and chose which targets to submit to the judges and which ones to "go up on," in the idiom, without approaching the court.

The NSA gave "the program" the code name Stellar Wind. It swept up vast amounts of digital information and voice communications, both abroad—where no warrant was needed—and inside the United States, where FISA required secret warrants and made every instance where a warrant was not obtained a felony carrying a prison sentence.

Records of suspected al-Qaeda operatives seized overseas—numbers called from their cell phones, for example, or contacts by their computers—were screened for numbers and e-mail addresses in the United States. As revealed a decade later in the numerous documents released by the young NSA contractor Edward Snowden, the agency was collecting virtually all such "metadata" inside the country—meaning phone numbers and the addresses and subject lines of e-mails—so its powerful computers could map the webs of contacts. A suspected terrorist abroad might have called or e-mailed someone in the United States, that person called and e-mailed others, and those numbers and addresses were available in the NSA's vast databases.

Impatient officials did not want to bother with what David Addington, counsel to Cheney, once called "that obnoxious court." Therefore, they evaded the judges, did the surveillance, and—because the fruits of illegal searches cannot constitutionally be introduced as evidence in criminal trials—later used some of the results in sworn affidavits to get legitimate search warrants, from judges in either the FISA court or an ordinary criminal court.

So Tamm's gnawing suspicions were right on target. After he was shut down by his supervisor, his next step was to Capitol Hill, where Sandra Wilkinson, a former colleague in death penalty litigation, "was on a detail to the Judiciary Committee, and I knew she would have a security clearance. So I went to her and said there's this thing called 'the program.' I just want to know if Congress knows about it. I waited several months and didn't hear anything from her. I e-mailed her and said could we get together for a cup of coffee? And she wouldn't tell me whether Congress knew what they were doing or not. She didn't tell me whether she even made any inquiries. She just said, 'Tom, whistleblowers frequently don't wind up very well.'"

Having raised the question inside the Justice Department and then with Congress, Tamm felt he'd hit walls he couldn't overcome. Looking back, he could see other roads left untaken. He might have tried the Justice Department's inspector general, an independent official who had done some candid, fearless reports, but Tamm had heard that the office did not have sufficiently high security clearances. He might have approached James Comey, then deputy attorney general, who—it was later learned—raised objections to some aspect of the surveillance and raced to Attorney General John Ashcroft's hospital bed to head off White House officials' attempts to get a groggy Ashcroft to sign off on the program. A decade later, Obama named Comey FBI director.

It now seems clear that no internal complaint would have made an impact. The program had President George W. Bush's approval; it was not as if some scandal were being revealed that would trigger a correction.

Upset by the illegalities and frustrated by the clerical nature of the work, Tamm wanted out of the secret OIPR and back to the Capital Case Unit, where he knew there was an opening and his old boss wanted him. But this was now the Bush administration, which politicized the Justice Department so thoroughly that when Tamm was discovered to have made a small contribution to John Kerry's presidential campaign, he was blocked from returning to his previous unit. His former boss called, "and she said, 'We're not bringing you back, and that's all I'm going to say.'"

So he moved to the U.S. Attorney's office in the District of Columbia, where he could prosecute cases and return to the courtroom, a place he loved to be. He was followed by his nagging anger at the administration's evasions of the FISA court. He could not escape what he had come to know. He felt distracted and ineffectual, especially after he took his next step and was, himself, consumed with fear.

Here he had kept the secret of the "rendition" of captives to countries known to practice torture, and then, the secret of the warrantless surveillance. And now reports were seeping out that American agents under the auspices of the CIA were, themselves, torturing prisoners. His cup of grief and anger was filling to the brim. It finally overflowed. And as it did, he kept his own secret, saying nothing to his wife, Claire, or his three children about what he had learned or his decision to move across a dangerous frontier from his controlled world of officialdom into the freewheeling universe of the press.

He considered whom to contact. "I didn't think the [*Washington*] *Post* would have the guts to run the story," he said, although he did admire Dana Priest, a *Post* investigative reporter who, later and without Tamm's help, revealed the CIA's rendition and black-site operations. "She was probably someone I should have gone to," he said years afterward.

"I tried to find Seymour Hersh on the Internet," Tamm recalled, but couldn't locate a phone number for the famous reporter who had exposed the My Lai massacre in Vietnam, the CIA's domestic spying on liberal groups, and other government wrongdoing. It turned out that "he's in the regular phone book in D.C.!" Tamm declared, enjoying a deep laugh at himself. "I didn't think to look in the phone book. I kept looking on the Internet—how do you get in touch with this guy?"

So he chose Eric Lichtblau, who covered the Justice Department for *The New York Times.* "I had read some stories that he'd written, and it seemed to me he had a pretty good handle on what was going on in the department," Tamm said. During a lunch hour he walked from his office, descended into the Judiciary Square Metro station, went to a pay phone, and punched in the number of the paper's Washington bureau. It was nine years before Snowden, in 2013, galvanized the world with his own revelations about the NSA.

Tamm had an appealing, self-deprecating style, picturing himself as a silly amateur taking ineffective precautions. "That's really kind of stupid in retrospect," he said of his pay-phone caper. But how else would he have done it? "Well, not stupid so much. But I was concerned that any government phone—at that time I was thinking, Maybe they're recording everything we do. I didn't want to use a cell phone, because those are clearly not as private as regular phones. And I clearly got to the point where, Well, are they gonna be able to trace the phone booth because they'll hear the rumbling [of a train] in the background, like a Sherlock Holmes or some Hollywood fantasy, and they'll be able to time it and stuff?" He laughed lightly. "I was uncomfortable making the contact with any of my colleagues around, and I didn't want to involve my family. So that was what I did."

When Lichtblau answered, Tamm remembered saying something general—"I want to talk to you about something at the DOJ"—and there was a pause at the other end of the line, then an indication of interest, and a suggested meeting place: a downtown branch of Olsson's, a small chain of bookstores no longer in business.

This was Tamm's account, because even though he had identified himself as the source, Lichtblau was unwilling to give confirmation. Tamm's recollections closely matched Lichtblau's description, in his book *Bush's Law,* of conversations with an anonymous official who began with a pseudonym and vague outlines of what he knew.

"When I first met with him, I tried to be kind of coy, and we danced around what it was," Tamm said. "He wanted to see something that made sure I was who I said I was, and I'd brought some credentials or some-thing." Gradually, Tamm got to the point and offered as much detail as he had about the separate track of surveillance that was being conducted.

Whistleblowers often feel as if they are flying solo, without land-marks or instruments, and certainly without wingmen or ground sup-port. They are completely alone, trying to convince a reporter that what they are telling him is, in fact, the truth. But here, "one of the things that was encouraging," Tamm remembered, was that Lichtblau told him, "You know, I have this other reporter who has these sources from other agencies," presumably the CIA and the NSA. If the reporters told Tamm what those agencies were doing, Lichtblau asked, could he tell them whether it was legal? Tamm said he could give his opinion, but not as a legal authority.

The other reporter was James Risen, who teamed up with Lichtblau in the end to break the story, which won a Pulitzer Prize. Tamm met with them seven to ten times, as he recalled, listened to what they were learning, and gave them explanations of the law under FISA. "They came back to me and said, 'We're hearing that they're doing data mining.' And I said, 'That's not legal. The way I read the statute, if you collect any electronic communications, it's got to go through this court.'" The law is very plain, actually. "It's direct," Tamm said. "It's why the whole court was formed in the first place."

It seemed that Tamm became a sounding board for *Times* executives' concerns, relayed from senior administration officials who were trying to prevent the paper from publishing. The officials told the executive edi-tor, Bill Keller, and the Washington bureau chief, Philip Taubman, that the government lawyers had judged the surveillance legal. But Lichtblau and Risen had in front of them a government lawyer who said the oppo-site, and he had actually prepared FISA warrant applications and had gone before FISA judges.

More than once the reporters asked Tamm, "Is there any chance this is legal?" he recalled. "I said, 'Look at the statute . . . They are going through the court, but they're gathering stuff before they go to the court.'"

And that illegality was precisely Tamm's motivation for alerting the press. "My view of what I did was trying to uphold the rule of law . . . It's a federal crime to conduct electronic surveillance without going through the court, and so each instance of that surveillance is a five-year felony . . . My entire motivation was that basically if we're gonna do this, it should be legal and it should be authorized by the Congress." He took a breath. "I think that my father would have understood that from that perspective."

There was a more serious administration argument that was making *Times* executives hesitate, which Lichtblau and Risen also presented to Tamm. "Most of their concern was, 'They tell us we're going to have blood on our hands. We're going to have blood on our hands. *The New York Times* is going to have blood on its hands.'

"I said, How? If the whole world knows that we listen to people with a piece of paper, how is it any different if we listen to people without a piece of paper? How does that extrapolate to blood on your hands? It's ridiculous. In the intelligence field we know bin Laden stopped using satellite phones and started using couriers and stuff. How is that going to impact bin Laden if we're listening to him and we don't have a piece of paper? And we can listen to him anyway when they're overseas—that's what the NSA does."

Lichtblau and Risen had the story nailed down before the 2004 election, but the *Times* held it for more than a year, until December 2005, just before Risen was about to publish it in his book, *State of War.* The long delay, the long silence, left Tamm—and other sources, presumably— suspended in anxiety.

After the story finally ran, and created an uproar, the FBI went into overdrive searching for the leakers. Agents fanned out through various agencies asking officials whether they had talked with Lichtblau or Risen. E-mail accounts were scrutinized, and perhaps phone records. At lunch with former colleagues from OIPR, Tamm learned that all of them had been questioned by an FBI agent named Jason Lawless. Tamm waited tensely for his turn. "Then I get the phone call, and I kept putting him off, putting him off, and I told him I wasn't going to interview." As a Justice Department lawyer, Tamm knew full well that if he were questioned, he would have to answer truthfully, for lying to a federal agent is a crime. It is an effective way to narrow down the list of suspects in such a case. "I've been told that at least one other attorney said they wouldn't talk to him, I guess just based on principle," Tamm said. "I knew at that point that I needed to contact a lawyer."

As the investigation gained momentum, Tamm happened to bump into a very nervous Lichtblau at a think tank discussion on legal issues. "Eric was totally shocked to see me, so we met afterward in some hallway, kind of like in the parking garage, and I told him, Look, if you get subpoenaed, tell them right away, just go ahead and reveal me, because you're not gonna go to jail over me. You're free to reveal my identity."

It was a noble gesture, one that very few leakers ever make, but the situation never went that far, because the FBI found Tamm without needing Lichtblau's testimony. It might have been that careless e-mail from his government computer to the congressional staffer, Sandra Wilkinson, asking to get together for coffee, Tamm thought. Of course the FBI questioned her, and of course—one assumes she answered truthfully— the agent learned that Tamm had asked her about "the program."

He shook his head at his own stupidity in contacting her through government e-mail. "When you get employed at DOJ, you get told the e-mail is not your personal property. It's the government's property. Be sure you don't put smut on there, use it for personal reasons, and stuff like that." On the other hand, he'd never really counted on escaping undetected. "I thought I would be found out at some point," he conceded, partly because of the very scope of the surveillance that he was exposing.

Anxiety was eating him. He was not concentrating on his work as a prosecutor. "The reality of it is, I probably was clinically depressed. I didn't do a good job at the U.S. Attorney's office. It wasn't horrible, but, you know, it wasn't what I could have done. I was preoccupied. Every couple of weeks the agent would come by my office or call, and I just thought that things were closing in."

So he resigned in late 2006, about a year after the *Times* story appeared. "I was pushed," he said at first, then made a revision: "We agreed that it would be a mutual leaving, essentially." Perhaps it was a little more complicated. Interviewed for a documentary, *War on Whistleblowers,* he said he had left voluntarily.

"Why did you say that?" he remembered his wife, Claire, asking him when she saw the film. "I said, 'Well, if I hope to become a judge or something, I don't want people to think that I was, like, fired.'" Yes, he hoped to become a judge.

After resigning, he looked for work at law firms and other government agencies but couldn't find a permanent job, although his role as a leaker was still not known. He borrowed money from his mother's estate to hire a lawyer, which cut into his inheritance. And his descent continued down to a place that he had seen firsthand but where he had never imagined himself being.

As a prosecutor, he had signed off on search warrants. He had gone along on some of those searches, and he had witnessed police officers crashing through people's doors, moving quickly throughout a house—they call it "tossing" a house—pulling things from closets and drawers, rifling through files, and marching off with computers and all manner of personal documents. Now it was his turn.

On the morning of August 1, 2007, Tamm drove his younger son to summer school, then went to the doctor for an injured shoulder. When he came back, he "saw twelve cars on one side of the street, and I thought somebody was having a party—until I noticed that one car was blocking my driveway. And my lawyer was there. I don't think he'd been at my house before."

Home searches are brutal violations of private space, no matter how legal. Unlike the FISA evasions that Tamm had disclosed, this one was based on a legitimate search warrant issued by a judge after seeing an FBI affidavit that there was probable cause to believe that criminal evidence would be found.

Some eighteen agents poured into the redbrick house in Potomac, Maryland, and into every room, including bedrooms where his two oldest children were sleeping—his teenage daughter, about to be a college freshman, and his son, a rising college senior. They "were awakened by strangers who were wearing guns," Tamm said coldly. The FBI took calendars, Christmas card lists, and everyone's computers—but made a gesture toward his older son, Terry, who "was in an a cappella group, and he was going to Scotland that night, flying out of Dulles, and they were nice enough to mirror his computer right there on the scene, however that's done," so he could take it with him. In the dark memories of that day, a small kindness glimmered.

People on his block had no idea what was going on. "The neighbors just assumed it was a drug raid, and my college-age kids must have drugs," he said. "I tried to disabuse them. There's probably some that still think that's what it was."

Tamm had not expected this invasion. Had he been home, he would have invited the agents in, he said, because there was nothing classified there, and he had not committed a crime. He had not given the reporters any documents, had not revealed the closely guarded "sources and methods" that are so jealously protected by intelligence agencies—not that he knew them in any case. He had not told the *Times* the targets of any surveillance or the reasons for it—only that it seemed to be occurring outside the law.

But the search of the house hit Claire very hard. Of all the fallout from his actions, Tamm said, "That's my biggest regret. You know, as a prosecutor you learn that burglary victims never feel quite the same way about their house, and my wife said that right away afterwards. She was really traumatized by it."

Soon, he and his lawyer were permitted to go to FBI headquarters to look through Tamm's computer for communications governed by attorney-client privilege. He had not been charged with any crime, but "two days afterwards they said that I could plead guilty to espionage, and the sentencing guidelines would contemplate that I would go to jail for a period of time." Espionage? *The New York Times* and its readers had evidently become the new enemies.

People who risk destruction to tell unwelcome truths usually have iron spines. For Tamm, the decision to speak was all about upholding the law, not violating it. So he was not about to plead guilty to anything. "I was convinced that I had not broken any laws," he declared. "I thought I would be charged, but I thought I would probably win a trial, and my biggest concern was whether I'd get out on bond or not."

Then nothing happened. Months passed with no charges being brought. Tamm was becalmed in a fog of perpetual anxiety as the FBI continued its questioning of various people around him. Hardly anyone reached out to offer concern or support, not even his brother, a retired FBI agent, "even after he had been interviewed by the FBI agents investigating me," Thomas said. "I would have thought if it were me that I would have called to say, How are you doing, and what can I do to help? And I never heard from him. So finally, when I called him, I was thinking, Is it possible that he doesn't know what had happened? And it turns out that no, he did, and had been interviewed, and he didn't approve." Evidently, the brother had taken a different lesson from their father.

"He basically let me know in no uncertain terms that he thought I should go to jail." Thomas paused for a few moments, as if reflecting on the notion that one brother should want another in prison. How was their relationship now? Thomas guffawed. "I'd say somewhat estranged. It's amicable. We're friendly, but we're not in touch a lot."

So it went. As word spread of the investigation, former friendly colleagues abandoned him. It didn't get better after he decided to reveal himself as a *Times* source, which he did in 2008 through a series of interviews with a *Newsweek* investigative reporter, Michael Isikoff. Criminal charges were still a possibility then, and so he was politically and professionally radioactive.

"I've never heard from the vast majority of people that I'd known in the Department of Justice," Tamm said, nor from those he'd known as a local prosecutor. "It's like I'm persona non grata."

One good friend in the Justice Department's division that does regular criminal wiretapping, a woman with whom he used to have lunch regularly, had not said a word to him for six years, until he contacted her from his rented law office across from the county courthouse in Rockville, Maryland. "I just sent her an e-mail about a law clerk here who's looking to work in the Department of Justice. I thought, you know, I'll just reach out to her and say here's this résumé . . . and she has a picture on the DOJ website, and I said, 'You're looking great, and here's this résumé, hope you're well,' and she said, 'Thank you.'" That was all. He laughed thinly.

How did he interpret the curt reply? He hesitated, cleared his throat, and rubbed his hands over the polished wood of the conference room table. "Well, I think that maybe I'm still a political hot potato." He continued, "I was hurt by that, the fact that a lot of people don't talk to me, and nobody's ever reached out to say how are you doing? It's possible that they may feel that that would jeopardize their position in the department. I'm not sure . . . I suspect there are a lot of people who don't approve of what I did."

How about his family? There was a long pause. "My two boys—at least my oldest—has said that he's proud of me. And I think my wife"—

again, a sparse laugh—"my wife has come around to—she's recently said that she's proud of what I did. I don't think my daughter's commented one way or the other. And I feel like my youngest also is proud, just maybe hasn't been as vocal about it as the older one."

He felt less isolated when he was given the Ridenhour Prize for Truth-Telling in 2009, joining a celebrated series of courageous officials, employees, and activists who had taken risks to speak out. It was "one of the neatest things and one of the almost kind of best days of my life," he said. A substantial audience had assembled at the National Press Club, "a large group of people that approved of what I did. And they told my wife, and it helped her immeasurably, to know that there are actually people out there that appreciate what I did. And we go back every year now. I think she likes to keep hearing that there are a lot of people that approve of what I did."

Tamm eventually learned that the FBI had assigned twenty-five agents to his case alone. "It's an unbelievable waste of tax dollars, time that could have been spent looking for real bad guys," he scoffed. "Twenty-five agents assigned to find out who leaked about the warrantless wiretapping!"

When Barack Obama took office in January 2009, Tamm allowed himself a moment of hope. "I was so naive and stupid, I actually thought that when there was a new administration that I might get a call and say, Hey, you know what? You did the right thing. You remember that position in the Capital Case Unit? Why don't you come on back. I actually thought that might happen. And in retrospect, that's just so naive and so stupid."

In fact, the lust for leakers was just gathering steam. It led the Justice Department to assign the same prosecutor—William M. Welch II—who had supervised a team that deliberately withheld exculpatory evidence in the corruption trial of the Alaska senator Ted Stevens, whose conviction was consequently thrown out by a federal judge at the request of the attorney general. That reversal came too late for Stevens, whose conviction had contributed to his failure to win reelection and who had then died in a plane crash.

The misconduct led to a scathing rebuke of Welch and others by a special counsel's investigation. Yet here he was, hunting down leakers and threatening them with the Espionage Act, rarely invoked and widely despised in legal circles as a political instrument that could be turned against a range of dissidents and government opponents, as it was when enacted under President Woodrow Wilson in 1917.

Welch summoned Tamm before a grand jury in 2011, assuring him that he would be asked about only one page in James Risen's book, in connection with another leaker case, and would receive immunity from prosecution for any grand jury testimony. Tamm knew nothing of Risen's sources. "It's kind of like secret compartmented information," he said. "I didn't know who he was talking to in CIA; I didn't know who they might have been talking to in the NSA."

But when Tamm got into the grand jury room, "They basically asked me about everything," he said. "He basically misled me and my lawyer." As Tamm finished testifying and started to walk out with a paper clip he'd been twirling in his fingers, he turned, went back, put it on the table, and told the grand jurors, "'I don't want to take any government property.' And they all laughed." But Tamm was angry until a few minutes later, when Welch came out, went up to his lawyer, and said, "There aren't gonna be any charges." Tamm had been twisting in the wind for about five years.

Oddly enough, the name Thomas Tamm is not widely known in Washington, D.C., even by journalists and lawyers who are well-informed, who have followed closely the unfolding story of the NSA's widespread surveillance. Perhaps because he was never charged, he didn't get much news coverage, and a good number of people gave me blank looks when I mentioned that I'd interviewed him. His relative obscurity also nourished small threads of hope that he might slide into a decent job without his background becoming an impediment.

When I first met him in the spring of 2013, he was eking out a living taking assignments as a defense attorney from the public defender's office in Montgomery County, Maryland, plus occasional cases referred by the federal public defender there. The pay was low, and private clients were few. He wasn't sure how his disclosure of the warrantless surveillance program was affecting his ability to attract business.

"It's fascinating to me how many clients do Google their attorney," he said, chuckling. "And they start talking about what I did, and I say, What are you talking about? We're here to talk about what you *allegedly* did." That infectious smile filled his face. "So it's interesting. Some clients who have maybe some mental health issues have been concerned that, if the government was so interested in kind of going after me and investigating me, whether I would be the right lawyer to represent them. Is the government going to hate me because of what I have done? And that has happened in a couple of the federal cases I've been appointed to. But I've tried to assure them that this is a separate part of the Department of Justice . . . 'They're just concerned with what you've allegedly been charged with, and I don't think that the fact that I'm your lawyer is either beneficial or not beneficial to you.'"

But he needed more lucrative, steady work. "I'm struggling financially," he said, and wasn't sure he could afford to keep his house. His wife had stepped up her part-time work as an actuarial assistant for pension plans.

He had applied to be a trial lawyer with the Federal Energy Regulatory Commission, which "is something that I wouldn't need a security clearance for." His name was on the Maryland governor's short list for a low-level judgeship in a court handling drunk driving, assault and battery, and small claims. "It's kind of a high-volume court," he said. "It used to be called the People's Court, and it still performs that function." But whether Governor Martin O'Malley, an avowed progressive, would shy away from Tamm because of his role as leaker, whistleblower, truth teller, or whatever title you wanted to apply was a question that hung in the air as we talked. Tamm wasn't chosen for either of two vacancies, but he remained listed as a candidate for future openings.

He asked one good friend at the Justice Department, who remained a friend, "if he would be a reference for me applying for this judicial position, and he said yes, but he said, 'You should know I don't approve of what you did.'"

5

Thomas Drake and Friends

Uncontrolled search and seizure is one of the first and most
effective weapons in the arsenal of every arbitrary government.
Among deprivations of rights, none is so effective in cowing
a population, crushing the spirit of the individual,
and putting terror in every heart.

—JUSTICE ROBERT H. JACKSON

Thomas Drake avoided taking showers at school. While the other
boys were stripping after physical education class, Drake stayed
dressed. He did not want the kids to see the welts and bruises from his
father's beatings.

The blows would come without warning. "Never could predict,"
Drake said, clipping his sentences as if he had to catch his breath between
each one. "You had to live a perfect life with him. He was defining what
'perfect' was. So there wasn't much room for error." Suddenly "a perceived infraction, not an actual, real one," triggered explosions. "It's
quite something when you're powerless, totally helpless. And you have a
primary figure in your life beating the shit out of you. To the point where
you turn into pulp. And you can't go anywhere. There is no escape." His
voice dropped nearly to a whisper. "The worst—the worst was when he
would take his belt off."

Drake paused. Silence lingered. Did he ever fight back?

"Never did. No, I never did. I couldn't." He meant that he was literally unable, as an "extremely sickly" boy with allergies and respiratory and immunity problems that frequently kept him out of school. His father "was a very strong man. I was extremely weak. I had no defense. So I just took it."

Eventually, as Tom Drake grew older and healthier, he stopped taking it. He no longer shrank from confrontation. At home, at school, and later in the wider adult world, conflicts sustained him with a sense of virtue. Wrongdoing collided with his steely righteousness, hardened during those chaotic and terrifying years growing up.

Following the 9/11 terrorist attacks, he exposed himself to abuse from his own government by disclosing—first to Congress, then to the inspector general of the Defense Department, and finally to the American public through the press—colossal wrongdoing by the National Security Agency, which had secretly spent billions on a failed computer system and, using another program, was illegally vacuuming up the phone and Internet communications of millions of innocent Americans.

Today, as lean and straight as an iron rod, Drake carries himself with military bearing, the legacy of his years in the Air Force and the Navy. His gaze is direct. His argument is pure. Less visible are his complications.

He appears casual in a collarless dark gray pullover and jeans. His face shows little affect. Steady and controlled at the outset of a conversation, he doesn't raise his voice above a funereal intonation, as if mourning for idealism and innocence lost. As he moves deeply into his story, however, a quiet tension develops. His voice fades until he is whispering, perhaps to dramatize, perhaps because he is treading stealthily through the intimate territory of his own emotions. He seems as taut as a wire. Especially when he talks about his childhood, he sometimes begins sentences without ending them. He gestures. His eyes redden. He circles around introspection, approaching it warily.

In his telling, several landmarks stand out: his mother's fears, an uncelebrated math prize, and the fence that he and his younger brother had to build on their land in Wells, Vermont. "He forced us to work," Drake said of his father, "though we got paid a quarter an hour. I remember one day we were out putting—these were locust poles—a fence in. I guess I was pretty weak. I didn't have strength. I couldn't—there were certain things I couldn't—I would collapse after a while. And I remember once he picked me up . . . and he got his fist and pounded me back and forth, called me a goldbricker, I'm not worth anything, a piece of shit son that he had brought into the world. Being pounded into such pulp I could literally not stand up. I remember crawling from the living room—I had to crawl up the stairs to my bed. I can't even begin to tell you."

He found his refuge in mental work, not physical. Math in particular "was an escape for me, because it was so ordered. There was no uncertainty." Computer language had the appeal of clarity, based on zeros and ones. "My body might have been failing, but I had a mind. My mind made me the best in the class. So I excelled in all academics. In high school I pretty much won every award you could win, including a very significant math award, which my father actually hid from me" before the awards ceremony. His father taught math at the school and after the presentation called young Tom into his office. As if he were somehow jealous or disbelieving, he told his son that he must have cheated on the test to have scored so high.

As in many abusive households, the only constant was utter vulnerability. "My mother abandoned me when I would speak up. She would console me later when my father wasn't around. But remember, we lived in terror. What does it feel like to live in terror? And there's no one there, there's no one there to rescue you, there's no one there." He paused, then whispered, "To protect you. No one there to protect you."

His father suffered from undiagnosed ailments never clearly labeled, "maybe bipolar disorder," Tom speculated. He did not drink heavily, Tom said, but his mother became an alcoholic—"drinking with a vicious disregard to moderation," she wrote in a memoir about her experiences as personal secretary to the author Pearl S. Buck. One day, after Tom had grown into a teenager with enough size that his father's beatings had gradually tapered off, his parents' loud and ugly confrontations reached a crescendo.

"I heard screaming, hollering, from my parents' bedroom," Tom recalled. "My mother herself would sometimes be on the receiving end of physical violence. I remember, I just said, There's no way anything's gonna happen, I'm not gonna let him. So I ran into the room." His father held a shotgun, and Tom stood between them. "I told him to drop it. 'You're gonna shoot me before you shoot her' . . . And the gun was pointed, he just held it. He dropped the gun. He dropped it. That began an incredibly dark period where he would disappear."

His mother described the episode in her book: "It was Tom who turned around that terrible incident so that we were not hurt, any of us, except in dreadful emotional scars which took a very long time to heal." Divorce followed.

In a community where nobody stepped forward to help, Tom was enfolded in cold loneliness. "Family friends and colleagues later came to me in private—this was when I was a late teenager—apologizing," he recalled. "I mean, the signs were there," but his father escaped reproach. "They protected him."

As Tom matured, "I found my voice, and I found my center," he said. "I was gonna stand up for—" His eyes teared, and he stopped for a moment. "I feel the emotion now." Again, that whisper. "That I would stand up for those who couldn't stand up, I would stand up for those who had no voice. I would stand up for those who are on the receiving end of all this abuse, no matter where it came from. So."

So, he exercised his rising voice in school, where "I experienced what happens when you speak and some adult doesn't like it and decides to punish you," he said. At Burr and Burton Academy, in Manchester, Vermont, he tried out his recalcitrance on teachers. In history, science, and other classes, he made waves by questioning constantly, whether it was a teacher's certainty about evolution or a textbook's version of the past: "One of the unfortunate things in history is those in power tend to dictate how it's written." In an English course, he rejected an assignment to write candidly in his journal, despite firm instructions from his teacher, Harvey Dorfman, a combative man who tried to trespass into Tom's protected territory of intimate reflection.

"I was an extremely private person," Drake explained. "The one place where I did write a lot was in my diary—my deepest thoughts, my deepest feelings. In the journal he wanted us to do that, and I refused. I didn't trust him. And he dinged me. I got a lower grade because I wasn't being open enough in my journal. You can't be open with somebody you don't trust. So I developed trust issues. That's a fact. I had major, massive trust issues, because my trust had been violated fifty ways to Sunday, OK? The only person I could trust is myself. All right? And a few select friends."

Once he flatly rejected Dorfman's order that students complete an intrusive personality survey. "I looked at it and said, 'I choose not to.' He said, 'You will, because I'm your teacher.' I said, 'Just because you're a teacher doesn't mean that I have to take the survey.' 'Yes, you do.' 'I won't.' So I actually got up from my seat and walked out of the room. I said, 'I refuse to take the survey. It has nothing to do with the class; it's for the benefit of yourself. You're using us.'"

Drake believes that his reduced grade knocked him out of the running for valedictorian, and he finished as salutatorian. He does not credit Dorfman for anything but unpleasant lessons in imperious adult behavior. Yet the teacher might have inadvertently done him a service by becoming a foil for the boy's newfound courage. An "incredibly egocentric man," as Drake described him, Dorfman was a sometime sports columnist who, after his teaching career, helped professional baseball players as a "sports psychologist," according to *The Washington Post,* by talking to them "bluntly about their lack of mental focus." With no formal training in psychology, he was nonetheless prized by major-league teams for his confrontational common sense. "He was straightforward, eyeball to eyeball, belly button to belly button," in the words of the New York Mets pitching coach Dan Warthen. "He wasn't a pat-you-on-the-back, go-get-'em-kid type of guy. He made you stand up for yourself."

Probably by accident, Dorfman made Drake stand up for himself. They tangled on the school paper, *The Octopus,* where Drake was co-editor and Dorfman, as faculty adviser, took a hatchet to Drake's effort at philosophical musing inspired by the appearance of a comet named Kohoutek. To accompany a photograph of the comet through the school telescope, Drake had composed a meditation on "taking ourselves beyond our space and earth," offering a "perspective given by something much larger," he recalled. Dorfman "completely changed it. All the stuff I had talked about in terms of comets and background and using that as an allegory to speak about larger perspectives—what if you were on the comet looking back here? I guess I was too poetic for his taste."

It sounded like severe editing; Drake called it "censorship," refused to allow the mauled version to run, and today cites the incident in his assessment of "adults who don't like what you're writing, and because of their power and authority they're going to try to prevent you from publishing it." The picture of the comet was printed without the article.

The telescope in question figured in another conflict over integrity: Drake's initiation in facing down institutional dishonesty. He was president of the astronomy club, which uncovered the school's failure to observe the wishes of heirs to Abraham Lincoln's son Robert Todd Lincoln, an amateur astronomer who had a palatial summer home nearby. His widow had given the school his telescope along with funds to build and maintain a school observatory. But the telescope had fallen into disrepair. The barrel was warped, the glass pitted, Drake said, because "the board of trustees had been routinely pilfering the fund for other projects."

The astronomy club asked the board for a new telescope. "We kept getting delayed," Drake said, but "we knew we had the ace," namely, a planned front-page exposé in *The Octopus*. "Adults intervened: You'll get your telescope, but the rest remains silent." And that is what happened: a new eight-inch telescope in 1974 in exchange for silence. Lincoln's instrument was later returned to the observatory that he had built on his estate, where it was refurbished and reinstalled.

Drake's other project in trying to set things right in high school was deeply secret. Rampant drug use in the early 1970s made Vermont a conduit for narcotics trafficking between New York City and Montreal, with Manchester as a transfer point. Classmates were overdosing. The town's police chief, Dana Lee Thompson, was shot and killed during a pharmacy break-in. "I saw this incredible loss of well-being" from heroin and other hard drugs, Drake said. "Kids coming to school high." The miserable and dangerous scene impelled him to begin helping his best friend serve as a police informant. Their surveillance on drug dealers yielded some convictions.

Clandestine work suited him, and computers fascinated him, eventually leading to a series of intelligence jobs as an air force crewman, a naval officer, a CIA analyst, and a senior official at the NSA. In the Air Force, serving as a crypto-linguist, he was introduced to advanced computer technology as he flew in RC-135 reconnaissance aircraft from Mildenhall air base in the United Kingdom, where his father had been stationed as an air force exchange officer years before.

Drake had a little whistleblowing practice on an air force base in Arizona, where he discovered that an excessive $40,000 had been budgeted to build a simple guard shack, the money used as a slush fund for other purchases. An investigation was done, but nobody was punished. Neither did he suffer any retribution.

Years later came his loudest blast of the whistle. This time, again, no punishment for the wrongdoers, but retribution in the extreme against the man who called the foul.

The headquarters of the NSA, sardonically called No Such Agency, are located at Fort Meade, Maryland, about twenty-five miles north of Washington, D.C. It is an agency of the Defense Department, founded to break enemy codes. Across the highway from its modern buildings, a mini-city of offices housing private intelligence contractors sucks in billions in tax money for technicians and analysts who move fluidly back and forth between government and company payrolls, often throwing business to their private colleagues and eventually profiting from their own contracting decisions after transferring into the private sector themselves. "They're outsourcing eavesdropping," says the author James Bamford, who has written several books on the NSA.

The symbiosis between the National Security Agency and its profit-making contractors troubled Drake, especially when he saw public funds being wasted on a computer system that didn't work. Code-named Trailblazer, it was supposed to upgrade and modernize the NSA's capability to sort and analyze huge quantities of digital data. The agency in 1999 had paid outside contractors several billions on the program. "Ultimately, they never got anything for it except a bunch of PowerPoint slides, a lot of rich contractors," Drake said. "It was an abysmal failure."

The "waste, fraud, and abuse," as he put it, only worsened after the terrorist attacks of September 11, 2001. "I can't begin to tell you how many millionaires and multimillionaires in the contracting space were made at NSA because of 9/11," he complained. "It's freakin' obscene."

Drake had worked for a private firm himself, as a software test engineer at a small dot-com company, Integrated Computer Concepts, under contract to the NSA. Then the NSA hired him in 2001 as a senior official in its Signals Intelligence Directorate. "My first day on the job was 9/11," he said, and being present at the agency that day was illuminating. "The workforce took 9/11 really hard, because they recognized that the NSA had"—and here he punched the table between each word for emphasis. "Failed. The. Nation. This national security apparatus which was put into place in [1952] had failed. It had not prevented the next Pearl Harbor."

But while "the workforce took it hard," he noted, "leadership took it differently. They took it as an opportunity." His boss called the attack "a gift to NSA," he said. "Not an opportunity to do a top-to-bottom review. It was 'a gift.' I remember hearing, 'We're gonna get all the money we ever wanted and then some.'"

Soon after settling into his new job, Drake realized that the NSA was doing illegal surveillance, inside and outside the United States, of "U.S. persons," which the law defines as any American citizens anywhere and foreigners who are legally resident in the United States. "Shortly after 9/11, people started coming to me in private, saying, Tom, what are we doing? Equipment that we normally use outward facing to collect foreign intelligence, I'm being now directed to take that equipment and put it on U.S. networks. This is just weeks after 9/11."

The massive surveillance program, which President George W. Bush had ordered without the required warrants from the Foreign Intelligence Surveillance Court, was called Stellar Wind, the same program that came to the attention of Thomas Tamm. "I knew there was a special component of it that was designed to target journalists and reporters and in particular to find their sources," Drake said. This discovery was an alarm bell, which he later failed to heed in his own case.

To make matters worse, in his view, the agency could have complied with the law by using another program, called ThinThread, which had been developed inside the NSA in the late 1990s for much lower cost but had gone unused. It could sift data in real time, separating potentially useful information from irrelevant records derived from web searches, bank and credit card transactions, e-mails, travel records, and other digital sources.

ThinThread also swept up communications that moved through the United States—as most global Internet traffic did—and because those interceptions were illegal without warrants, the program team built encryption into the software to block access to any transmission deemed to involve a U.S. person. It also "anonymized" the data by masking individual names. The NSA, the FBI, or other government agencies could have read the content of Americans' traffic and identified the individuals only by means of a key provided by the FISA court as it issued a warrant. Furthermore, as a check on abuse, ThinThread would have tracked government analysts to be sure they weren't gaining unauthorized access to the communications. It would have come close to being an auto-

matic method of observing the law—"a phenomenal program," Drake
called it.

As a contractor for a dozen years before joining the NSA, he had met
"the brains of ThinThread," an NSA crypto-mathematician named William Binney, and others on the development team inside the agency.
Then, as an agency official himself after 9/11, Drake reconnected with
the team, became executive program director for ThinThread, and three
weeks after the attack went to his boss, the chief of the Signals Intelligence Directorate, Maureen "Mo" Baginski, to suggest that it be used.
"She rejected it out of hand," Drake recalled. "I said, 'Why?' She says,
'They've gone with a different solution. We don't need that anymore.' "
The different solution was the warrantless surveillance program Stellar
Wind.

Drake persisted. "I did everything I could to get ThinThread deployed
out onto the operational system," he said. "NSA management and leadership, through Mo, refused." She finally threw him a bone by letting
him direct ThinThread in a kind of test against the NSA's single largest
database of communications and digital transactions that had been collected but not analyzed. The results were startling.

"Without giving anything classified," he explained, "let's just say that
ThinThread in the umpteen terabytes of data that NSA had stored, both
pre- and post-9/11, discovered actual intelligence regarding al-Qaeda and
associated movements that had never been discovered: critical, action-
able, additional intelligence never known prior to 9/11 . . . This gets into
NSA's huge challenge problem. How do you make sense, how do you find
intelligence in the presence of massive amounts of data, unprecedented
amounts?"

So, he concluded, "NSA had credible intelligence that was never
shared, critical intelligence that was never discovered, critical intelligence that they ignored. And if it had been shared, had been discovered
and shared, it could have easily have stopped 9/11 all by itself." This was
not what NSA wanted known, he said, and ThinThread "was turned
on once and shut down." The 9/11 Commission never investigated this,
never interviewed Drake, and essentially gave NSA a pass.

On both his concerns—the billions in waste and the violations of
the Fourth Amendment's restrictions on government searches—Drake

followed the rules by trying to work inside his agency. He first went to Baginski. "I said, What are we doing, Mo? I've got people coming to me saying that we're in violation of the Fourth Amendment." She directed him to one of the NSA's lawyers, Vito Potenza, who later became the agency's general counsel. "So I confront him on the phone. He says, Tom, it's all legal . . . We are the executive agent for the White House. The White House has approved it," an apparent reference to an authorization issued by President Bush and renewed every forty-five days. "He made it clear," Drake said of Potenza. "Don't ask any more questions, Mr. Drake. You don't want to go there."

But Drake did ask Potenza more questions, and he got a troubling answer to one of them. He suggested that if the law was so inadequate that it was being evaded, Congress should be asked to change it. "You know what I was told?" Drake reported. "They'll say no. Not only had the wheels come off the Constitution," Drake asserted, "we were in an entirely different vehicle I no longer recognized. It was secret government by executive fiat."

Potenza might have had his own doubts, though, for he was later reported to have tried to inspect the Justice Department's internal legal opinions upholding the program. He was angrily denied access by Vice President Dick Cheney's counsel, David Addington.

Nevertheless, Drake found his conversation with Potenza "chilling, absolutely chilling. I realized in that moment, I could remain silent—I would be complicit in the subversion of the Constitution—or I could say something. And I chose to say something."

As he tells his story, Drake repeatedly cites the oath that he took four times, when being sworn into the Air Force, the Navy, the CIA, and the NSA, to "support and defend the Constitution of the United States against all enemies, foreign and domestic." He saw domestic enemies of the Constitution inside his own agency.

"The guys I worked with on ThinThread weren't gonna stick around," Drake said. "There was actually a bet that I would last three months, and I'd take a hike. I guess I was kind of stubborn. And I guess I realized I was gonna do everything I could within the system. The last thing that crossed my mind was going to the press, 'cause I would have been fired immediately."

But "the system" was not responsive to his complaints. In fact, even as he tried to work within the approved channels, he came under suspicion from his NSA superiors. Getting nowhere inside the agency, he went to Congress and cooperated fully with the congressional committees that were investigating 9/11. He testified in closed hearings of a subcommittee chaired by then representative Saxby Chambliss, Republican of Georgia, and of the joint inquiry conducted by the Senate Select Committee on Intelligence and the House Permanent Select Committee on Intelligence.

"In order to deal with Congress, NSA actually set up a war room," Drake recalled. "They commandeered the SIGINT executive briefing room. They commandeered it, it was an air-gap system [immune to eavesdropping], and all of it was dedicated to combating the congressional investigation. The joke was, Who are we at war with? The terrorists or Congress?"

Then he further antagonized the NSA brass by cooperating with an investigation by the inspector general of the Defense Department. Every federal agency has an inspector general, nominally independent, to whom employees are obliged to report "waste, fraud, and abuse" across a broad range of wrongdoing. They can do so anonymously, and Drake chose that route; in a formal complaint, he was identified only as a senior official. Four others who felt safer, having resigned, signed their names to the complaint: Binney, J. Kirk Wiebe, and Ed Loomis, all formerly of the NSA; and Diane Roark, a former staffer on the House Intelligence Committee.

But Drake's participation was hardly hidden. The inspector general established an office on the NSA campus to do interviews. "I became the primary witness," he said. "Many, many trips. I lost count. Tens of thousands of pages of documentation, if you count the physical that I would carry over in courier bags as well as electronic. Every time I went over there, it almost became comical. As soon as I'd come through the turnstile, the guard would pick up a phone." And he was certain that the room was bugged. This was inside the National Security Agency, after all.

In December 2004, the inspector general issued a report, classified top secret, with a heavily censored version released nearly four years later. A great deal of the print was blanked out by rectangles of white—called "redaction" in the euphemism of the intelligence world—so it's hard to tell how severely the agency was criticized. It may be that the most damning findings were deleted from the public copy. The surviving passages appear to confirm Drake's basic allegations about both Trailblazer and ThinThread—the first as a case of wasteful spending, the second a rejected method of making surveillance legal.

Despite his vindication—or because of it—Drake was stripped of his duties step-by-step. "They took away all my money, all my staff, even took away my functional position. It was weird. It was like you have no—a man without a job, a man without an agency." He laughed dryly. "You're in a purgatory, you really are. You have a desk, you have a phone, I still had my computer. I had a flag in my office. I could go talk to people."

He was not the first in the NSA to have this experience. "This has happened in the past. You cause too much trouble; you were perceived as not a team player. It's a sad history in terms of culture. In the end, even I could not stand the bureaucratic assault. They pick away at you."

So he applied to teach, under NSA auspices, at the National Defense University in Washington, D.C., which enrolls senior military, diplomatic, and intelligence officials. He began in August 2006 and loved "teaching strategic leadership, information strategies, ethics."

But he was being scrutinized. The previous December, *The New York Times* had published its blockbuster investigative piece disclosing the NSA's warrantless surveillance. Drake was not a source, but since he had been a burr under the saddle for a while, he was seen as a prime candidate by the FBI team investigating the leaks. Their suspicions were raised further by a series of articles beginning in the spring of 2006 by Siobhan Gorman in *The Baltimore Sun*.

Drake had not talked to the *Times* reporters, but he said he did contact Gorman in late February 2006, anonymously at first through e-mails encoded by an encryption service, Hushmail, whose server was located in Canada. He began to feel watched. "I could tell from attempts to intrude into my personal computers. Later on, I was physically surveilled, I was tracked, monitored . . . I'd get pulled aside, these random inspections, right there in front of the guard station, they're opening my car doors. They would hold me there, they would slowly come out, it was like they were making a lesson of me."

Gorman's articles described the costs and failures of Trailblazer, detailed personnel disputes and internal politicking, and reported ThinThread's having been shelved despite—or because of—its ability to encrypt Americans' information pending a warrant. She quoted "an intelligence officer familiar with the program."

According to Drake, it was a full year before Gorman knew his name. "She had no idea who I was, although editors started getting antsy," he said. It's not clear how she verified his authenticity. Perhaps, as a court document later asserted, he had contacted her at the suggestion of a congressional staffer, who vouched for him. (Following journalistic ethics in refusing to name anonymous sources, she would not confirm that she had communicated with Drake, even though he had identified himself.) In any case, her stories appear to have relied heavily on the information he provided by anonymous e-mail.

He thought a personal meeting with her would be foolhardy, especially at her office building in downtown Washington, where visitors were recorded by closed-circuit cameras and a sign-in sheet at the desk. "This is 2006," he noted, and in the wake of the *Times* story, "there's this massive national criminal security leak investigation going on. I knew that from inside NSA . . . The order had come down from Cheney: Find and fry them, no matter who it is. We're gonna put their heads on a platter. They were totally ticked off."

But in 2007, with "the noose tightening," Drake sensed, "I needed to make direct contact with her, although I knew that that was even more fraught with risk. I found out later from the FBI, as I suspected, that they were hot on my trail . . . I went there [to her office] six times, OK? The FBI actually asked me about how did I get away with that without being detected. And I take some pride in the fact that I was able to throw off their tails, although it took a lot, on all occasions except the very last meeting—except the very last one." He knew how to lose the agents "because of where I used to work, in the CIA." His success in eluding the FBI "ticked them off. It really ticked them off."

His wife, Karen, knew nothing of this. An NSA contractor herself, she needed true deniability, Drake felt. Practicing family secrecy is typical for those who disclose facts the government wants contained, and even though the silence is designed to protect spouses from criminal charges of conspiracy, it can drive wedges into marriages, as it did in his.

At 7:05 a.m. on November 28, 2007, Karen learned something of what her husband had been up to. She was getting ready to take their twelve-year-old son to school on her way to work at the NSA when a dozen agents streamed across the front yard.

"I'll always remember this rather loud knock," Drake said. "They told me later that if I hadn't responded—I was upstairs—if I had not answered the door, they were going to break it down."

They sent a couple of agents around back in case he tried to run out, and the lead agent, Paul Maric, presented him with a search warrant. "I had the presence of mind to ask them for their identification," Drake said. "That was a bit of a moment, 'cause he was ready to come in the door, and he has to stop and pull out his badge. He did not like that at all."

Drake seems still haunted by "the look in my spouse's eyes, as well as my son's." He searched for the right word. "Scared is an understatement. Fear is an understatement. Their looks, their looks are frozen." He added, "In that moment I knew that our life was forever altered . . . They told her that they were going to talk to her later when she got to work." And they did, after she went through the routine of dropping their son at school and driving to the NSA, where the FBI interrogated her for a couple of hours.

"My spouse did not take any of this very well at all," Drake said. She did not applaud his courage or integrity but rather believed that "because she worked at the NSA, I'd jeopardized the entire future of the family," he explained. "I understand." She was not fired, but "they were screwing around with her security clearance and threatening because of her association with me."

Tom and Karen were separated for nearly a year. "It's still not the same," he said. "It just isn't."

The search tormented and exhausted him, but it did not surprise him. He had been waiting for it, as if he could see a tornado aimed unerringly at his house. It had been telegraphed several months earlier, when searches had been done at the homes of all who had signed the complaint to the inspector general. Binney, who had developed the ThinThread program, was in the shower, and they pulled a gun on him—a "real dangerous" character, James Bamford said mockingly. "What? Is he gonna hit him with a code? Throw a piece of software at you!"

Drake soon heard about the searches. "Two of them came to me a couple of days later: Tom, you need to know what happened to us. You're next. They were asking about me . . . I was prepared to look out my window one day or come home to see my house wrecked."

When they finally came, the agents spent all day at Drake's, from early morning until about 5:00 p.m., and "shredded the house," he said. "They went through everything, I mean everything." They passed metal detectors over the backyard to hunt for hidden metal boxes. They searched for secret compartments and wall safes inside. "They went through every book in my library, they looked behind it, they were opening up books in case I had secret compartments in books. They went through every dish in the kitchen." They probed a false ceiling in the basement, setting off old mousetraps that he'd put there years back, the clack, clack, clack bringing a trace of comedy to a day of dismal tension.

"Something that was really chilling about what was on the search warrant was that it particularly listed Jim Risen's book, *State of War,* as if having possession of a book would be evidence of a crime," Drake said. When he asked why, he was told, "It's been our experience in terms of history that spies will often use secret codes in their books, and we need to check, just in case you have some other secret language." The warrant also listed copies of *The New York Times* and *The Baltimore Sun* as potential pieces of evidence to be seized.

As agents searched his house, Drake was questioned and kept mostly at the dining room table, where he was given the *Miranda* warning on his rights to silence and an attorney—although he was not formally in custody. He answered openly. "The reason I cooperated is that I reported high crimes and misdemeanors. It was yet another opportunity—this was the FBI. But they were not there to hear about high crimes and misdemeanors committed by the White House and the NSA . . . Paul Maric at one point during the cooperative interview said, 'Who did you piss off?' . . . I had pissed off the government. And they were just serving as bootjack henchmen. They really were. The men in black had shown up. This is the police state. How do you capture this? I lived what a police state would look like, on a very personal level. I don't want any American—that's why my speaking out gets stronger, and I've become a First Amendment activist, a constitutional activist, a freedom rights activist, a human rights activist. I don't want my fellow Americans or anyone else in the world to live what I had to live. I'm fortunate in that I remain free. But, wow."

The "wow" came from the drawn-out experience that followed the search, several years punctuated by interrogations and a grave threat in April 2008. He remembered the investigator's words this way: How would you like to spend the rest of your life in prison, Mr. Drake, unless you start cooperating? We have enough evidence to put you away—permanently.

That turned out to be a bluff, which ultimately collapsed under what Drake called "the weight of the truth."

He was indicted by a grand jury in 2010 under the infamous 1917 Espionage Act, which had been passed to facilitate the prosecution of opponents to American entry into World War I. About 2,000 antiwar activists, including socialists, anarchists, labor leaders, and German Americans were among the targets at the time. Socialist newspapers were barred from the mails.

Until the Obama administration, the law had been used mostly to prosecute spies, rarely leakers. Daniel Ellsberg was an exception, charged under the Espionage Act for giving the Pentagon Papers to *The New York Times* in 1971; charges were dismissed because of government misconduct. Samuel Loring Morison was convicted in 1985 of selling pictures of a Soviet aircraft carrier to the British journal *Jane's Defence Weekly;* he was pardoned by President Bill Clinton in 2001. Two officials of the pro-Israel lobby the American Israel Public Affairs Committee (AIPAC), Steven Rosen and Keith Weissman, were charged under the act for giving information to the Israeli embassy; the charges were dropped in 2009.

Then a flurry of leaker/whistleblower prosecutions using the Espionage Act began under Obama: Shamai Leibowitz, an FBI translator, was sentenced to twenty months in prison in 2010 for giving a blogger classified documents about Israeli diplomats. Stephen Kim, a State Department contractor, was charged in 2010 under the act for telling Fox News that North Korea planned a nuclear test in reaction to new sanctions. Also in 2010, Jeffrey Sterling, a CIA employee, was indicted under the act for allegedly leaking to James Risen details of a botched CIA effort to sabotage Iran's nuclear research. John Kiriakou, formerly with the CIA, pleaded guilty and was sentenced to thirty months after being charged under the act in 2012 for e-mailing a reporter the name of an undercover officer who supervised prisoner interrogations.

The army private Bradley Manning (now Chelsea after gender reassignment) was convicted by a military court-martial in 2013 and sentenced to thirty-five years for dumping a huge trove of classified documents onto WikiLeaks. In the same year, after a broad subpoena of phone records of the Associated Press, the Justice Department charged an FBI contractor and former agent, Donald Sachtleben, with violating the act by telling the AP about a foiled plot in Yemen to bomb a plane bound for the United States. He pleaded guilty. And Edward Snowden, the NSA contractor, was charged in 2013 under the Espionage Act for his disclosures about NSA surveillance to the British newspaper *The Guardian.*

Drake's 2010 indictment alleged "retention" of classified documents: that he had brought them home; that he had e-mailed classified material to "Reporter A" (Siobhan Gorman), and that he had made false statements to FBI agents by denying that he had done anything more than cut and paste unclassified sections of files into Word documents. This is a little trick FBI agents often use: If you haven't committed a crime and tell them you haven't, they charge you not only with that crime but also with lying to them by professing your innocence. Instead of cooperating, Drake might have been better off if he had invoked his Fifth Amendment right to silence.

However, silence is exactly what whistleblowers reject. They tend to think that they are doing the United States a service by disclosing wrongdoing, that they are helping America be the just, moral, and self-correcting place it aspires to be. In that regard, the section of the Espionage Act, 18 U.S.C. § 793(e), under which Drake and some others have been charged, contains a passage that seems like an escape clause. It criminalizes disclosure of classified information that the defendant "has reason to believe could be used to the injury of the United States or to the advantage of any foreign nation." Drake had no reason to believe any such thing. He thought he was doing his duty out of loyalty to his country.

In pretrial hearings before the judge, the government finally admitted that none of what Gorman had written was classified. Furthermore, Drake insisted, "There was no classified anywhere in my house." The bulk of the seized material duplicated what he had turned over to the congressional and Defense Department investigators, minus the classified documents that he had provided them but had not taken home. "How ironic that they used the very evidence that I had given in cooperation with official government investigations, used that against me as the basis, as the core charging document basis, for each of the felony counts, as the basis for criminally indicting me."

Significantly, the man who supervised the prosecution, beginning in 2009, was William M. Welch II, the zealous prosecutor who went after Thomas Tamm, and had himself come under unflattering scrutiny, as head of the Justice Department's public integrity section. He left the department for private practice in 2012.

His espionage case against Drake, which drew extensive press attention for its aura of exaggeration, simply unraveled. Welch rationalized the end of the prosecution by asserting that classified information would have to be disclosed in court to go forward. But it became clear that the material he was citing had been improperly classified. That fact was sworn to by the government's former classification czar J. William Leonard, who drew from his experience as director of the Information Security Oversight Office to describe a widespread pattern of overclassification. Prosecutors had contended that one key e-mail, for example, "'reveals classified technical details' of NSA capabilities," Leonard noted. "This explanation is factually incorrect," he countered. "It contains absolutely no technical details whatsoever."

In the e-mail, later released under the Freedom of Information Act, only names of NSA employees were blanked out. The rest was an embarrassing rhapsody of praise for the team on a troubled program called Turbulence, which was supposed "to continuously troll cyberspace to sniff out threats from terrorists and others, then rapidly tip off analysts who can mobilize defenses," Gorman wrote in the *Sun*. "Delays, technical problems and what critics call a vague game plan have sparked rising skepticism inside the agency and in Congress," she reported. Nevertheless, the unidentified author of the e-mail, titled "What a Wonderful Success!," gushed about the team's demonstration of the program to the NSA director: "You should be extremely proud . . . everyone in the room associated with TURBULENCE was just BEAMING with pride (especially me!)." Only later, Drake noted, was this burst of ecstasy given a "Secret" classification.

"They couldn't demonstrate to the judge that any of it was classified," Drake said. So prosecutors changed tactics. As the trial date approached in June 2011, nearly four years after his house was searched, they adjusted the charges and pressed him to plead guilty. He firmly resisted until the government dropped all felonies and offered the mildest slap on the wrist: a misdemeanor known as "exceeding the authorized use of a government computer."

He pleaded guilty to that simply because the government could have stretched out the process and the uncertainty. It could have appealed the judge's rulings that no classified information was at play. It could have refiled with different charges. Drake could have been left for years in limbo. "If you play that chicken, who's gonna blink?" he asked.

Drake won a certain vindication at sentencing for the misdemeanor, where Judge Richard D. Bennett excoriated Welch and the government. He cited the "extraordinary delay" of two and a half years between the "extreme experience" of the home search and the indictment, and a total of "four years of hell that a citizen goes through" before the government finally drops the case. "When these kinds of cases are brought I think the government has an obligation to stick with it or make amends very, very quickly," the judge declared from the bench. "It's up to the judicial branch to note the impropriety of it. It was not proper. It doesn't pass the smell test . . . I find that unconscionable. Unconscionable. It is at the very root of what this country was founded on against general warrants of the British."

Judge Bennett rejected the prosecution's request for a fine, noting that Drake had been driven out of the NSA just five years short of eligibility for his government pension and had spent $80,000 on a lawyer before being provided with a federal public defender at government expense. "There has been financial devastation wrought upon this defendant that far exceeds any fine that can be imposed by me," the judge said, "and I'm not going to add to that in any way."

Instead, he pronounced a sentence of a year's probation and 240 hours of community service, which Drake spent interviewing veterans of World War II, Korea, Vietnam, the first Gulf War, Afghanistan, and Iraq for an oral history project by the Library of Congress. It was a fascinating experience, and he allowed himself a smile as he described this "punishment," which turned out to be a contribution to his country's archive of memory.

The judge was right about the financial devastation. Drake lost his position at the National Defense University. Strayer University, where he also taught a course, fired him. He went into debt, took a second mortgage, and had to pay tax penalties for withdrawing half the money in his retirement accounts.

Before he qualified as indigent and got free representation by the public defender, he hired Tony Bisceglie, a private attorney who charged him $500 an hour. "Over the period of two years, let's just say that I pretty much exhausted all of my liquid assets and I incurred a number of other expenses, because I had no income. I had no means by which I could carry my other obligations," Drake said. "This is part of breaking and bankrupting, and that's part of the government's intent, is to flatten you as an individual."

Bisceglie estimated that it would have cost $700,000 to $1 million for a private legal defense, so he tried to get a couple of law firms to defend Drake pro bono. Drake said that they declined because they also represented defense contractors and senior government officials and did not want to jeopardize those relationships. "So I'm the sacrificial lamb," Drake remarked. "Who's Tom Drake? I'm no sugar daddy, I'm no millionaire, I don't have any other means at my disposal. I'm just an American who just happened to work as a senior executive and discovered what I discovered, and I reported it."

Bisceglie gave a different version. He approached a couple of lawyers who "would have enjoyed both the cause and the client," he said, but the firms' committees that decide what pro bono cases to take had different priorities. Some "dedicate their pro bono resources to mortgage or indigent criminal defense. I didn't see any inclination by any firm on the basis of the subject matter." It would have been expensive and high profile, but he didn't hear that they declined because they represented defense contractors.

Drake suffered lasting professional and personal costs as well. He went from a $150,000 senior government job to work in the Apple store in Bethesda, Maryland, for about $50,000 a year—a job he loved.

He once sold a computer to the daughter of a cabinet secretary, whom he asked to remain unidentified. And he once noticed Attorney General Eric Holder in the store. "He had to approve the indictment," Drake said. "He was there with his entourage, his security detail, and he was looking at iPhones, and I was with a customer about six feet away from him, and I excused myself temporarily and I introduced myself to the attorney general and said, 'Do you know why they're coming after me?' There was that moment, and he looked at me and it dawned on him who I was, and he said, 'Yes, I do.' And I said, 'But do you know the rest of the story?' He didn't answer me. He just looked down, and shortly thereafter he walked out of the store with his security detail." (Scott Shane of *The New York Times* told me, "Holder's told associates that he regrets having signed off on the Tom Drake prosecution.")

Two decades earlier, well into adulthood, Drake had managed to reconcile with his father. So after speaking unwelcome truths about the NSA, Tom felt the need to fly to Texas, where his father had retired, to explain what he had done on principle to provoke such aggressive retaliation. His father, a World War II veteran, had been a career air force logistics officer, a "brilliant mind," Tom now says admiringly, who "struggled for a long time attempting to get his hands around why would the government come after his son. That took several trips down to Texas, two extended trips to stay with him, to help him understand what had happened . . . My father's a very complex individual, but one of the things that I still remember from growing up is that he always said honesty is the best policy. And I told him, 'I was just honest, Dad, with the government, and they criminalized my honesty.'" So, in sum, "We actually talked through all this," Tom said. "It was not easy, but we did."

However, no conversation can ease the burden Drake carries about the spillover onto former NSA colleagues. Some were dismissed; others abandoned their friendships with him. "They choose not to associate with me because I'm radioactive," he said. "As one explained to me very honestly and openly, he said, Tom, I agree with everything you did. I wouldn't have done it, but I agree with everything you did. But I've got kids in college, I have a mortgage, I've got government retirement. I do not want it jeopardized. Nor do I want to lose my job, and I'm afraid that if I continue to associate with you, that's gonna happen. Or I'll be threatened with that. So I have to keep my distance."

Drake's voice finally rose, more animated by his indignation. "There's only two people left that have any contact with me from all of my time, both as a contractor and as a senior executive at NSA. That life is no more. That life is all history. That's the price, OK?"

One of those two is Les Richards, aged fifty-nine, an electrical engineer who worked as a principal program analyst for an NSA contractor. He specialized in electronic warfare, which involves analyzing and jamming enemy radar, communications, and equipment used for tracking. His extensive résumé is full of arcane acronyms and vocabulary, impenetrable by a layman.

His talents did not protect him from being tainted by his association with Drake. In 2009, at the height of the Drake investigation, "I get a phone call, a message from an FBI agent," Richards said. He thought nothing of it, because "you're always being interviewed by somebody about other people's clearances."

Two agents, a woman from the FBI and a man from NSA counterintelligence, met him in the NSA's investigative room. "She didn't read me my rights; she didn't tell me I needed to talk to an attorney. She started to ask me questions. So several hours they're grilling me about stuff in the [news]papers, and it looks like my writings, and I said, What the hell. I sent that stuff to so many people internally I couldn't even begin to tell you who got it. And they're trying to pin down that I'm the one leaking this stuff to the press.

"So we go on for hours. The thing started about nine, and about twelve, one o'clock I was let go. I was told to go back to my desk, and I went on about doing my job," which was for the Army. "The stuff I had written had to do with all the horrendous mistakes NSA was making after Congress had told them to get their act together. At no time did I think it was being done maliciously. I thought it was incompetent." In fact, he wrote a long paper and gave it the title "Incompetence!"

One issue he raised involved the insecurity of the NSA's computers. "Every electronic device has an electronic signature, even some stuff that unintentionally radiates," he explained. "Everything's leaky. That's one of those things that I was screaming about: When they changed to PCs, they were not properly shielded. If you're not careful, the PCs can put data on the power supply. Do you know where their PCs are from? China. They buy Dells and stuff. They're contaminated."

One day, the NSA's turnstiles wouldn't let him leave after a meeting. He was directed to the counterintelligence agent, who questioned him for four or five hours and accused him of including a top secret paragraph in an eighty-four-page paper on incompetence that he'd written and given to Tom Drake, among others. Richards quoted the agent as telling him, "We need to control the truth."

Finally, the NSA "yanked my access, got me to sign a nondisclosure agreement, and escorted me out of the building." His analysis: "They literally picked targets based on whoever Tom was talking to . . . I became a target because Tom was a target. Who's Tom talking to? Plus, there was stuff pulled from my documents that ended up word for word in her [Gorman's] stories. Remember, everything I wrote went to lots of people besides Tom."

Although his security clearance wasn't revoked, Richards could not get a job in his field. "I went to every freakin' place. Job fairs. People trying to do something with multimedia. I went to an interview all the way to San Diego with Raytheon, interviewed with nine people. They said you're the first person who ever came to us who knew about ELINT [electronic intelligence]. And then Raytheon fell off the planet. They didn't respond. The paranoid side of me says that someone is calling them about me." Previously, "all I had to do was throw my résumé out and I'd get fifteen offers."

He couldn't afford to stay in Maryland, so he moved to Wyoming after his wife got hired there as a physician's assistant. "There's hardly any work out here," he said. "It's all about the coal and oil and gas out here. I have applied to the five major companies out here but haven't heard anything back."

Once the curtains of silence and isolation have divorced whistleblowers from their professions, their former colleagues, and occasionally their friends and family, they have various reactions. Some withdraw unhappily, such as Thomas Tamm. Others, such as Thomas Drake, seek new zones of comfort, often within a burgeoning subculture of leakers and their defenders. It is a natural inclination for people to gravitate to others like themselves, and Drake has settled inside a circle of activism nourished by the Obama administration's zealous prosecutions. Those aggressive crackdowns on whistleblowers have given Drake a continuing cause.

In that subculture, he has found a kindred spirit in another whistleblower whose hard childhood also forged a tough rectitude: Jesselyn Radack, a former Justice Department lawyer whom he likes having by his side when he gives interviews. As Drake talks, Radack jumps in to punctuate his story with her own.

"We both grew up in very dysfunctional, very abusive households with abusive men and alcoholic mothers, actually quite similar in a number of respects," Radack explained. In high school, she moved out to live with family friends of her guidance counselor's. "You come out either completely screwed up, or you come out stronger, and I think with a deep sense of wanting to protect people. I know for me, and I think for Tom, too, it contributes to kind of wanting to devote your life to justice and sticking up for the small guy or sticking up for the underdog, which becomes more complicated when suddenly you're the underdog."

She became the underdog after she was asked for an opinion, as an official in the Justice Department's ethics unit, on whether the FBI could question John Walker Lindh, an American Taliban fighter captured in Afghanistan, without the attorney that his parents had hired for him. Given the Sixth Amendment, which guarantees the right to counsel, she and her supervisor agreed that questioning was prohibited, and Radack e-mailed her advice to the lawyer in the counterterrorism unit, using Lindh's middle name. "We don't think you can have the F.B.I. agent question Walker. It would be a pre-indictment, custodial overt interview, which is not authorized by law."

That was on a Friday. On Monday, Radack learned that the FBI agent in Afghanistan had gone ahead with the interrogation anyway, under coercive conditions that she is certain would have made Lindh's statements inadmissible had his case gone to trial. She wrote that his statement might have to be sealed or used for intelligence purposes only, not in a criminal prosecution, since the Fifth Amendment protects a defendant from being compelled "to be a witness against himself."

Lindh was read the *Miranda* warning and waived his constitutional rights to silence and to counsel, but courts have held that waivers are invalid if given unwillingly, under duress. Suffering from a leg wound and acute hunger, he was being held incommunicado in a freezing metal shipping container. The FBI agent made no recording of his statement, and his written summary was challenged by Lindh as inaccurate. Further, Lindh had been prevented from knowing that his parents had hired a lawyer, whose letter informing him, sent via the Red Cross, had been blocked from delivery by American authorities.

But Radack knew that Lindh had counsel, and she failed to fall obediently into line. She followed up with more than a dozen e-mails, pointing out that he needed medical care and that his treatment looked like torture. She questioned the Justice Department's plans to have him tried in eastern Virginia, the Pentagon's neighborhood, rather than in his home district on the West Coast.

Given the charged post-9/11 atmosphere in an area where so many residents worked for the Defense Department, the jury pool would not have been sympathetic. So with a life sentence or possibly execution looming, Lindh, his parents, and his attorney calculated that a plea bargain would be a safer bet. He got twenty years. Therefore, his treatment during interrogation never came before a court for judgment.

In any event, Lindh's guilt or innocence was not the issue before Radack when she was asked for her advice about questioning. The Constitution was the issue. And she was not a lone wolf. She consulted with colleagues all along the way. The attorney in the counterterrorism unit "agreed that it was a problematic interrogation," she recalled. Yet her persistence earned her a scathing performance review and a suggestion that she look for another job, shortly after she had received a merit raise.

She did not go job hunting until, a month later, she was stunned to learn from the federal prosecutor that only two of her e-mails had been submitted to the judge, who had ordered that all internal Justice Department documents be turned over so the court could decide whether any should be provided to the defense. She had written not two but at least a dozen, so she questioned her supervisor, who told her that everything in the file had been sent to the court. "I found the file," Radack said, "and it had two pieces of paper in it, both innocuous."

It had been purged, in the judgment of a colleague, a senior U.S. Attorney, who inspected the file at her request. She had no copies; she had erased the e-mails from her computer. What should she do? Her colleague urged her to see if they could be resurrected by the department's technicians, who were able to do so. Radack notified her supervisor, who asked why they weren't in the file. Radack had no idea, but "it was an obvious cover-up," she noted. "I said, 'I'm giving you two weeks' notice.

If the court knew how this guy was interrogated, there was no way this case could go forward.'"

The e-mails should have formed the basis of a huge scandal involving dismissals and perhaps indictments of Justice Department officials for evidence tampering and defiance of a court order. Instead, Radack became the target.

She landed a position at a Washington law firm but could not let the matter rest. She leaked word of the episode and some of her internal e-mails to *Newsweek,* prompting the Justice Department to convene a grand jury, inform the firm that she was under criminal investigation, and move (unsuccessfully) to have her disbarred in Maryland and the District of Columbia.

"They had a grand jury on me," Radack said, "and the night I was told that I was going to be arrested by my attorney, I was pregnant at that time, and I ended up having a miscarriage that night. I can't causally say, Oh, because of that. But I have no doubt in my mind that that was why. And I try to focus on the silver lining of that, which is that I now have a beautiful daughter that wouldn't have happened if not for that turn of events. But it was very, very—" She was looking down at the table, struggling for composure. "It's hard to put into words what it does to you physically and mentally." Drake looked on, tense and quiet.

No charges were brought in the end, but the law firm put her on administrative leave, paying her salary for only a couple of weeks, then suspending her pay and leaving her in what she calls "purgatory for a couple of months." She applied for unemployment benefits, and the firm packed up her office, but the partners never explicitly fired her, perhaps in recognition of a D.C. law that prohibits dismissal of someone for being a whistleblower. Her career was effectively derailed.

No refuge existed for her except one. "I was in the wilderness and was unemployed and unemployable, because that's what it does to you when the government calls you a traitor and a turncoat and a terrorist sympathizer . . . You become radioactive. It doesn't matter that you went to all these great schools"—in her case, Brown University and Yale Law School—"and have all these great degrees and background. Once you've been labeled that by your government, no one wants to touch you."

So she was propelled into the profession of perpetual whistleblower, free-speech advocate, antisecrecy campaigner. She found a place at the

Government Accountability Project, a nonprofit that helps whistleblowers in their defenses and presses for government transparency. She and Drake have become a traveling duo, flying all over the world lecturing together and heralding those who expose government wrongdoing. They visited Julian Assange of WikiLeaks in his sanctuary at the Ecuadorean embassy in London (after which she was subjected for a while to extra security checks at airports), and they presented an award in Moscow to the NSA leaker Edward Snowden, who won temporary asylum in Russia, where he was stuck when the United States revoked his passport as he tried to change planes en route to Latin America.

The dramatically diverging trajectories of those involved in whistleblower cases are like diagrams of speech and retribution, reward and punishment. Reporters usually fare well, unless they are subpoenaed and ordered by judges to divulge their sources and face jail time if they refuse. That did not happen in the Drake case. His leaks helped Siobhan Gorman win a prestigious Sigma Delta Chi Award for her stories on the NSA and propelled her into a top job covering intelligence and counterterrorism for *The Wall Street Journal*.

Drake's boss, the head of the NSA's Signals Intelligence Directorate, Maureen Baginski, did quite nicely also, much better than those who spoke out in an effort to improve the NSA's economy, efficiency, and legality. She found the key to self-preservation by sliding away from controversy and keeping her head safely down.

While Drake was being ruined financially and professionally, Mo Baginski transferred from the NSA to the FBI, where she was named executive assistant of intelligence. She then moved to the lucrative private sector, where she rose to chief executive officer of National Security Partners, which contracts with intelligence agencies. In 2012 she was named chair of the board of visitors of the National Intelligence University in Washington, D.C.—a training institution at the Defense Intelligence Agency—whose announcement of the appointment called her "one of the nation's most respected intelligence professionals."

Tom Drake, who should be one of the nation's most respected intelligence professionals, continued working in the Apple store in Bethesda, Maryland.

6

The New War Correspondents

Find the man with the unhappy look on his face.
—JAMES RESTON

J ournalists have always danced an awkward minuet with their sources. They devise levels of attribution in exchange for receiving information: "on the record" (for quotation by name), "background" (for quotation anonymously), "deep background" (for use as a statement of fact without attribution), and "off the record" (for facts not to be mentioned at all).

Each of these categories may contain subcategories of refinement: Can the anonymous source be called "a White House official" or "a congressional staffer," or must the identification be less precise to avoid giving investigators a lead? Does information provided on "deep background" have to be confirmed with a second or third source before use? Must it be written in the passive voice, e.g., "It is understood that . . ."? Does "off the record" have an escape clause that allows the disclosure to be reported if someone else, besides the original source, tells the journalist the same thing under looser ground rules?

These intricate conditions are all subject to negotiation and verbal agreement between news organizations and the officials who offer information to the public through the press. The understandings rely on trust. The reporter must trust the official to be knowledgeable and truthful. The official must trust the reporter to respect the ground rules by concealing the source's identity, even if subpoenaed.

The informal bargains, made daily in Washington over the decades, have opened windows onto policy debates, wrongdoing in various forms, and outright illegality. Without the arrangements, reporters would lose their ability to give Americans certain facts and insights that the government does not want known. And today, in the long aftermath of 9/11, a curtain would descend across the secret war against terrorism, a subject few officials are willing to discuss on the record.

Journalists who cover that conflict, who write about national security from the safety of their desks in Washington, have become a new breed of war correspondent. "Everything you're writing about is secret," observed James Risen of *The New York Times,* who faced the prospect of jail time for refusing to identify a source. So the new war correspondents dodge surveillance instead of bullets. They calibrate their movements and their contacts with care. They think about security. They try to avoid leaving digital tracks that can be followed. They camouflage their encounters.

Beginning in the Obama administration, the aggressive prosecution of leakers cast a pall of anxiety over communications between the government and the Washington press corps. Not just whistleblowers but also conforming officials who used to brief journalists on national security issues grew so fearful and reticent that the flow of unauthorized information seemed likely to dry up. In practice, however, the impact on reporters' ability to tell Americans about their government's behavior has been inconsistent. Of the war on terror, citizens have learned more than government would like and less than they need if they are to manage their democracy sensibly.

"You'd be hard-pressed," said Risen, "to find any significant fact, any major significant fact about the war on terror that hasn't been revealed, disclosed first, in the press, rather than voluntarily disclosed by the government. And so it puts an enormous burden on the press that we've had only mixed results on. But it also shows the importance of the fight against—to stop this oppressive campaign on leaks. Because that's the only way, the absolutely only way the American public has found out the details of the war on terror, has been through leaks of classified information through reporters."

The country has a stark choice, he believes. "Do you want to give up aggressive investigative reporting in order to . . . fight terrorism? It's a fundamental philosophical issue . . . The basic issue is whether or not you can have a democracy without aggressive investigative reporting, and I don't believe you can."

Correspondents use various methods to conceal the identities of officials who don't want their names in print or on the air. It's no longer enough to promise sources anonymity, given the government's capacity for electronic monitoring. Cumbersome precautions are required instead, circuitous tricks and evasions that may slow government investigators but also impede reporters. The practices make investigative journalism even more time-consuming and expensive than it has always been, in an age when financial hardships and shrinking news budgets are forcing cutbacks.

One technique can be witnessed by sitting long enough with Jesselyn Radack, the former Justice Department lawyer and whistleblower who now represents other whistleblowers. On a weekday morning in her office, her cell phone rang. She glanced at the screen, saw a row of ones on caller ID, and guessed immediately that it was a reporter. "Every time I get a phone call from 1111111, I know it's a journalist with that throwaway cell phone," she said. They're using "drug-dealer tactics . . . meeting and moving in multiple places, not communicating by phone, not giving information other than in person, never e-mailing anything of importance."

A prepaid, disposable phone, also known as a burner phone, has the advantage of a number that cannot be traced to an individual, at least in states where you don't have to show an ID to buy one. The phone's number might be revealed on caller ID if it's not blocked, but if it is, the display shows something like "Unknown Caller" or that row of ones that Radack saw. The trouble is, the number expires, so it's not practical for maintaining long-term contacts. Eric Lichtblau of the *Times* used one for a brief period but gave it up because its temporary number made it hard for sources to reach him. "It makes it very difficult to communicate after a time," he noted.

Snail mail has become popular—and frustrating. In earlier years, tipsters just phoned. "Now you're getting anonymous letters in the mail where there's no way of tracing them," Lichtblau said. "They're guarding their identity to a reporter. I got one a week ago with some intriguing stuff [saying], 'Hoping you can smoke it out on your own.'" That can be a dead end, because "there's not even any way of following up."

Some reporters avoid typing notes into their computers, preferring to write them out in longhand so they're safe from electronic spying and can easily be destroyed. Some encrypt their e-mails, as Thomas Drake of the NSA did with Siobhan Gorman of *The Baltimore Sun.* Lichtblau has used anonymous e-mails, too, but with diffidence because of "the ethical question," he remarked. "Are we trying to evade law enforcement? You're trying to use the same tactics as terrorists."

If reporters and their sources meet, they often pay for coffee or lunch with cash, not credit cards, to prevent government investigators from mining records to locate the journalist and the official at the same spot at the same time. They find places for face-to-face conversations that are hard to monitor: loud restaurants, for example. Radack prefers her porch at home "with a bunch of noisy children running around," instead of her office building in downtown Washington, D.C., an area with ubiquitous security cameras, both above ground and below. "It doesn't feel safe to meet here on K Street, where you're surveilled at every single [Metro] stop and in this building," she said.

An exclusive venue is favored by James Bamford, the author of immaculately researched books on the NSA. He is a dapper fellow who fits nicely into the rarefied ambience of the members-only Cosmos Club, an ornate turn-of-the-century mansion on Embassy Row in Washington where he invites his sources to lunch. There, amid Beaux Arts extravagance, well-guarded information is passed across the table. "I never communicate in e-mail with sources," he said over a relaxed meal at the club. "I do it here. The FBI can't get in here. They're not members." He smiled. Besides, he added, "there is club discretion: You don't gossip about who you're here with."

Routes to information, once fairly straight, are often cursed by self-imposed detours. Typical is the third-party approach to officials or government contractors. "You find their friends," said Jane Mayer of *The New Yorker,* who has written extensively on torture and surveillance, "and then you ask their friends to contact them and ask in a more roundabout way whether they might meet you."

Mayer is among the most probing and intrepid Washington journalists, seemingly unstoppable in her drive to dig and expose with exactitude. Yet her concerns about the well-being of her sources color her calculations.

In the United States and abroad, reporters have traditionally left to their sources the critical decisions about what chances to take, figuring that the disgruntled official, the political dissident, or the corporate whistleblower is better positioned than the journalist to assess the risks and figure the odds of the gamble. That is not universally correct, however. Sometimes journalists are more savvy than their sources. No official's willingness to talk relieves a responsible reporter of the burden of worry.

Mayer feels this acutely. The fear of "putting sources in just hideous jeopardy," she said, had weighed on her work. "In writing about the torture program, there was serious intimidation of some of the people who wanted to speak about it," she noted. "There were all these national security taboos. There were literally laws that they could break if they talked." Even those who were scrupulous in staying on the legal side of the line were targeted.

"I had sources who were very careful about what they said so they didn't reveal any national security secrets, but nonetheless, they were being investigated by the Justice Department for talking. And the effect of that ruined people's lives," she observed. "It cost tons of money for them to hire legal counsel. They were threatened with being charged with being traitors, facing very serious legal repercussions. These were people who had careers working for the United States government and were very dedicated to it, and the reputational damage could be terrible.

"The cliché is 'a chilling effect,'" she continued, "but it's not metaphorical when you're dealing with it. It is for real, because what it means is that you literally can't contact people who you know know things without putting their legal lives in jeopardy. You can't check things. You can't warn them of stuff you've heard. You can't continue your reporting. And so it chills the story to a deep freeze. It just ends the ability to cover something."

Furthermore, precautions are often taken in vain. "There are officials who are very high up and basically kind of authorized to talk to the press," said Scott Shane of the *Times*, "who instead of responding to the message left on their work phone will call your cell from their cell. They're trying to reduce the footprint a little."

It seems a futile evasion, for even an innocuous phone message can whet prosecutors' appetites, as in one instance that Lichtblau remembered, where "they tried to make a case on a voice mail saying, 'Hey, give me a call.' It makes it very difficult to do your job."

The precautions can also backfire. The very fact of concealment, such as encrypted e-mail, may eventually be cited by the government to claim that the official knew he was transmitting classified information. That was done in the case of Thomas Drake of the NSA, who used Hushmail with *The Baltimore Sun* but gave nothing classified, and Stephen Kim, a State Department contractor who adopted a pseudonym in e-mails with a Fox News correspondent, James Rosen, and was sentenced to thirteen months after pleading guilty to revealing classified information. Fox had reported the existence of CIA "sources inside North Korea," from which the United States concluded—mistakenly, as it turned out—that North Korea was likely to respond with more missile and nuclear tests to a UN resolution of condemnation.

The landscape is so tough to navigate that news organizations are often at a loss. "We've had whole meetings about this in the Washington bureau, with lawyers and security guys," Lichtblau said. "Should you e-mail? What kinds of conversations should you feel comfortable having? At the end of the day, a lot of reporters threw up their hands and said, Almost anything you do is going to be detectable in some way or another."

The technology that has facilitated the leak prosecutions is a double-edged sword. While it has allowed more thorough government surveillance of both reporters and officials, it has also eased access by low-level officials to classified information that would have been safely locked beyond their reach in the old days of paper.

In a couple of cases, this has been a boon to the press and alarming to government. The first dramatic example came when Bradley (now Chelsea) Manning, as a lowly army private, managed to acquire troves of diplomatic cables and other documents and transfer them to WikiLeaks for the world to see—an indiscriminate "document dump," as critics called it. Manning was sentenced to thirty-five years in prison.

Then came the telling NSA documents, released more judiciously by Edward Snowden, who galvanized Washington and other capitals with his evidence that the NSA was scooping up virtually all Americans' phone and e-mail contact information. His material went on to show that the NSA had tapped into the main links between Yahoo! and Google data centers to collect information from hundreds of millions of user accounts of Americans and foreigners. The agency was also watching and listening to friendly foreign leaders as they used their electronics.

Veterans in journalism have not yet been put out of business by the leak investigations. Information still gets to Seymour Hersh, the indefatigable investigative reporter. Known for hectoring his sources until they feel a guilt they can alleviate only by talking to him, Hersh was working on a book amid the prosecutions. "The guys I deal with," he said, are officials troubled by what they see but unwilling to throw their careers away. "Don't underestimate the impact of people on the inside who aren't whistleblowers. Some colonel wants to be a four-star. He can't stand what's going on there, but he doesn't want to be a whistleblower."

Bamford, too, seemed little affected, and he took a long view. "There are ebbs and flows in all this consideration of secrecy. Every time there's a new prosecution, there's a chilling effect," he said. "But I see ripples more than waves."

"I think it's mixed," James Risen observed. "There are some people who are obviously afraid to talk. You don't know how many of those people there are, because they don't call you or don't return your calls." In other words, you can't know how many miles of a cave are unexplored. You can't know what stories you're not hearing.

Yet some officials have come forward specifically because they watched Risen fight a legal battle for years against a subpoena to testify in the trial of a CIA case officer, Jeffrey Sterling. Again and again, Risen declared calmly that he would go to jail rather than identify a source. The more strenuously the government pursued his testimony, the more people came to him. "They say, I'm willing to talk to you because I know you're willing to protect your sources," Risen reported. "Some of them will call me or they'll contact me and they'll say, I really appreciate the way you've fought, so I want to come to you instead of somebody else."

Others have pulled back, though. Congressional staffers, once chatty about national security, are "mindful about not disclosing classified stuff," Lichtblau said. Scott Shane has found that officials who could provide context and perspective, and even press spokesmen for the CIA and other agencies, have grown reluctant.

"The border between what's classified and unclassified is this huge gray zone," Shane noted, and "where officials before were willing to meet you in the gray zone, so to speak, now many more people, maybe rank-and-file folks more than many senior folks, just don't want to enter the gray zone: What's in it for me to risk a leak investigation to help you get your stupid story?"

When I was starting out in the newspaper business, the columnist James Reston gave me this advice for getting a story out of government: Find the man with the unhappy look on his face. The technique still works, up to a point.

"There will always be people who are on fire for some personal reason, political reason, policy reason, who will be willing to talk, who are either reckless about the risks or see themselves as dissidents who are willing to take the risk," Shane observed. "But that's a small minority of folks who we deal with. You can't earn a living off those folks."

Outside the Washington Beltway, the term "classified information" has the authoritative ring of mysterious importance. But inside, everybody who deals in government understands very well the huge extent of over-classification, which encompasses so much that "nobody knows what's secret anymore," James Bamford observed.

"It's a joke; it's always been a joke," Risen remarked. "For about thirty years, from the mid-1970s," he said, "there was an unspoken agreement between the government and the press about leaks. It's kind of like that scene in *Casablanca* with Claude Rains, I'm shocked, shocked that gambling goes on here. We would get a story, we'd write it, the CIA or the FBI or somebody would get all upset about it, they would start a leak investigation, and then nothing would happen . . . Inside the government it was known as kind of a joke. The FBI agents who were assigned to a leak investigation hated it; they didn't want to do it. The internal security people at the CIA knew that they had better things to do . . . I think the problem is that this unspoken agreement has broken down."

Risen dates the breakdown to the investigation during the Bush administration into who leaked the name of Valerie Plame Wilson, an undercover CIA operative. The aggressive pursuit by a zealous special counsel, Patrick Fitzgerald, whose subpoenas of reporters and their notes held up in court, revised the unwritten rules. "Ever since the Plame case," Risen said, "every new prosecutor thinks they're going to be Pat Fitzgerald, so they're all eager to get involved in leak investigations, and they're subpoenaing reporters, including me."

The next milestone came in early 2010, about a year after Obama moved into the White House, when Private Manning contacted Wiki-Leaks. (A *Washington Post* reporter hadn't taken her seriously, she later wrote, and *The New York Times* never returned a message she left on voice mail.) Her mass disclosures stunned officials across the federal government and generated immense pressure from intelligence agencies on the Justice Department to get tough with leakers. The young president, a supposed liberal who had taught constitutional law, found himself suddenly at a crossroads. He could map out a nuanced, carefully balanced policy aimed at protecting both press freedom and truly essential secrets, or he could unleash relentless investigators to punish and suppress. He chose the latter.

Republicans' success in labeling Democrats as soft on national security surely contributed to Obama's impulse to prove otherwise. He turned out as more centrist than liberal on such matters, with aides reluctant to oppose the military and intelligence establishment. "So for political reasons they want to salute and say, Yes, this is very important," Mayer observed. "They don't want to take risks. They don't want to be blamed if something goes wrong, and so there's a real diminution of protection for civil liberties, I think. It's fascinating."

Mayer was offered an insight into the reasoning. "I was talking to a very top White House person right when Obama came in about whether they were really going to look back and hold anyone accountable for the CIA's torture program," she said. "The official told me that the last thing a young president with no national security experience needs is what he called 'a rogue CIA' coming after him. And so they were afraid themselves about the CIA. I thought it was kind of amazing."

Previously, Scott Shane explained, if the FBI had a sense of who had leaked information, "in most cases they'd go by and question and scare the hell out of them and nothing more would happen. In some cases they'd be suspended without pay, in some cases, I think, there've been some pensions docked. Or been hauled into the agency and read the riot act, just various administrative measures." That's what happened to an official he knew of at the NSA, which "didn't want to have a long, drawn-out trial making some guy a hero. So it remains a little bit of a puzzle as to what changed."

But change it did. Jesselyn Radack believes that after 9/11 the combination of increased surveillance and escalating government secrecy "inverted the usual paradigm under which our personal lives were private and the work of the government is open." Increasingly, she said, "the workings of the government became secret, and our personal lives became public."

The new climate has fostered techniques of evasion familiar to reporters who have worked in dictatorships abroad.

Mayer has been taken back to her worries in 1989 writing about the Stasi, the East German secret police: "It's a very intimidating feeling to be watched. It's inhibiting. You feel you're going to hurt people by contacting them."

"Don't get me wrong," she added. "We're nowhere near what East Germany was. But that was the first time I'd ever reported in a place where you felt you were being monitored and watched." Back then, she thought to herself, "Gosh, it's so great that the United States isn't anything like this." And now? "The thing about the national security surveillance potential in this country now is you can be surveilled without knowing it. And I'm not saying that everybody is, but the capacity exists in a way that didn't exist in 1989. And when you're reporting on people who are being surveilled, you're going to be in that net, too."

In other countries, some of the surveillance was more obvious but less extensive in the days before e-mail, cell phones, texting, and social media. Interviewing former political prisoners in South Vietnam, I had to break off meetings if I couldn't shake the secret police tails, which were not always skillful enough to be invisible. In Moscow, we correspondents assumed that our phones, offices, and apartments were bugged, and when we were followed, it was sometimes noticeable, even ostentatious, as if to intimidate us.

In the late 1970s, the Soviet Union was a place of burgeoning dissent by democracy advocates, Protestant fundamentalists, workers' rights activists, unorthodox artists, and Jews who sought to emigrate to Israel and the United States. The authorities operated against them unpredictably, issuing departure visas to some, leaving some alone, and staging political trials of others who were then imprisoned or exiled to Siberia. Many of them, thinking that they would be protected by having contact with American journalists, were not trying to conceal their meetings with us. Still, to avoid placing the less open activists at risk, we tried to be careful. Sometimes it was a bizarre game.

One rainy night in Minsk, I went down to the hotel lobby on my way to visit a Jewish dissident who had not made himself public. Seated there, pretending to read a newspaper, was a young blond man, in a light-colored sport jacket, who had been shadowing me all day. Every so often he looked over the edge of his paper. Then he stood and walked to a kiosk to feign fascination with a sparse display of pathetic souvenirs, turning periodically to glance in my direction as I stood by the door, as if waiting for the rain to abate.

I was actually waiting for a chance to evade him. There was a rhythm to his observations: looking away for a few seconds, then looking around, then looking away. I entered the vestibule and joined a crowd crammed between two sets of doors in anticipation that the downpour would ease. From the crowd I watched my watcher, who had not come prepared for the rain, and when he looked back toward his souvenir display, I knew I had a few seconds and squeezed through the outer door, then ran across the street to a bus stop, where I merged into a cluster of commuters.

Moments later, the blond man in the sport jacket—without an umbrella, poor guy—dashed out of the hotel into the dark rain and jogged down the block to a restaurant where I had eaten the night before. After he disappeared inside, the bus came. I boarded, rode away, and felt a surge of satisfaction that can come only from eluding the KGB.

The sad part of the story is that I'm reminded of my days in Moscow as I talk with national security correspondents in Washington today. Some of their precautions are reminiscent of those we used: placing calls from pay phones, not on home or office lines; avoiding substantive conversation on any phone; meeting in person, preferably outside, where microphones were presumably less effective; and checking to see if we were being followed. While in our offices or apartments, we were careful to avoid mentioning the names of dissidents we planned to visit; we used hand signals or Magic Slates, which erased the writing when a plastic overlay was lifted.

In general, reporters in Washington are not aware of being under real-time surveillance themselves. From what we've learned in leaks by Snowden and others, it seems that the massive data being collected on virtually everyone—records of phone numbers called, e-mail contacts, credit card transactions, travel information, and the like—are stored and then examined after the fact, once a story is written and investigators begin looking for the leak.

Physical surveillance seems more selective and inconsistent. Risen was surprised when I told him that when Drake and Radack met with him, they had noticed a "minder," presumably an FBI tail. "He always has a minder," Radack told me.

"It was too obvious," said Drake, the former CIA hand, who can spot tails.

"I had a minder?" Risen said. "Somebody was following me?" Yes, I answered; according to Drake and Radack, somebody was following him. "Really?" He seemed taken aback.

"You weren't aware?" I asked.

"No."

"Have you ever been aware?"

"Well, there have been occasions where I've heard about it afterwards. You know there were two grand jury investigations of my work. One was about my book. The other was about the NSA story that appeared in the *Times*. Those were going on in parallel for quite a while. And they never—they finally dropped the NSA investigation, never prosecuted anyone or indicted anyone. They never subpoenaed us in that case. My view is they didn't want to go after *The New York Times* on that story. I think they realized it would lead to a kind of a Pentagon Papers battle, a constitutional battle. And they were on very bad legal grounds given that the program itself was illegal, or arguably illegal. And so I believe that they decided to come after me on my book because they could isolate me from *The New York Times*. They could find something besides the NSA story.

"And so I know for a fact that they went through my book and investigated a whole range of leaks," he continued, "and finally decided on the one on Iran. But that wasn't the only one that I know that they investigated. And so there were a lot of FBI agents assigned to me and my work, I know, for a while. And I've heard different anecdotes about that . . . I heard that one of my sources was told that the FBI had physical surveillance of our meeting, or whatever. But I've never confirmed that. So, you know, you hear different things."

Extensive monitoring of Risen is documented in the government's legal filings in the case of Jeffrey Sterling. The brief demanding Risen's testimony makes clear that the authorities had sifted through more than the phone numbers and e-mail addresses with which Risen had been in contact. Content, at least of e-mails, was also obtained; direct quotes from Risen's messages are included. The government also inspected his credit card transactions, credit reports, and travel records. "I have no doubts that I've been under some kind of surveillance," Risen said. "I just don't know the extent of it."

On one occasion, I was certain that he was not being tailed: the day I met him at his house in suburban Maryland, on a quiet and sparsely populated street where physical surveillance would have been hard to hide. No mysterious car was lurking nearby, and nobody followed us as we drove in my car to a café that happened to be closed, then to another restaurant for coffee, and back to his house. Maybe the FBI had found more important threats to national security.

In fact, officials have told some journalists that there is no longer any need to try to force reporters to identify their sources, so sweeping is the surveillance of communications. At one meeting with intelligence officials, Lucy Dalglish, then executive director of the Reporters Committee for Freedom of the Press, remembered, "One of them was taunting me, saying, You've seen your last subpoena. We don't need your people." It sounded logical. "If you're in the Justice Department and you go after a journalist," she said, "you're committing to a two- or three-year delay in your case. So if you can build your case without going to get the reporter, you've just saved a lot of time and money."

But Risen doubts that the electronic data obviate the need for reporters' testimony. "They've been able to narrow down suspects in these leak investigations through e-mail or phone records," he explained, "and they can get indictments sometimes. But basically all they're getting is circumstantial information or circumstantial evidence from that kind of data. What they can't do is go to trial with only that . . . If you look at the government's strategy on the other cases, in which they've gotten convictions, they haven't taken any of them to trial." Instead, "they use that circumstantial evidence to pressure people to cut deals . . . and the people who they're targeting don't have the resources to fight long legal battles against the government." The result has been one guilty plea after another. Sterling became an exception.

As every reporter who has quoted anyone anonymously knows, masking the identity of a source requires withholding information: the name, of course, and the person's position and sometimes her government agency. But in addition, some journalists show a source in advance what they've written, or they discuss the wording and agree to delete or blur details as requested. This is unorthodox in normal reporting but seems reasonable when someone's freedom is at stake.

"I will take every precaution I can to protect the source, sometimes to the point of not reporting something," said Siobhan Gorman, who covered intelligence for *The Wall Street Journal.* "I would err on the side of protecting the source as opposed to getting it in the newspaper."

Others do the same for national security reasons, or—anticipating later court battles—to burnish their credentials as responsible citizens who respect government's legitimate interests in keeping certain secrets, such as the names of spies and detailed methods of intelligence gathering. "Every book I've done, I've held back stuff," said Bamford, who criticized Private Manning for her huge document dump.

Reporters and editors with a major story based on classified information routinely notify senior officials and sometimes delay or scuttle publication, or leave out certain facts, if they can be convinced that more than simple embarrassment to the government would result. The *Times* has a standing policy of not naming any undercover CIA agents who are in a foreign country, for example, as in the case of Craig Osth, who was identified as CIA station chief in Pakistan by a Pakistani political party protesting drone strikes. The *Times* withheld his name even as it was published by foreign news organizations.

Times editors listen seriously to official objections, perhaps too seriously. When Risen came up with the story that led to Jeffrey Sterling's indictment—that the United States had given Iran flawed blueprints in February 2000 that were designed to lead nuclear weapons technicians astray—the paper acquiesced in the requests of National Security Adviser Condoleezza Rice and the CIA director, George Tenet, not to publish, lest a "human asset" be placed in jeopardy and national security damaged. Three years later, Risen told the story in his book, *State of War.*

In fact, Risen's account reveals the plot as remarkably dangerous and foolhardy and raises the strong possibility that the CIA inadvertently helped Iran acquire a critical piece of technology for building nuclear bombs. No wonder the government wanted the public kept in the dark, and no wonder it then launched a vindictive prosecution to punish the CIA case officer suspected of disclosing the boondoggle.

The CIA had obtained, from a Russian defector, authentic blueprints for a TBA 480 high-voltage block used to trigger a nuclear chain reaction, Risen writes. The plans were then doctored to introduce subtle defects that would make the device harmless. However, the flaws were immediately detected by the man assigned to convey the plans to Iran—another Russian engineer living in the United States. He had not been told that this was a huge trick, so when he traveled to Vienna, where he was to leave the plans with Iran's mission to the International Atomic Energy Agency, he took it upon himself to insert a cover letter into the envelope indicating that the blueprints should be studied carefully. He warned, "If you try to create a similar device you will need to ask some practical questions," and he could provide the answers, for a price.

Whether Iranians ever contacted him Risen didn't know, but they might not have needed to, because with Pakistani weapons designs already in hand, and with Chinese and Russian expertise available to them, Iranian technicians could have rectified the plans and used them to build the trigger. The CIA had no way of monitoring their work to learn how the blueprints were used.

The most vehement government appeals to editors have been the assertions that grave damage to national security will result. But the true cost may be reckoned in the damage to the reputations of those who laid plans that were illegal or ill-conceived. Because they cross a thresh-old of acceptability or good sense, they flunk the front-page test, which every official who thinks up every bold caper should consider: Would I be comfortable seeing this on the front page of *The New York Times*? If the answer is no, then perhaps it shouldn't be done.

There are exceptions for spying scenarios, undercover operations, and military movements, but in such instances, where legitimate secrets are at stake, the more respectable response by editors is usually to delay, not cancel, the publication or broadcast or to delete details judiciously. In my five years of experience dealing with Israeli censors, who examined stories about military and national security issues, I learned that their concerns were tightly focused on very specific, minor facts that might point toward the sources or successes of their intelligence gathering. The deletions the censors demanded—in one case, the model number of a Soviet-built helicopter the Syrians were flying—did nothing to under-mine the story, which remained largely intact.

If Israeli censorship operates with a scalpel, American officials prefer a chain saw. They do not have the tool of censorship, of course, and it's hard to get the courts to order prior restraint of publication, given the Supreme Court's refusal to do so in the Pentagon Papers case. So officials can only plead with editors for self-censorship, often on a grand scale aimed at killing entire investigations, not just excising a stray fact here and there.

For thirteen months, through the presidential election of 2004, the *Times* sat on the Risen-Lichtblau story revealing the NSA's warrantless surveillance, in part because editors believed what White House officials told them falsely: that there was unanimity among government lawyers that the program was legal.

Actually, there was neither unanimity nor legality. As the reporters themselves knew from their contacts with the Justice Department attor-ney Thomas Tamm, there were divisions of opinion inside government. Furthermore, the Foreign Intelligence Surveillance Act was plainly writ-ten; even a layman could see that domestic surveillance without war-rants issued under the act was a felony. The *Times* published only when Risen's book, disclosing the eavesdropping, was about to appear. And Michael V. Hayden, then the NSA's director who pressed vehemently against publication, admitted to the *Times*'s public editor in November 2013 that he could not prove any harm, then or now, to national security.

The newspaper's delay was cited by Edward Snowden as a reason for funneling his NSA documents mostly to Glenn Greenwald of *The Guardian,* who broke the first story by publishing the FISA judge's broad order authorizing the collection of all of Verizon's metadata on phone and e-mail contacts. Laura Poitras, a filmmaker, and Barton Gellman of *The Washington Post* were also favored by Snowden, who said later, "The bottom line is that sources risking serious harm to return public information to public hands must have absolute confidence that the journalists they go to will report on that information rather than bury it." The *Post* and *The Guardian US* won the Pulitzer for their NSA stories. Only eventually did Snowden allow a large number of his documents to be provided to the *Times,* whose Scott Shane used them to write the most searching, well-reported piece on the NSA's foreign surveillance done to that point.

Suppression by editors of information uncomfortable to the government must be fairly widespread, given the instances that have come to light. In his sweeping NSA story, Shane mentioned that some facts had been withheld. When *The Washington Post* in 2005 reported the existence of CIA "black sites" overseas where suspected terrorists seized abroad were being interrogated and tortured, the paper omitted the names of the European countries that were providing prison facilities. There was no evident reason to do so other than the diplomatic upsets that would have ensued. The countries were later identified in reports by human rights and other news organizations.

On the other hand, certain delays are defensible. In 2013, Bill Keller of *The New York Times* revealed this incident as he wrote of government entreaties not to publish, lest lives be lost or intelligence sources exposed:

> We listen respectfully to such claims, and then we make our own decision. If we are not convinced, we publish, sometimes over the fierce objections of the government. If we are convinced, we wait, or withhold details. The first time I ever faced such a decision was in 1997 when I was foreign editor, and a reporter learned of a dispute between Russia and Georgia, the former Soviet republic, over what to do with a

cache of highly enriched uranium left behind after the breakup of the Soviet Union. The dispute was interesting news. But when the reporter checked, it turned out the stockpile was completely unsecured, available to any terrorist interested in constructing a dirty bomb. We were asked to hold the story until the material was fenced and guarded—and we did so. It was not a hard call.

But it is hard to know when officials are in a mode of hysterical exaggeration about the fallout from a story. In May 2012, the White House tried mightily to dissuade the Associated Press from running a piece about the CIA's interception of an underwear bomb in Yemen, newly designed without metal parts to avoid detection by airport screenings. The device, to be worn by a passenger on a flight bound for the United States, was believed to be the work of Ibrahim al-Asiri, the master bomb maker of al-Qaeda in the Arabian Peninsula. The explosive was intercepted before the would-be suicide bomber had bought a plane ticket. Other news organizations later reported that the supposed bomber was a double agent, working for the CIA.

The revelation contradicted the Obama administration's political story line, during an election year, that no al-Qaeda attacks were being planned against the United States. That was part of an effort to portray the terrorist group and its offshoots as debilitated. In addition, intelligence officials might have believed that they could keep secret the CIA's ability to place an operative with the Yemeni terrorists, even after disrupting the plot.

The AP sat on the story for several days at the government's request, "because the sensitive intelligence operation was still under way," the news agency reported. But once it became clear that publication was going ahead, the White House flipped, decided to take credit for foiling the plot, and asked the AP to delay until a press conference announcing the development could be held on Tuesday, May 8. Assisting the administration's public relations effort did not seem an adequate reason for further postponement, and the AP posted the piece on Monday, May 7.

The government then followed with the most extensive sweep of journalists' records in American history. Data were collected on twenty AP telephone lines to determine the numbers of all calls made or received by the home and cell phones of reporters and of the AP offices in Washington, D.C.; New York City; Hartford, Connecticut; and the House of Representatives. That provided information on about 100 staffers' calls. The FBI also interviewed 550 officials in an unprecedented effort to track down the leaker. In the end, a former FBI agent and bomb technician, Donald Sachtleben, pleaded guilty to providing classified information, and also to a child pornography charge.

Risen is highly impatient with the government's admonitions against reporting classified information. "I don't think anybody can point to a single story in recent history that's really damaged national security," he said. "Embarrassment. Political damage. Diplomatic damage. If you look through the whole WikiLeaks thing, I read through a lot of those cables, there's nothing in there that hurt national security. All it was was kind of embarrassing. But actually," he continued, "after reading a bunch of them, you know what this does is give me a lot more respect for the Foreign Service. They're more intelligent, better writers, and less stupid than I thought."

He was right. The cables sent back to Washington by various embassies were often erudite, sophisticated, witty, and perceptive about the countries being observed.

Further, reporters who are asked to suppress a story cannot accurately predict the impact of doing so or of going ahead and publishing. Nor should they try.

"I remember the one real lesson I had on this," Risen said, "was about a year or two before 9/11. I found the CIA had a team of agents, officers in northern Afghanistan, working with [Ahmed Shah] Massoud of the Northern Alliance to try to go after bin Laden. And I called the CIA for comment, and George Tenet called me personally and said, Don't run that story, my guys will get killed. And so I didn't run the story.

"And then 9/11 happened, and I finally wrote the story after that. And as the investigation of 9/11 went forward, I realized the whole failure of the CIA before 9/11 to do anything serious about going after bin Laden was at the whole entire heart of the 9/11 investigation, and that Tenet had repeatedly rejected a more aggressive approach in going after bin Laden in Afghanistan, and the operation I'd found out about was all they were doing—five guys sitting and drinking tea with Massoud in the north.

"And I often thought after that that if I had written that story and forced a more open debate about what to do about bin Laden, and brought congressional attention openly to what do we seriously want to do about Osama bin Laden, that that story might have helped. So that, ever since, has colored my view whenever they argue about the national security implications of a story."

Therefore, Risen squirms when asked to withhold. "I've been in a lot of those meetings on a lot of stories where they've asked. I don't like doing it; I've never liked doing it. As you know, the problem is, a lot of times it's not your decision. It's the editors' decision."

The most famous and catastrophic case of journalists' abandoning their role in getting the facts out was the *Times*'s decision to water down advance information on the Bay of Pigs invasion of Cuba. After the invasion's spectacular failure, President John F. Kennedy said that he wished the publisher had ignored his appeals to withhold details; a full-throated disclosure might have derailed the plan, saving lives and preventing a humiliating defeat.

That incident is taken by many journalists as a lesson in unpredictability and as a reinforcement of their ethics, which require the news to be reported boldly. "You can't worry about the impact of a story," said Risen. "You've just got to write it to the best of your ability under the conditions that you're operating on when you're writing it. You can't worry about having an impact, because then you're more of a social worker than a journalist."

It would be reassuring, though, to see action taken when the press exposes wrongdoing. Reporters work in the realm of pure speech. They can only report. Then it's up to others—those in office—to pick up whatever astonishment and outrage the injustice generates and make corrections. To state the obvious, journalists cannot make policy. They cannot pass laws or issue regulations. They have no subpoena power, so their investigations are limited to what they are told voluntarily. They can do no more than define and document a problem, which may or may not be enough to mobilize those with the authority to enact solutions.

At least in the beginning of their careers, professionals in the news business tend to have a lot of faith that turning a problem into the sunlight will lead to its cure. This is especially so in an open democracy, whose capacity for self-correction is nourished by information. They soon learn that sunlight is necessary but not sufficient, that the link between the diagnosis and the will to heal can be tenuous.

Muckrakers who have made an impact are lonely figures against the sky, standing out as exceptions in American history. Upton Sinclair, a journalist and socialist, did it in a 1906 documentary novel, *The Jungle,* written after spending a couple of months in the meatpacking plants of Chicago. His ruthless descriptions of filthy conditions triggered widespread disgust, most importantly in one of his readers, President Theodore Roosevelt, who ordered an investigation that led to the Pure Food and Drug Act of 1906, the federal government's entrance into the regulation of food safety.

In 1962, Michael Harrington, also a socialist, provoked policy change with his book *The Other America,* which confronted a materially comfortable political class with the specter of deep poverty. The volume, amplified and publicized by a lengthy, admiring review in *The New Yorker,* is credited with having influenced President Lyndon B. Johnson in devising the Great Society programs that included Medicare, Medicaid, Head Start, Job Corps, and the War on Poverty.

In the same year, *Silent Spring* by Rachel Carson documented the harmful effects of pesticides and led to the banning of DDT. In 1971, the publication of the Pentagon Papers by *The New York Times* helped undermine the government's credibility and feed the flames of protest against the Vietnam War by disclosing previously untold bits of history both distant and current: that the post–World War II Truman administration had assisted in France's reconquest of its colony, for example; that Johnson had waged covert warfare against North Vietnam for years before openly sending ground troops; and that the American intelligence community had predicted in 1965 (correctly) that bombing North Vietnam would not force Hanoi to abandon its support of the Vietcong and its fight against South Vietnam. Johnson ignored the secret intelligence and went ahead with years of bombing that devastated but did not dissuade.

The Pentagon Papers displayed truths the government did not want told, in keeping with the noblest purpose of a free press. So it was also with *The Washington Post*'s coverage of the Watergate scandal of 1972, in which President Richard Nixon's aides engineered, and then tried to cover up, a break-in to spy on the Democratic National Committee headquarters. The young reporters Bob Woodward and Carl Bernstein relied mainly on a single source, called Deep Throat and identified thirty-three years later as Mark Felt, No. 2 in the FBI. The stories led to Nixon's resignation in the face of probable impeachment.

Seymour Hersh, who had broken the story of the massacre by American troops of women and children in the South Vietnamese village of My Lai, wrote a front-page blockbuster for *The New York Times* in 1974 about the CIA's domestic spying. Combined with other reporting, the revelations led to several investigations, culminating in the voluminous, thoroughly documented findings of a Senate select committee headed by Senator Frank Church. Today this stands as the most solid examination of intrusive surveillance of Americans by the CIA, the FBI, the IRS, and other federal agencies, which were monitoring leaders of the antiwar and civil rights movements, including Martin Luther King Jr. Government operatives who found out about King's womanizing tried to humiliate him into committing suicide. The FBI tried to provoke violence between a street gang and the radical Black Panthers. Agents attempted to break up Panthers' marriages by sending their wives concocted letters as if written by their husbands' mistresses.

The disclosures resulted eventually in an array of privacy laws enacted to regulate intelligence gathering inside the United States, capped by the 1978 Foreign Intelligence Surveillance Act. It was this law whose restrictions were compromised after 9/11 by the Patriot Act of 2001 and the 2008 amendments to FISA.

The subsequent revelations by journalists about the NSA's massive surveillance, some of which clearly violated FISA, had virtually no impact initially in the realm of policy making. Indeed, the 2008 amendments were designed by Congress effectively to legalize the violations by the Bush administration, to make FISA into a permissive statutory platform from which the government could look down into the private lives of Americans who were suspected of absolutely nothing.

So, unlike the disclosures by Upton Sinclair, Michael Harrington, Rachel Carson, Bob Woodward, Carl Bernstein, Seymour Hersh, and other hard-digging writers over the decades, those by James Risen and Eric Lichtblau did not lead to reforms. These abortive investigations have been called "frozen scandals" by Mark Danner.

"We remember, many of us, a different time," Danner lamented in *The New York Review of Books,* "the climax of a different time of scandal that ended a war and brought down a president. In retrospect those events unfold with the clear logic of utopian dream. First, revelation: intrepid journalists exposing the gaudy, interlocking crimes of the Nixon administration. Then, investigation: not just by the press—for that was but precursor, the necessary condition—but by Congress and the courts . . . And finally expiation: the handing down of sentences, the politicians in shackles led off to jail, the orgy of public repentance."

Expiation takes time, and the post-9/11 game is not over. Beginning in the spring of 2013, when the sensational documents from inside the NSA were disclosed by Edward Snowden, a drip, drip, drip of exposés came through *The Guardian* at first, via Glenn Greenwald, then through *The Washington Post, The New York Times,* the *Los Angeles Times,* the Associated Press, and various other publications abroad. When Snowden's documents revealed that the German chancellor Angela Merkel's cell phone had been tapped, and President Dilma Rousseff of Brazil canceled a visit to Washington to protest the monitoring of her Internet activity, the ensuing uproar abroad drowned out the milder protests that had been voiced inside the United States. The White House and Congress responded more seriously to the offenses against foreign leaders than to those against ordinary, innocent American citizens.

Obama appointed a couple of committees to investigate. Senator Dianne Feinstein, chair of the Senate Intelligence Committee, displayed her first stirring of concern by denouncing the Merkel taps. A bill was introduced to prohibit the mass collection of Americans' phone and e-mail contacts, require a modicum of transparency by the FISA court, and create an advocate who could argue secretly in closed hearings against the government's warrant applications. It died in Congress.

As in previous deviations from constitutional liberty in the name of national security, the post-9/11 offenses seemed unlikely to end without an end to the threat—of terrorism, in this case—or an egregious violation so spectacular that the public and its legislators would rise up. At the time of this writing, neither had occurred.

Obama accepted some of his blue-ribbon panel's recommendations. The House passed a bill to leave metadata in the hands of communications companies—which would be required to keep the files—to be acquired only with court orders. Some companies began to respond to their customers' concerns by imposing security protections to thwart government snooping. But on balance it remained to be seen whether the Snowden disclosures, by continuing to animate opposition to broad surveillance, would reach a critical mass, enough to drive demands by well-placed Americans for a return to constitutional norms. The question turned on whether there were enough reporters who could dig deeply and dare to report what enough brave people dared to disclose.

Some writers confessed to a reluctance to tackle certain subjects because of the surveillance, according to a survey by the PEN American Center, the literary and human rights organization. The poll was taken by e-mail in October 2013 following months of disclosures by Snowden about the NSA's collection of communications information.

Of more than 520 American writers surveyed, 16 percent said they had avoided researching, writing, or speaking on particular topics, and another 11 to 12 percent said they had seriously considered such avoidance. The subjects included "military affairs, the Middle East North Africa region, mass incarceration, drug policies, pornography, the Occupy movement, the study of certain languages, and criticism of the U.S. government." Nearly one-quarter said they had stayed away from certain subjects in e-mails or phone conversations, and 28 percent had cut back or stopped their use of social media.

One writer, quoted anonymously, dropped an idea for a book on civil defense preparedness during the Cold War, saying, "What would be the perception if I Googled 'nuclear blast,' 'bomb shelters,' 'radiation,' 'secret plans,' 'weaponry,' and so on?" Another respondent, after writing an essay about a poem found on a Libyan jihad site and expressing "some sympathy for young men on the other side of the world who are tempted into jihad," reported having been put on some U.S. government list and subjected to searches for cocaine and explosives upon returning twice from Mexico.

Such reactions of extreme caution may look like paranoia, but a corrosive feature of invisible surveillance is its ability to appear in the imagination as ubiquitous and omniscient.

Insiders know its inefficiencies; intelligence analysts understand its limits. But if you are a target who minds being monitored, you are not likely to find much comfort in hearing about the inadequacies in sifting and sorting huge quantities of data. The likelihood that the watchers will overlook you may not undo the uneasy sense of nakedness. You watch yourself as you think you are being watched. You picture your words on an agent's screen and wonder how they will appear, out of context. You consider how your visits to certain Internet sites may be interpreted, and how, if you contact sketchy people "of interest" to the authorities—no matter how legitimately your journalism carries you into their orbits— you will then occupy a place in the suspicious web of connections being mapped by NSA computers.

For a man who was likely to go to jail, James Risen seemed oddly placid. Tall, strapping, in jeans and an old sport jacket, he looked as solid as an oak. He did not wince at his own predicament or doodle nervously or twist uncomfortably as we sat over coffee in a suburban café. If you'd turned off the volume and watched only the impassive expression on his face, you would never have guessed at his acerbic determination. He derided the government's assertions that news stories had compromised national security. He called intelligence officials' claims that their massive surveillance had saved the country from attacks "all bullshit—it's total bullshit."

And when it came to the government's subpoenas, and federal prosecutors' demands that he testify about his sources in the trial of Jeffrey Sterling, Risen was a bulkhead, immobile and reinforced by principle. Whatever anxiety he felt had long since abated. "I was concerned about it at first but not anymore," he said evenly. "It's been going on for five years," through one appeal after another. "It doesn't bother me anymore. I'm not nervous about it anymore. I've just gotten used to this part of my life. It's been going on forever, so I do other things. It's a marathon."

Is it enervating? "It was for a while, but it's not anymore. When the ruling [by the Fourth Circuit, denying his appeal] came out this summer, everybody was like, Oh, that's terrible! Of course they hadn't been paying attention for five years. To me it's just another day in the case that's been going on forever."

The law did not favor Risen. The press is mentioned explicitly in the First Amendment, and journalists had long argued that their ability to report freely, and therefore the constitutional right to freedom of the press, were damaged when they were forced to violate their pledges of confidentiality to sources. But the Supreme Court had never agreed.

In the controlling case, *Branzburg v. Hayes,* a 5–4 majority ruled in 1972 that the First Amendment conferred no testimonial privilege before a grand jury investigating a source's crime. A reporter who witnessed a crime had the same obligations as any citizen, the court found.

Paul Branzburg was a reporter for the *Courier-Journal* in Louisville, Kentucky, who had written about the drug scene, first a story describing the synthesis of hashish from marijuana, and later about marijuana smokers he had interviewed. He was ordered to identify the drug manufacturers and users, whom he had promised anonymity as he assembled a portrayal of the narcotics problems in the area.

The cases of two other reporters were combined with *Branzburg.* One, a television newsman and photographer, Paul Pappas, had been admitted to a Black Panther Party office in New Bedford, Massachusetts, on the condition that he photograph only an anticipated police raid (which never occurred) and not report on anything else he saw and heard inside the building. He kept his word when subpoenaed to testify before a grand jury.

The other was Earl Caldwell of *The New York Times,* an African-American reporter who argued that even stepping behind the closed doors of a grand jury room would make him suspect in the eyes of the Black Panthers, whom he was assigned to cover, "driving a wedge of distrust and silence between the news media and the militants." He had been issued a very broad subpoena, demanding that he testify and provide notes and recordings of interviews with Panther leaders about the organization's purposes and activities.

"We cannot seriously entertain the notion that the First Amendment protects a newsman's agreement to conceal the criminal conduct of his source, or evidence thereof, on the theory that it is better to write about crime than to do something about it," the Supreme Court majority declared. But stories such as Branzburg's drug investigations may actually help law enforcement "do something about it" by illuminating a hidden social situation. And insights into a radical movement are helpful to a public that needs schooling in the trends of its own society. This cannot be considered anything but useful to a democracy.

The Court expressed skepticism, however, about the dire predictions that sources would be silenced by demands for journalists' testimony. "Only where news sources themselves are implicated in crime or possess information relevant to the grand jury's task need they or the reporter be concerned about grand jury subpoenas," the majority wrote. "Nothing before us indicates that a large number or percentage of all confidential news sources falls into either category and would in any way be deterred by our holding that the Constitution does not, as it never has, exempt the newsman from performing the citizen's normal duty of appearing and furnishing information relevant to the grand jury's task." The justices added, "From the beginning of our country the press has operated without constitutional protection for press informants, and the press has flourished. The existing constitutional rules have not been a serious obstacle to either the development or retention of confidential news sources by the press."

But this is small comfort to journalists, who are always looking ahead. After all, it is crime, or the prosecutor's definition of crime, that is most sensitive to a source's desire for anonymity and to a reporter's pledge. The alleged offense in the Sterling case was the transfer to Risen of classified information, so Risen emerged as a critical witness to the supposed crime, probably the only witness besides the source—who was, perhaps, the defendant himself.

Since the ruling, lawyers for the press have hung their hopes on a slender hook provided in a concurring opinion by Justice Lewis F. Powell Jr., who signed on as the majority's deciding vote but then issued this apparent contradiction: "The Court does not hold that newsmen, subpoenaed to testify before a grand jury, are without constitutional rights with respect to the gathering of news or in safeguarding their sources." He wrote vaguely in support of striking "the proper balance between freedom of the press and the obligation of all citizens to give relevant testimony" on a case-by-case basis and concluded, "The courts will be available to newsmen under circumstances where legitimate First Amendment interests require protection." What that meant has been a matter of debate for more than forty years.

A hint of Powell's thinking can be found in his papers at Washington and Lee University, which include his notes on the justices' closed conference following oral argument in the case. "We should not establish a constitutional privilege," Powell wrote. He cautioned that one problem was defining "newsmen," an uncertainty even more acute today, in an era of bloggers and amateur witnesses who can elevate their observations into something approaching electronic journalism. But he also wrote this in his conference notes: "There is a privilege analogous to an evidentiary one," similar to those enjoyed by spouses, doctors, lawyers, and priests.

That analogy never made it into his concurring opinion, however. Instead, Powell disputed Justice Potter Stewart, who worried in a dissent that the Court was allowing law enforcement authorities to turn the news media into "an investigative arm of government." That possibility worried journalists as domestic protest boiled up during the 1960s and 1970s, when some police and prosecutors were using the subpoena to fish through news organizations' raw reporting. Knowing that anything a reporter saw or heard could end up being used against them in a court of law, dissident groups could hardly be expected to welcome the press into their midst. Closing off access would impoverish Americans' understanding of important developments in their country.

The concern prompted a flurry of shield laws passed by the states to require that prosecutors meet several conditions before demanding reporters' testimony. These usually included direct relevance to a criminal investigation, a showing that all other possible sources of evidence had been exhausted, and a balancing test in which a judge must weigh the harm the silence would do to the prosecution against the harm the testimony would do to the ability of the press to meet its obligation as a conduit of vital information to the public.

No such shield law exists at the federal level, despite four decades of congressional dithering about whether to pass one. The epidemic of leak investigations revived the idea, but the proposed legislation circulating as Risen awaited his fate displeased him mightily, for its protection excluded anything involving national security, the only area in which the government was issuing aggressive subpoenas.

"I think there is a need for a shield law, but the shield law they're talking about would be terrible," Risen said. "Virtually every leak case is about national security, so basically you're writing a shield law that will have zero effect on 99 percent of the cases that might come up." The result of such legislation would be "to create a legal definition of what is acceptable journalism and what is not acceptable journalism for the first time in American history. It would put government parameters around what is acceptable national security coverage, so I think in a weird way it would create a back-door official secrets act."

Consequently, he has no patience with media organizations pressing for such a shield law. "None of them know what . . . they're talking about in national security reporting," he said, and he fulminated about a "transparency" award given in 2011 to Obama (in a closed-door meeting) by a small constellation of groups that advocate open government, including the Reporters Committee for Freedom of the Press. "They've got, like, Stockholm syndrome," Risen declared.

Because of *Branzburg,* most lower federal judges, even those sympathetic to reporters' claims, have been boxed in by their obligation to follow precedent and have not been able to find a First Amendment right for the press to conceal a source's name in defiance of a judicial order. That's why Judith Miller of the *Times* went to jail for eighty-five days in 2005 after she lost in the lower courts and the Supreme Court refused to hear her appeal.

She had declined to identify I. Lewis "Scooter" Libby, Vice President Cheney's chief of staff, as having named Valerie Plame Wilson as an undercover CIA agent. (Miller never wrote the story, but the columnist Robert Novak did.) The disclosure was part of a tangled game of dark retribution against Wilson's husband, Joseph Wilson, who had helped give the lie to the Bush administration's concoctions about weapons of mass destruction in Iraq. Wilson, a retired diplomat, had been asked by the CIA to investigate reports that the Iraqi dictator, Saddam Hussein, was attempting to buy uranium from Niger for nuclear weapons. Wilson found absolutely no evidence, reported as much, and then wrote an op-ed piece essentially accusing the Bush administration of fabrication.

Miller was cited for contempt of court, and there was no limit to her incarceration. She got out only after Libby released her from her vow of confidentiality. He never served a day behind bars, however, because his thirty-month prison sentence was commuted by President George W. Bush.

Risen won his argument with the trial judge but lost on appeal in the Fourth Circuit. His petition to be heard by the Supreme Court was declined. That left intact the Fourth Circuit's order to testify. The only escape would be if the Justice Department decided to drop its demand that he testify, and that seemed possible when Attorney General Eric Holder told a group of journalists in May 2014, "As long as I'm attorney general, no reporter who is doing his job is going to go to jail. As long as I'm attorney general, someone who is doing their job is not going to get prosecuted."

Otherwise, Risen was ready to go to jail. "I'm willing to do it," he said. "I'm not going to give in. I'm going to keep fighting, so it depends on what the government wants to do. I'm not going to talk. I'm going to protect my sources. I'll always protect my sources."

When Risen was finally called to the witness stand, at a pretrial hearing in January 2015 to explore what questions he was willing to answer, Holder had already instructed his prosecutors to avoid asking for the name of Risen's source. But the reporter drew his line of resistance farther out, making it clear that he would not be a helpful witness for the prosecution at Sterling's trial.

"I am not going to provide the government with information that they seem to want to use to create a mosaic to prove or disprove certain facts," Risen told the court. So he jockeyed contentiously with the prosecutor, even over answers he'd given years before in a sworn submission: that he entered into confidentiality agreements and that he had interviewed Sterling, who is black, for an unrelated article about a racial discrimination lawsuit the case officer had filed against the CIA. Risen finally confirmed those earlier answers but would not say whether he had promised confidentiality to a source for the relevant chapter of his book. "In my stories or my book," he declared repeatedly, "where I say I had unidentified sources, I had unidentified sources."

The prosecutor could not get anything more. Risen did not budge. He was just the kind of reporter you'd seek out if you didn't want your life ruined for telling a significant story of wrongdoing to the American public. Therefore, the government didn't bother calling him to the stand in the trial itself, relying instead on records showing that he and Sterling had phoned and e-mailed each other. The circumstantial evidence, which lacked the content of their conversations and messages, was enough for the jury, which found Sterling guilty. Data collection overcame Risen's resolve.

PART III

Stereotypes

7

The Cultural Limits of Bigotry

I am not racist.

—DIANE FEDELE, president of a
Republican women's club in California

David Marsters, a retired police officer, was fed up with Barack Obama. "One man ruined the whole country," Marsters declared by phone a few days after being interrogated by the Secret Service. "I voted for him the first time. He's conned everybody in the nation that he's gonna change this or change that."

But the only change that Marsters saw from his rural town in Maine was a shift toward the revolting, which he watched through the peculiar lenses of Fox News, Glenn Beck, and other right-wing polemicists.

"It's getting disgusting, the whole country," Marsters said. "He's given away the country—food stamps, all that. Nobody wants to work anymore. He always blames everybody else." And Obama "was blowing smoke from marijuana" during the first presidential debate in 2012, Marsters imagined. "He was high as a kite. With Romney. That's what I feel. I got a right to my feelings."

Indeed he does. He also has a right to his speech, which he exercised in a galvanizing way in late August 2013. As the rest of his disgusting country was marking the fiftieth anniversary of the March on Washington and hearing again the ringing cadence of Martin Luther King Jr.'s inspiring call, "I have a dream," a different phrase altogether came to David Marsters, and he did not keep it to himself.

Before his line is quoted, Marsters should be allowed to make his case: "I'm not prejudiced against blacks or anything. We have many black friends." A black Baptist church was his place of worship, in the Roxbury section of Boston, before he and his wife moved to Maine. "We traveled twenty miles to go to church," he said, and loved it, at least as a social spectacle. "The service would last four to five hours, all great people. They had a band there, jambalaya, dancing around. They knew how to live. Their kids were very well trained, sat there for four or five hours, all well dressed."

This shield of non-racism did not protect him. It was quickly pierced by three words, which he posted on his Facebook page with a link to a Republican congressman's call for Obama's impeachment. "Shoot the nigger," Marsters wrote. Imagine. While much of the country was thinking, "I have a dream," Marsters was typing, "Shoot the nigger."

The landscape of free speech is vast in America, but there are boundaries, often invisible to the unwitting, who trip over the unseen taboos and then fall, bewildered, into disrepute. The list of the self-wounded is long enough, and prominent enough, to suggest that despite all that the society has learned about the traditional patterns of stereotyping, there are plenty of tone-deaf Americans. They do not hear themselves. They do not recognize the old, unpleasant discords of prejudice in their remarks, their jokes, their accusations. They surely believe what they say: that they are not racist, not anti-Semitic, not biased along the lines of ethnicity or religion. Often they are sincerely stunned when their innocent words, lighthearted words, strong words, yes, but principled words of legitimate criticism, are turned around and used to brand them as bigots.

Marsters felt the repercussions immediately. He was a relative newcomer who had come just three years earlier, at the age of sixty-five, from Malden, Massachusetts, to the village of Sabattus, which straddles the Maine Turnpike south of Augusta. He noticed, with annoyance, that Sabattus residents who were not willing to serve in town offices were nonetheless "the first to bitch," so he volunteered and was seated on the Ordinance Review Committee, the Budget Committee, and the Charter Commission.

Amid a rash of home break-ins, he made a stir by proposing a law that would have required every household to own a gun; it was voted down. He also set his sights on a run for selectman. All this made him a quasi-public figure, ripe for unwelcome press coverage, all the way from the *Bangor Daily News* to the New York *Daily News,* when his terse remedy for the Obama problem went up on Facebook.

First, the local government forced him to resign from the committees, with the town manager, Andrew Gilmore, calling his Facebook remark "deplorably hateful, dangerous, and exactly opposite of all this country and the town of Sabattus stands for."

Then, Marsters recalled, "My police department where I live called me up and [said], Dave, come down at two o'clock. We want to talk to you about it." When he walked into the office, in the one-story, cream-colored municipal building, he saw "a guy there with civilian clothes on. I knew he was Secret Service. I'm a retired cop, and I can smell 'em a mile away . . . He's a young kid, fresh out of the academy, stationed up here in Maine."

The fledgling agent was obviously interested in only one of the two components of the Facebook post—not the racist epithet, but the apparent threat. "It's against the law to threaten the president of the United States," Marsters acknowledged. "People took it as a threat. I talked to many people who didn't take it as a threat," and he said he didn't mean it literally. He meant "do something about it. Impeach him . . . They've been trying to get rid of him. They've been talking about it for two years now." In the immediate clarity of hindsight, he called his typed sentence a "slip of the finger."

The agent issued Marsters the *Miranda* warning about his rights to silence and counsel and asked Marsters for his name, his date of birth, his children's names and addresses, his educational background, and his military service. "Have you ever been to Washington, D.C.?" Marsters remembered being asked. "Did you ever go to any rallies for Obama?" No. "Ever go to rallies around here for Obama?" No. He took Marsters's picture and asked for consent to search his house for weapons.

The retired cop knew the routine very well, and he gave consent, thereby waiving his Fourth Amendment right against a search without probable cause, which would have required the agent to get a warrant from a judge. Marsters told the agent up front that he had one weapon, a handgun. "I showed it to him before he searched the house," Marsters said, and then, accompanied by local police, "he searched the house for more weapons."

He found nothing else and left the gun. "I had a concealed weapons permit," Marsters said. "Three days later the chief of police wrote me a letter and revoked it, said I was not of good character."

The Secret Service agent interviewed his wife and neighbors and required Marsters to sign an affidavit stating that he had not been hospitalized for mental illness and was not taking drugs for any psychological ailment. He told Marsters that the agency would check, and "if you lied, we'll come back to you again."

As a former law enforcement officer, Marsters voiced no complaint. "They have to do their job, that's how I figure," he said. "They took it as a threat. The town manager took it as a threat, the police chief took it as a threat, the sheriff took it as a threat." But Marsters wasn't worried. "They can't find a black mark against me. I never had a parking ticket, haven't been arrested, was a cop, thirty years in the military."

Under federal law, it takes less to activate an investigation into threatening words against the president than it does, say, against your boss or your neighbor. Pure speech, even ugly speech, is protected by the First Amendment unless it crosses limits into criminal conspiracy or incitement. So police departments usually don't act on stated threats alone without accompanying action that rises to the level of harassment or imminent danger.

The president, however, enjoys special protection under the statute, which states, "Whoever knowingly and willfully [makes] any threat to take the life of, to kidnap, or to inflict bodily harm upon the President of the United States . . . shall be fined under this title or imprisoned not more than five years, or both."

But what constitutes a threat? The Secret Service uses a three-pronged test before bringing charges: Agents must determine that the person in question actually made the statement, did so "knowingly and willfully," and meant it as a true threat. No proof is needed that the individual intended to carry it out.

"The Secret Service is interested in legitimate information relating to threats, plans or attempts by individuals, groups or organizations to harm Secret Service protectees," the agency says on its website. "However, the agency does not desire or solicit information pertaining to individuals or groups expressing legitimate criticism of, or political opposition to, the policies and decisions of the government or government officials."

Marsters portrayed himself as fitting into that second category. "It wasn't very appropriate," he admitted, but he wasn't really calling for violence. The Secret Service didn't seem to think so, either, because in the following months—after the agent told him that a report would be made to higher officials in the agency—no further questioning occurred and no charges were brought. "They'll be keeping an eye on me," Marsters figured. "They'll watch me for a while." Would it affect his behavior? "No, I say what I want." And he didn't feel alone, because he'd tapped into a small subculture of like-minded Americans, some of whom had called him from far and wide offering to donate to his defense fund, should he need one. "These are high people, too," he said cryptically, refusing to name them.

Marsters had trouble deciphering the codes of racial interaction and stereotyping. He was puzzled and indignant that blacks could use the word "nigger" but whites couldn't. "Our [black] friends say, if he's no f—in' good, he's a f—in' nigger." (Marsters was fine with "nigger" but couldn't bring himself to say "fucking.") He continued, "They call us white niggers. They can call us niggers, but we can't call them one? That's reverse discrimination. They can call us white niggers and white trash, and what else do they call us? But we don't say nothing about it. It seems to me that white people are afraid of black people."

This is a familiar refrain from certain whites, and Marsters, despite his black friends and Sundays in a black church, had not acquired a keen ear. For blacks who use the word, it stays within the family, so to speak. They may call each other "nigger" as an affectionate ribbing, a friendly insult, a rough way of teasing or joking. Or they may fire it as a nasty epithet of denunciation, usually of other blacks, more rarely of whites they detest. For some, adopting the word is a way to expropriate it, control it, and defuse its terrible racism. This is nonetheless denounced by many African-Americans who see its casual use by blacks as a kind of psychological self-oppression, a symptom of white racism internalized by the black minority. "You can only be destroyed by believing that you really are what the white world calls a nigger," James Baldwin once said.

In any event, when whites say "nigger," blacks hear something very different and very particular: ugly echoes of America's long legacy of racial hatred and degradation. The "nigger" is a slave, a sore, a speck, a specimen despised. The label cages a person hopelessly.

So it was that Michael Richards, the white comedian who played Cosmo Kramer on the *Seinfeld* television show, practically destroyed his career after exploding at an African-American heckler during a night-club routine in 2006: "Shut up! Fifty years ago we'd have you upside down with a fucking fork up your ass!" Richards worked himself into a fury, shouting with abandon, "Throw his ass out! He's a nigger! He's a nigger! He's a nigger! A nigger! Look, there's a nigger!"

For seven years afterward, Richards virtually disappeared, and not until the end of 2013 did he win an ongoing role in *Kirstie,* a series on TV Land.

"I busted up after that event, seven years ago," he told his friend and colleague Jerry Seinfeld in a short taped piece they did together. "It broke me down. It was a selfish response and I took it too personally and I should have just said, 'You know, you're absolutely right. I'm not funny. I think I'll go home and work on my material, and I'll see you tomorrow night.'" His face twisted in pain as he told Seinfeld, "And thanks for sticking by me. It meant a lot to me, you know. But inside, it still kicks me around." Seinfeld told him he'd been carrying that baggage long enough; the time had come to put it down.

No hint of such regret or introspection was betrayed by "Dr. Laura" Schlessinger, a brash conservative who spews tough advice to listeners. In 2010, when a black woman called to complain about her white husband's friends using "the *n*-word," Schlessinger shot back, "Black guys use it all the time. Turn on HBO and listen to a black comic, and all you hear is nigger, nigger, nigger. I don't get it. If anybody without enough melanin says it, it's a horrible thing. But when black people say it, it's affectionate. It's very confusing."

The caller chided "Dr. Laura" for uttering the word, but Schlessinger held firm in their back-and-forth, refused to accept the woman's discomfort, and finally taunted her: "Nigger, nigger, nigger is what you hear on HBO." Schlessinger added, "Don't take things out of context. Don't NAACP me." After the listener left the line, Schlessinger kept on: "If you're that hypersensitive about color and don't have a sense of humor, don't marry outside of your race."

The next day, after an uproar, Schlessinger apologized. She then left her show when her contract expired. Profits usually prevail in the end, however, and several months later she had a multiyear deal with SiriusXM satellite radio.

David Marsters wasn't rewarded. As he was writing "Shoot the nigger," he was also circulating a petition to get on the ballot for selectman. He collected fifty-five signatures, thirty more than he needed, to give himself a margin of safety in case some wanted their names removed after the Facebook post. None did.

Sabattus, Maine, is home to just under 5,000 residents of the second-whitest state in the Union, after Vermont. At the last census, 5 black people lived in town. It's not a wealthy place. Along the main road, clusters of quaint old houses give way to newer mobile homes parked permanently on cinder-block foundations. Some front yards are adorned with rusting vehicles. Modest lakeside cottages crowd the shores of Sabattus Pond, and a collection of small industries is marred by an abandoned factory, a relic of a better time. The median household income in 2011 was $52,310; the median house or condo value was $139,282.

In 2012, voters in Sabattus went for Obama over Romney, 51 to 46 percent. The local, off-year election of 2013 brought a low turnout, and the few who bothered to go to the polls, approximately two months after the Facebook post, handed Marsters a resounding defeat. Of six candidates for two vacancies on the town's governing council, he came in a distant last with only 52 votes; the winners had 396 and 348, respectively. His analysis? "To begin with, I'm an outsider. I'm from Massachusetts. A lot of people say, Move back to Massachusetts. Go back where you came from." He added his wry consolation: "Fifty-two people like me, anyway." The next year he was back on the Budget Committee, though, after running unopposed and getting 1,586 votes.

Marsters had issued so many clarifications and explanations of his offending sentence that he'd seemed poised to wish he could go back and hit the delete button. So the natural question was, what did he wish he'd written instead? He barely took a breath to consider. "The way things are going now, I'd leave it the way it was," he replied, sweeping aside all regret. His sources of information were still pumping him full of bile: Glenn Beck ("He tells it the way it is"), Sean Hannity, Bill O'Reilly, and Rush Limbaugh. Oh, and the primitive corners of the Internet, where he read—and believed—that generals had launched a movement for Obama's impeachment. "I'm against him as a person," Marsters said, "not as a black person."

And therein lies the rub. How much of the extreme criticism of Obama turns on his race, and how much on his policies and his performance? Some lines of attack are blatant and explicitly racist, others are subtle and hard to decode, and a good many seem race neutral, applicable to any president in disfavor, white or black. Obama is both white and black, it might be remembered, the son of a white mother from Kansas and a black father from Kenya, a multiracial man who has chosen to accept the "black" label that American society attached to him as he grew up in a culture obsessed with racial categories.

Needless to say, Obama is not smeared for being white—unless you count the few black intellectuals who have slammed him for not being "black" enough because of his reluctance to speak vigorously on race relations. But he is routinely smeared for being black. The criticisms with the most staying power and the widest support are those that rest on a legitimate policy complaint embellished with racial innuendo. The racial component is often encrypted, as most prejudice is nowadays.

Racially inspired comments run the spectrum from the obvious to the camouflaged. Sadly, Obama's election gave new currency to the most blatant. Rather than snuffing out stereotypes, the elevation of a black man—a biracial man—ignited the furies of hatred, now fueled with the speed and reach of the Internet.

Consider the many caricatures of Obama as an ape, Photoshopped pictures that have been widely circulated online. One shows Barack and Michelle Obama standing together, their noses, lips, and chins altered to look like monkeys'. On Biseor's Madness, a website indulging in profane, anti-Semitic, anti-Arab, and racist images and commentary, a chimpanzee with Obama's face is pictured hanging from a rope above the word "HOPE" in big, bold letters. The site carries an ape-faced Obama portrait headlined "Hail to the Chimp!!!" It promotes a video game called *Muslim Massacre*. Another site sports a doctored photograph of Obama beneath the headline "Primate in Chief." A T-shirt labeled "Hail to the Chief" shows a chimp behind a lectern bearing the presidential seal, and the same image is available on a baby's pink onesie. Another depicts an ape speaking behind a sign that reads "More Taxes."

And so it goes through an online gallery of vile images. From Chimpout, a white supremacist site: a pair of naked primates with the faces of Barack and Michelle, and another of President Obama in suit and tie, his nose and lips like a gorilla's, his mouth of scraggly teeth open in a horrifying yowl. From Stormfront, another "white pride" forum: a takeoff on the film *Planet of the Apes* picturing monkey-faced Barack and Michelle beside a ruined Statue of Liberty; a couple of little videos, photo portraits of the president and the first lady that gradually morph into the faces of chimpanzees; a T-shirt bearing Obama's face, with huge ears, and the legend "I fling poo too."

The primate image was used against President George W. Bush, as well, by hostile Photoshoppers who pictured him as an ape of primitive stupidity. The reaction might have been the same in a perfectly ahistorical world free from bigotry. But in our world, the connotation was entirely different. The caricature is deeply embedded in the country's racial history as a shorthand depiction of blacks as subhuman. It has pernicious resonance, absent when used against a white. So while Bush's supporters surely took offense, they couldn't argue racism. The images of Bush flowed around the Internet without generating the same indignation.

The obnoxious is now so easy to manufacture and distribute technologically that it reaches broad audiences, including malleable children who have not yet learned the country's terrible tradition of antiblack stereotyping. The vast majority of the graphic inventions are created and perpetrated anonymously, so the authors and messengers escape responsibility and opprobrium. The people who run into trouble are the ones who forward them under their own names. Their standard cover is to insist on their own ignorance (and therefore their innocence) as they circulate the material, which they profess not to recognize as racist, at least not until it's pointed out to them. That raises a question: Is something racist if you don't know it is? Is naïveté a legitimate excuse?

The "I'm not a racist" defense was attempted with moderate success by Marilyn Davenport, a retired Christian book publisher and a Tea Party member of the Republican Central Committee of Orange County, California. She forwarded what she thought was a humorous e-mail of a doctored photograph. It showed two adult chimpanzees and, supposedly, their baby bearing Obama's face. The title read "Now you know why—no birth certificate!"

If you're even a minor political figure such as Davenport, you can no longer just wink and nod and be offensive with a few trusted people. Her transgression swept through the Internet like a windstorm and swept her up as well. She fumbled. In interviews with reporters afterward, she seemed alternately contrite and confused, insisting that she didn't see Obama as a black man, wasn't racist, and thought the picture was a funny way to comment on his policies. It's hard to believe, but it may be true, that the traditional derogation of blacks as subhuman, animal-like, and akin to primates had not occurred to her. "Before I sent that e-mail," she eventually conceded, "I should have stopped to think about the historical implications."

Enough Republicans—not all—were concerned about the stain on the party to want her off the central committee. The Republican county chairman demanded her resignation. But she refused, citing messages of support from her constituents. By law he couldn't force her from her elected position, so the executive committee had to settle for a motion of censure, which passed by a vote of 12–2. She remained a central committee member through 2013.

Another California politician did resign—sort of—after e-mailing a cartoon showing the White House lawn as a watermelon patch and the title "No Easter Egg Hunt This Year." (For the uninitiated: Blacks have long been ridiculed as simple-minded country bumpkins who sit around lazily eating watermelons.) Dean Grose, the Republican mayor of Los Alamitos, was quoted as saying that he was unaware of the stereotype; that might have been true, because he included a black councilwoman among the e-mail's recipients. So he stepped down as mayor. But he remained a member of the city council and in 2012 was reelected councilman.

That's the way it usually goes: Immediate outrage and sometimes ouster, and then the person bobs to the surface and continues on, perhaps more carefully.

For example, Diane Fedele remained on the board of a Republican women's club five years after she resigned as president in a bizarre incident that tested the concept of racist intent. In 2008, before Obama won election, Fedele—who headed a local club in California's San Bernardino County—spotted what she thought was a witty cartoon online and included it in a newsletter she sent to 200 members.

The drawing, shaped like a $10 bill, bore a caricature of a grinning Obama as a Democratic donkey surrounded by a watermelon, ribs, and fried chicken beneath the label "United States Food Stamps." She saw it as a clever riposte to Obama's remark that he didn't look like any of the presidents on U.S. currency.

After she was attacked, Fedele professed to have no idea that the foods were used in stereotypes of African-Americans. "Everyone eats those foods, it's not a racial thing," she told the *Los Angeles Times*. "If I was racist, I would have looked at it through racist eyes," she insisted. "I am not racist, which is why it probably didn't register." It did register on a black member of the club, who told the paper she was so shocked when she saw it that she turned the computer screen away from her sixteen-year-old daughter.

After Fedele had resigned, the story took a curious twist. It emerged that the drawing had actually been done by a Minnesota Democrat, Timothy Kastelein, not to denounce Obama but to make fun of "fringes of the Republican Party who fear a black president." So a Republican used an Obama supporter's satire of Republicans to satirize Obama.

The boundaries between acceptable and unacceptable speech can be about as logical as Texas gerrymandering, and the morality about as pure. The unappointed guardians who police the lines and punish the trespassers are not without self-interest. What counts in politics, more than racial propriety, are the votes. What counts in business, more than racial rectitude, are the dollars.

Don Imus, the shock jock radio host, was given a two-week suspension by CBS in 2007 for calling the championship Rutgers women's basketball team "nappy-headed hos." (Eight players were black; two were white.) But as protests rose in volume and advertisers fled, CBS discovered that the statement was somehow growing more and more grotesque. The suspension was expanded to dismissal, and Imus was off the air—but only for eight months, until ABC picked up his morning program. In 2009 he signed a contract for national syndication by the Fox Business

Network. By 2012 his listeners numbered 2.25 million a week, compared with 14 million to 15 million for Rush Limbaugh and Sean Hannity, who favor less crude racial stereotyping that is closer to the end of the spectrum where camouflage prevails.

Glenn Beck, the conspiracy theorist and libertarian enthusiast, left his daily show on Fox News after an accumulation of extreme comments. Fox never specified the reason for his departure, but it occurred after he provoked an opposition movement that claimed to have pressed more than 300 advertisers to drop his program.

Beck called Obama a racist who hated white people. He conjured up the primate image after showing Obama, denouncing special interests, at a union event. Beck held his head, wailed, and poked the AFL-CIO logo behind Obama on the screen. "Special interests!" Beck raged. "What planet have I landed on? Did I slip through a wormhole in the middle of the night? And this *looks* like America. It's like the damned Planet of the Apes!"

The line was not impromptu, obviously, because Fox's studio engineer was ready with an immediate clip from the movie, a scene of apelike men surrounding a white man captured in a net, who was shouting, "Get your stinking paws off me, you damned, dirty ape!"

Beck survived comfortably after leaving Fox, though, with his own subscription service and talk show, streaming successfully online and carried by some cable services.

A young California woman, Denise Helms, had no such luck. She didn't get to keep her job after posting, "Another 4 years of this nigger. Maybe he will get assassinated this term." She was amazed by the inevitable uproar. "Apparently a lot of people in Sacramento think I'm crazy and racist," she wrote on Facebook. "WOW is all I got to say!! I'm not racist and I'm not crazy. Just simply stating my opinion!!!"

For "simply stating" her opinion, she was fired by the ice cream store where she worked, Cold Stone Creamery, whose director, Chris Kegle, called her comments "disgusting" and said angry "community feedback" had been decisive. "When your community does not like you because of an employee, that's bad," Kegle noted. "We have a business to run." In other words, dollars.

Twitter was ablaze with "nigger" and "monkey" references on election night 2012, especially from teenagers who used their real names. A football player at Xaverian High School in Brooklyn tweeted, "No nigger should lead this country!!!" according to the website Jezebel. "Only thing black people are good at is basketball. #run #shot #steal." A high school hockey player in York, Pennsylvania, wrote, "About time we get this monkey out of office #GoBackToTheZoo." He added, "Hope Obama dies." A football player at West Islip High School in West Islip, New York, wrote, "When in doubt kick the nigger out #Romney!!"

It's hard to determine how many of these words will come back to haunt these youngsters as they apply to colleges and seek employment. It is well established that digital trails never quite melt away, and some admissions officers and employers look at online postings. Because many of the students bragged about being on school sports teams, Jezebel contacted some of their schools and learned that a few of the kids had run afoul of administrators who denounced the remarks and promised unspecified discipline. The tweets were deleted, accounts were taken down, and several students then claimed that their accounts had been hacked and that someone else had written the offensive rants.

That may be. People's reputations are easily damaged in this ethereal world of the Internet. An accomplished Australian photographer, Ted Szukalski, began getting e-mails in 2008 accusing him of racism over a picture bearing his copyright designation. It showed Sarah Palin sitting on a stool while her black high-heeled shoes were being polished by Barack Obama. In fact, Szukalski insisted that he had nothing to do with the photograph, which was a doctored version of the one he'd actually taken of a homeless man named Bryan, his face hidden by long, stringy hair, shining the shoes of an unidentified woman on a street in Sydney. The Photoshopper had left Szukalski's name on the image.

He was indignant. "This image is an unauthorised and unlicensed plagiarism of original photograph," he wrote on his website. "My photograph of Bryan and his customer, at least to me, is one of a positive attitude and enterprise. Bryan, down on luck, does not beg for money. He puts [in] a solid day's work to earn his living." Szukalski wrote that he was "trying so hard to defend my name against this plagiarised image" but did not know its originator.

Mainstream political cartoonists, whose job is to create caricatures, have usually drawn Obama without exaggerating the facial features that would implicate them in racist stereotyping: no thick lips or broad nose, for example, and a smile that may be toothy but stops well short of the goofy, obsequious look of the minstrel. Obama's ears are easily exaggerated, and they are cartoonists' favorite feature for making fun. In real life they stick out prominently, and in cartoons they stick out even more, enough to be comically large. Here is the invisible line. Ears are not regarded as a racial trait, so they're fair game.

An exception to the unwritten rule governing Obama cartoons in the mainstream press was drawn by Sean Delonas and published in the *New York Post.* A policeman, who has just shot an ape on the street, says, "They'll have to find someone else to write the next stimulus bill." The paper's editor justified the cartoon as "a clear parody of a current news event, to wit the shooting of a violent chimpanzee in Connecticut. It broadly mocks Washington's efforts to revive the economy."

Given that blatant racial slurs are broadly unacceptable in twenty-first-century America, you could say that freedom of speech has its limits, restrained here not by law but by culture. And the punishments are inconsistent. People may lose jobs, promotions, reputations, and their chances for political office—or they may not. They can't predict with confidence. Therefore, either instinctively or deliberately, people inclined to indulge in racial stereotyping find ways to disguise their messages in raceless terminology.

That leaves much room for disagreement over what is really being said. Is it encrypted prejudice or honest commentary? Which criticisms of Obama should be taken at face value, and which reverberate with echoes of age-old racial contempt? How can hidden implications be identified? Bias is agile and from time to time shifts into keys that sound race neutral to some Americans but are "dog whistles" audible to those who hear the notes of bigotry.

So, in polite company you cannot say that Obama is an "uppity" black, but you can call him "arrogant." You can't say derisively that Obama's got rhythm, but you can accuse him of empty eloquence. You can't say that he's dumb or lazy—his obvious brilliance can even seem threatening—but you can say again and again that he has to read speeches from a teleprompter, an accusation not made against previous presidents who used the tool routinely. You can say he's incompetent, but you can't say that his blackness makes him so. Instead, you can say that his blackness got him elected to a job that's over his head—a kind of political affirmative action by voters who didn't want to oppose him for fear of seeming racist. Rush Limbaugh has actually made this argument.

You can't tell whites that Obama will mug them because he's black, but you can stir fears of black danger by saying, as Limbaugh has, that he hates whites, that he "has disowned his white half, that he's decided he's got to go all in on the black side" of his father. You can't conjure up the scary image of an angry black man, but you can imagine that he's Muslim, which today is code for menacing.

You can't say explicitly that he is not "us." You can't say that he is really "other" and doesn't know his place. You can't say that he "doesn't belong" in mainstream America because he's black, but you can say that he wasn't born in this country, that he's a closet socialist, that he doesn't understand or value what is authentically American. You can't say that his race makes him a dark, frightening mystery, but you can say (again, as Limbaugh has) that we know less about him than we've known about any president—although, in fact, we know much more, owing to his autobiographies, *Dreams from My Father* and *The Audacity of Hope*. In other words, you can find ways to accentuate the sense of distance that many whites already feel from African-Americans.

If many of these lines of attack seem ridiculously contrived, it's because Obama has carefully avoided playing into the old stereotypes. He does not display public anger, so as not to trigger the "angry black man" alarm, and to such an extent that some of his supporters fault him for being too conciliatory with conservative Republicans. Nor does he talk much about race, and he's been pummeled from the right on the few occasions when he has. "He has become the most successful black politician in American history by avoiding the radioactive racial issues of yesteryear," writes Ta-Nehisi Coates, "and yet his indelible blackness irradiates everything he touches." His reticence, which annoys some blacks, is a loss for a country that would have much to learn from Obama's compassionate insight into the complex racial dynamics that course through the society. As Coates observes, "Obama is not simply America's first black president—he is the first president who could credibly teach a black-studies class."

The winding, indirect route of stereotyping is illustrated by the word "arrogant," applied so frequently to Obama. He doesn't strike me as arrogant, but he gives that impression to a good many others. It may be the upward tilt of his chin or his lecturing cadence when he's exasperated with people who don't see his positions as self-evident. If you Google "images for Obama arrogant," you get a block of pictures showing him with his chin raised and his eyes half closed, a mannerism that a former campaign aide described as appearing to add to his already considerable height, as if he were looking down at you.

It's worth noting, however, that arrogance can be perceived in someone with undeserved power, and a black man is still placed in that category by certain circles far on the right. To some minds, an African-American with authority is an anomaly; a white behaving in the same way would not trigger the epithet "arrogant." As a white woman in Alabama once told Richard Arrington, the first black mayor of Birmingham, "Our parents would always say, If you don't get your lessons done and you don't do this, you'll end up with a nigger for your boss one day." She added, "For us, that was the worst thing that could happen."

Discomfort with blacks in power is surely dissipating as more and more African-Americans rise to supervisory positions in schools, workplaces, politics, and the armed forces. But the aversion remains acute in some quarters. Since it can't be expressed so explicitly, the concern has to be blurred and reshaped into terms that sound reasonable. "Arrogant" slips past the guardians of political correctness by entangling the racial motive in the thicket of political argument, where it cannot easily be isolated and examined. What one person sees as obvious another dismisses as fantasy.

Those who are accused mount counterattacks on the accusers for playing the "race card" to delegitimize criticism that could justifiably be made against a president of any race. That happened to Oprah when she commented that the "disrespect for the office . . . occurs in some cases and maybe even many cases because he's African-American." She was jumped on by the right as a chorus of Fox News commentators distorted her remarks to make them sound categorical and extreme. The result is a shouting match, not the useful dialogue that should happen in the regions of racial nuance.

Most examples of Obama's supposed arrogance are less than persuasive. The "nine most arrogant quotes of the Obamas" listed by a conservative website, Independent Journal Review, include his observation that change would "take time because we've got this big, messy, tough democracy." It cites his assertion that "anger is exploited by politicians, to gin up votes along racial lines, or to make up for a politician's own failing, and occasionally it finds voice in the church on Sunday morning," a time, he noted in paraphrasing Martin Luther King Jr., that had been called the most segregated hour in America. How are these remarks arrogant?

Only two of Obama's statements in the list come close to sounding superior. At a 2008 fund-raiser, he disastrously played pop psychologist while speaking about small towns where jobs had been lost and "bitter" residents "cling to guns or religion or antipathy to people who aren't like them or anti-immigrant sentiment or anti-trade sentiment as a way to explain their frustrations." He sounded bitter himself, and dismissive, about ordinary Americans he was supposed to be wooing.

And according to a secondhand account, when he interviewed Patrick Gaspard before hiring him as his campaign's political director, Obama allegedly said, "I think that I'm a better speechwriter than my speechwriters. I know more about policies on any particular issue than my policy directors. And I'll tell you right now that I'm gonna think I'm a better political director than my political director." On the website the comment is illustrated with a picture of Obama with his chin raised. What we can't see is whether, when he uttered these words, he had his tongue in his cheek.

Inexplicably, the list of arrogant quotes also includes remarks by Michelle Obama that her husband never takes a day off, is always ready to listen to good ideas, and thinks there's no such thing as "us and them."

Of course Obama has an ego; you can't get to the White House without one. The subjective issue—and it is subjective—is whether his ego is large enough to reach arrogant proportions and whether it would be considered overly developed if he were white. Because we've all watched Obama for years, we're all entitled to our assessments. Mine holds that the word "arrogant" slips off the tongue too easily and is mostly misapplied, primarily by conservatives who have not been champions of racial justice and are hypersensitive to an African-American with power.

"It's arrogant, it's arrogant," said the right-wing commentator Pat Buchanan. He was attacking Obama's speech defending the Affordable

Care Act as its rollout was tripped up by multiple website and policy glitches. "I watched that speech from beginning to end," Buchanan fumed. "It was really a smugness, arrogance, and self-confidence despite the fact . . . that he deliberately deceived and misled the American people for three years."

"Arrogant-in-chief" was how Obama was labeled by Tom DeLay, the former Republican majority leader of the House, who suddenly resurfaced after his money-laundering conviction was overturned. He fulminated on CNN after the October 2013 government shutdown, when Obama pleaded, "All of us need to stop focusing on the lobbyists, and the bloggers, and the talking heads on radio, and the professional activists who profit from conflict, and focus on what the majority of Americans sent us here to do." DeLay called the statement "the height of arrogance and incompetence."

The phrase "arrogance and incompetence" was tossed around as if it had been distributed as a script. It turned up in a headline on Fox News, over a column by Michael Goodwin of Rupert Murdoch's conservative *New York Post:* "ObamaCare Glitches Perfectly Reflect President's Arrogance and Incompetence."

According to Murdoch, Mayor Michael Bloomberg of New York City said of Obama, after a fifteen-minute conversation with him about the economy, "I never met in my life such an arrogant man," Jake Tapper of ABC News reported. But Bloomberg endorsed Obama's reelection!

After Syria used chemical weapons in its civil war, Michelle Malkin, on *The Sean Hannity Show,* called Obama "flippant, arrogant, contemptuous" for planning a retaliatory attack without UN or allied backing and without congressional approval. Presumably, he then became the model of humility when he decided to ask for authorization from Congress, which was not given. (With less frequency, President George W. Bush was called arrogant—his smirk became a favorite irritant to the left—for taking the United States into Iraq without broad international support.)

"Does Obama's Arrogance Have Any Limits?" asked *The Loft,* part of GOPUSA. "The Arrogance of the Obama Administration Will Bankrupt Us," said the headline in *Forbes* over an opinion piece. When the presidential seal fell off Obama's lectern and he joked, "That's all right, all of you know who I am," the quip was cited as a case of his "arrogance problem" by a liberal-bashing blogger named Jonah Goldberg.

The word has grown ubiquitous. Ken Mugler, a Pennsylvania resident, posted, "We have never, ever had a president who is so arrogant and constantly talks down to people." Betsy McCaughey, a writer for *Investor's Business Daily,* chastised Obama for using an administrative fix to allow Americans to keep substandard health insurance policies for a year after they were outlawed. "Amazingly," she wrote, "our arrogant president says he will veto" any legislation that would permit the sale of such policies indefinitely.

If you have a flimsy argument, you can infuse it with vigor by using subtle racial stereotyping: Obama as all show and no substance, Obama as incompetent, Obama as deceptive, Obama as dangerous, Obama as not truly American. Deeply ingrained doubts about African-Americans, long embedded in the majority white culture, seem to have an amplifying effect on certain criticisms.

In any given case, however, it's an open question whether the purveyors of prejudice themselves are fully aware of what they're doing, especially if they're not well versed in the long legacy of antiblack images. The calls to bigoted thoughts are often so encrypted that they require some key of knowledge to unlock the code. Even listeners who can't do that—who can't clearly identify a statement as racially biased—may be subliminally affected by the racial message.

The result is a curious paradox: that such commentary can seem both benign and pernicious, that it can appear racially neutral and yet stir inchoate racial aversion. It would be simplistic, therefore, to brand someone like Rush Limbaugh an avowed racist, even as he plays on the stereotypes. Is he cunning or just unknowing?

Intentionally or not, he and others on the right trade in charges against Obama that probably wouldn't stick if he weren't black. Many of their accusations just don't compute for most Americans, because the images stand so far from what the general public sees in the president. He has been under close scrutiny since 2008, after all, and widened his margin of victory in his 2012 reelection. So the extremists have to reach for timeworn racial assumptions designed to generate contempt and fear. The hard rightists accuse him of laziness, for example, and of fostering violence—two of the most durable antiblack labels in American history.

The dread of rage and brutality derives from the time of slavery, when it seemed only logical that those who lived under the whip would, if they could, rise up in rebellion and revenge. Thomas Jefferson imagined ominously that if blacks were freed, as he believed they should be, racial coexistence would succumb to racial war. He proposed instead that a colony for freed blacks be established on the coast of West Africa. "Deep-rooted prejudices entertained by the whites," he wrote in *Notes on the State of Virginia,* "ten thousand recollections by the blacks, of the injuries they have sustained; new provocations; the real distinctions which nature has made; and many other circumstances, will divide us into parties, and produce convulsions, which will probably never end but in the extermination of the one or the other race."

Even at today's distance from slavery, vestiges of the images and fears survive in some quarters of white America, and they are handy for rightist commentators. Limbaugh, America's master propagandist, skillfully strikes those chords of anxiety. In a 2010 monologue nimbly touching on the indolent, the unpatriotic, the arrogant, and even the sexually uninhibited, Limbaugh said,

> Let me focus mostly on the lazy . . . He's on his sixth vacation, he really doesn't appear to work very hard, gets to the Oval Orifice [yes, that's what Limbaugh said] at 9:30 in the morning . . . Obama is late, he doesn't spend a lot of time in there. I don't think it's laziness. I think it is arrogance. I think Obama thinks of himself as above the job . . . I don't think he likes the White House. I think he looks at the White House as confining . . . He and his wife do not like living there. To them the White House is not a great place of honor, it's a prison, and a lot of presidents have felt that it's a prison, but to them it's like some African-Americans, "Fourth of July ain't no big deal to me, yo."

Limbaugh went on, in a rare violation of the unwritten cultural rule against the word "uppity": "Obama is uppity, but not as a black. He is an elitist. He does think he's smarter and better than everybody else. That's what he was taught. He's a Harvard man." Later, Limbaugh also accused

Michelle Obama of "uppity-ism" because she flew separately to a vacation in 2011.

Obama's supposed anger, as one of Limbaugh's favorite themes, surely strikes the nerve of those listeners who share many whites' low threshold of tolerance for black men's rage. "I think he's motivated by anger," Limbaugh said of Obama in 2012. "He's got a chip on his shoulder, a number of them." (The "chip" turns up regularly in Limbaugh's comments.) "The days of them not having any power are over, and they are angry," he said in June 2009, four and a half months after Obama's inauguration. "And they want to use their power as a means of retribution. That's what Obama's about, gang. He's angry; he's going to cut this country down to size. He's going to make it pay for all the multicultural mistakes that it has made—its mistreatment of minorities. I know exactly what's going on here." Two years later, Limbaugh predicted racial violence as "part of the program," saying, "There are going to be race riots, I guarantee."

To drive home the terror that whites should feel, Limbaugh pictures a vast policy conspiracy driven by black grievances. "Obama has a plan," he said in January 2012. "Obama's plan is based on his inherent belief that this country was immorally and illegitimately founded by a very small minority of white Europeans who screwed everybody else since the founding to get all the money and all the goodies, and it's about time that the scales were made even. And that's what's going on here." What's more, he and Michelle Obama view the presidency "as an opportunity to live high on the hog without having it cost them a dime. And they justify it by thinking, Well, we deserve this, or we're owed this because of what's been done to us and our ancestors."

Soon after his inauguration in 2009, Obama was branded by Limbaugh as "more African in his roots than he is American." This implication of "otherness" has animated the right. It recalls the historical ethnocentrism of this land of immigrants, which has marginalized and disqualified one group after another, from one era to the next: Chinese, Italians, Eastern Europeans, Jews, Latinos, blacks, and on through the phases of decades.

In the case of Obama, born in Hawaii of a mother from Kansas and a father from Kenya, the drive to make him seem part of "them," not "us," took several forms: He was falsely portrayed as a "socialist." He was pictured as threatening the American way by favoring a redistribution of wealth. He was targeted by a disinformation campaign asserting that he was a Muslim. And of course he was dogged by the wacky "birther movement" that questioned his place of birth.

To rummage around in the subject online is like stepping into a dizzying fantasy of bad satire. Then you realize that the people writing this stuff take themselves seriously. And they have an impact. A Pew poll in July 2012 found 17 percent (and 34 percent of conservative Republicans) believing that Obama is Muslim. In a 2011 CBS poll, 25 percent of the total sample, and 45 percent of Republicans, said that Obama was born outside the United States and so didn't meet the Constitution's requirement that the president be a "natural born" citizen. (Even if he had been born abroad of his American mother, however, he might be considered a "natural born" American in constitutional terms; legal scholars disagree on the matter.)

The birther allegation has murky origins—possibly with a Hillary Clinton supporter in Texas named Linda Starr—but its wide promotion was clearly the work of another Clinton partisan, Philip J. Berg, a Pennsylvania Democrat who sued in an effort to get Obama out of office. He has a website he calls ObamaCrimes.com. The movement then gained momentum in the hands of the Tea Party and other conservatives.

It's hard to imagine that any such serious doubts would have been directed against Obama had he been white. Many Americans felt cleansed by electing their first African-American president, and a good number of commentators rhapsodized about the country's supposedly entering a post-racial era. It was a mirage that quickly evaporated as the hard right mobilized.

A few public figures, trying to make a name for themselves, demanded Obama's birth certificate. When he produced it, several of them pronounced it a fake. Again, however, some extremists tripped over an uncharted boundary into their own demise. The persistent skepticism helped torpedo the clownish presidential aspirations of Donald Trump, the real estate mogul, who kept at it even after the 2012 election, saying on NBC, "Was there a birth certificate? You tell me. Some people say that was not his birth certificate. I'm saying I don't know. Nobody knows."

When the argument finally died off except at the distant fringe, the line of attack shifted from Obama's place of birth to his place in American values.

The president is not "a real American," said Mike Coffman of Colorado, a House Republican, at a fund-raiser during his 2012 reelection campaign. "I don't know whether Barack Obama was born in the United States or not, but I do know this: that in his heart, he's not an American. He's just not an American." The audience reacted with a moment of silence, then with a smattering of desultory applause.

Later, following criticism over his comment, Coffman issued the pretense of an apology while reframing Obama as unenthusiastic about his country. "I have confidence in President Obama's citizenship and legitimacy as President of the United States," Coffman's press release declared. "However, I don't believe the President shares my belief in American exceptionalism. His policies reflect a philosophy that America is but one nation among equals." Perhaps if Obama had gone around the world touting American exceptionalism, he would have been condemned as arrogant. In any event, Coffman seemed out of step with the constituency in his district, who gave Obama a five-percentage-point victory over Romney. Coffman won reelection, though, by two points.

Relying on partial quotes and manufactured attitudes, rightist commentators have been eager to drive home this notion of Obama as standing somewhat apart from the country he leads. In 2009, for example, Sean Hannity of Fox News broadcast a fragment labeled on screen in bold type, "OBAMA ATTACKS AMERICA." In the excerpt from a speech in France, Obama was heard to say, "In America, there's a failure to appreciate Europe's leading role in the world. Instead of celebrating your dynamic union and seeking to partner with you to meet common challenges, there have been times where America's shown arrogance and been dismissive, even derisive."

That was where the clip ended, allowing Hannity to come on camera indignantly. "And the liberal tradition of blame America first, well, that's still alive," Hannity sneered. "I resent this," considering "all we have done in just the last century alone to save Europe from themselves."

What Fox viewers didn't get to hear were Obama's next sentences: "But, in Europe, there is an anti-Americanism that is at once casual but can also be insidious. Instead of recognizing the good that America so often does in the world, there have been times when Europeans choose to blame America for much of what's bad. On both sides of the Atlantic these attitudes have become all too common. They are not wise, they do not represent the truth." It was an evenhanded, uncontestable appraisal of relations in early 2009, coming off the Bush administration's anti-European posture. But the omitted quote, the full balance of Obama's analysis, would have spoiled the pitchman Hannity's insinuation of Obama's questionable loyalty.

Omissions, silences, selective facts—these are the stuff of propaganda, which a Soviet academic once described this way: You tell a truth, a truth, a truth, and then a lie. By the time you get to the lie, you have caught the listener in a sequence of truths from which only the well-informed mind can escape before being captured by the lie as well. The comedian Stephen Colbert mocks the squishy relationship between the lie and the fact as "truthiness."

Not all victims are equal. Some get more protection than others. And not all perpetrators are equally punishable. Some are more profitable than others. So the penalties for crossing the vague line of acceptability are inconsistent. They depend on what is said about whom by whom. The cunning and the agile, such as Limbaugh and Hannity, usually escape retribution because they attract a large enough fraction of the public to garner advertising dollars. And their employers are mostly impervious to catcalls from the left. Others, clumsier and less discerning about their targets, are more vulnerable.

The targets are a key variable. Slights and smears aimed at some victims trigger sharp reactions, but not when directed at others. Some racial, ethnic, religious, or other groups have been brought under the society's informal umbrella of defense; there, they are granted immunity from overt expressions of prejudice. Violators may be punished with a chorus of loud complaints, and possibly a job dismissal or an election defeat.

While Obama is a magnet for bigotry, blacks in general have been under this shield of protection for a while, and so have Jews, at least where the racism or anti-Semitism is blatant and indisputable. Arabs and Muslims have been mostly outside the defenses and are just beginning to find their way into the peripheral zones of protected status. Negative generalizations about them are sometimes, but not always, condemned. The same is true for gay, lesbian, bisexual, and transgendered Americans, who are newcomers to the sphere of immunity, arriving during the speedy revision of social attitudes and expanding legal rights to enter into same-sex marriages, to serve openly in the military, and to be free from discrimination in many walks of life.

A measure of the shifting, unresolved attitudes on sexual orientation occurred in 2013, when the A&E television network suspended Phil Robertson, the star of the popular reality show *Duck Dynasty,* after he made antigay remarks in an interview with *GQ* magazine. At sixty-seven, Robertson was a long-bearded evangelical Christian and the patriarch of a Louisiana family that manufactured duck calls used by hunters. His defenders pushed back hard. Christian organizations and right-wing politicians and commentators, including Sarah Palin and the Louisiana governor, Bobby Jindal, accused the network of assaulting Christian values and freedom of speech. Some called for a boycott of A&E.

In the *GQ* interview, Robertson said this: "It seems like, to me, a vagina—as a man—would be more desirable than a man's anus. That's just me. I'm just thinking: There's more there! She's got more to offer. I mean, come on, dudes! You know what I'm saying? But hey, sin: It's not logical, my man. It's just not logical."

He went on: "Everything is blurred on what's right and what's wrong. Sin becomes fine . . . Start with homosexual behavior and just morph out from there. Bestiality, sleeping around with this woman and that woman and that woman and those men. Don't be deceived. [Here he paraphrased 1 Corinthians:] Neither the adulterers, the idolaters, the male prostitutes, the homosexual offenders, the greedy, the drunkards, the slanderers, the swindlers—they won't inherit the kingdom of God. Don't deceive yourself. It's not right." This paragraph of comments later disappeared from *GQ*'s online version of the interview.

An A&E executive told *The New York Times* that Robertson had been suspended because of his explicit language and the association he'd made between homosexuality and bestiality. But the network was also hedging its bets. Apparently, it calculated that its audience had little tolerance for homophobic remarks, yet it didn't say how long the suspension would last; nine of the following year's ten episodes had already been recorded, so viewers wouldn't actually notice his absence for some time, if at all. The show had 14 million viewers and brought in huge revenues, from both advertising and such related merchandise as T-shirts and lawn ornaments.

In the end, his suspension lasted all of one week. Inundated with online petitioners and a threat by the rest of Robertson's family to bail out of the lucrative show, A&E executives had a change of heart. In business, hearts pump money.

Interestingly, neither the network nor most news coverage cited Robertson's assertion, in the same interview, that blacks had been happy under Jim Crow segregation. During his youth in Louisiana, he told *GQ*, "I never, with my eyes, saw the mistreatment of any black person. Not once. Where we lived was all farmers. The blacks worked for the farmers. I hoed cotton with them. I'm with the blacks, because we're white trash. We're going across the field . . . They're singing and happy. I never heard one of them, one black person, say, 'I tell you what: These doggone white people'—not a word! . . . Pre-entitlement, pre-welfare, you say: Were they happy? They were godly; they were happy; no one was singing the blues."

It's a good practice to fasten your seat belt when somebody says, "I'm not a racist" or "I'm not a bigot" or—as Richard Nixon declared shortly before resigning—"I'm not a crook."

The journalist Juan Williams of National Public Radio began a fateful remark on Bill O'Reilly's Fox News show by declaring, "I mean, look, Bill, I'm not a bigot." He must have figured that what he was about to say might be taken that way. Williams is black, a former *Washington Post* reporter who wrote a biography of the Supreme Court justice Thurgood Marshall and a companion book to the public television documentary on the civil rights era *Eyes on the Prize*. He is no stranger to the intricate dynamics of bigotry.

He reinforced his credentials with O'Reilly: "You know the kind of books I've written about the civil rights movement in this country. But when I get on the plane, I got to tell you, if I see people who are in Muslim garb and I think, you know, they are identifying themselves first and foremost as Muslims, I get worried. I get nervous."

Those were the lines that got the most news coverage. But he had actually gone on to quote President Bush as stressing that this war was not against Islam. As O'Reilly began talking over him, Williams tried to make the point that not all Muslims should be classified as extremists, noting that Christians weren't blamed for Timothy McVeigh's bombing of the federal building in Oklahoma City. Williams had trouble negotiating through O'Reilly's bombast, and he was never able to complete what seemed to be his argument against generalizing about whole religious groups, as he himself had just done. But he also passed up numerous opportunities later in the show to acknowledge that he had indirectly legitimized the fiercest stereotypes of Muslims as violent.

Williams was summarily fired by National Public Radio, with no chance to defend or explain himself. His dismissal ignited passionate debate about whether he had simply made an accurate observation about anti-Muslim feeling in the country or had crossed a line by buying into the crude assumption that self-identification as a Muslim implied a propensity for terrorism. Putting aside the absurdity of his statement—the fact was, the nineteen hijackers on 9/11 were not in "Muslim garb" but sought to blend unobtrusively into American society, as any skilled terrorists would—NPR thought that Williams had disqualified himself as a fair-minded commentator.

The result was messier, though. Williams was unapologetic, writing the next day, "NPR fired me for telling the truth," which was "not a bigoted statement. It is a statement of my feelings, my fears after the terrorist attacks of 9/11 by radical Muslims." He insisted, "I revealed my fears to set up the case for not making rash judgments about people of any faith." Fox commentators defended him loudly, and Fox awarded him a $2 million, three-year contract as an analyst and columnist.

Furthermore, the veteran NPR editor who did the firing by phone, Ellen Weiss, was forced to resign after an internal investigation, and NPR's chief executive, Vivian Schiller, was denied her annual bonus after she supported the dismissal by saying gratuitously that the feelings Williams "expressed on Fox News are really between him and his psychiatrist or his publicist, or take your pick." She insisted that Williams, also a Fox News contributor, had been told repeatedly that as an analyst for NPR he should avoid stating his personal opinions on Fox. She did not survive. The following year, after an underground video caught an NPR fund-raiser disparaging Republicans, Schiller was out as well.

If there is any pattern here, it appears to preserve the voices of the Limbaughs, Hannitys, and Becks who repeat their innuendo day in and day out for millions and to penalize those, such as Williams, who make a single remark. It's a bit like taking low-level drug dealers off the street while leaving the kingpins alone.

But of course speech is not a crime, even offensive speech. On the contrary, turning bigoted speech into the sunlight is much more curative than keeping it under wraps, because out in the open it can be countered and rebutted. Communist dictatorships generally prohibited the overt expression of bigotry against various ethnic groups, but the bigotry thrived underground all the same until, when the autocracies collapsed, the interethnic tensions and hatreds sprang to the surface. The Soviet Union divided peacefully into fifteen countries along ethnic boundaries, Czechoslovakia broke peacefully in two, Yugoslavia tore itself apart in an explosion of warfare and genocide, and other Eastern European nations struggled in their newfound freedom to manage strong aversions across the lines of difference. Eliminating the speech did not eliminate the hatred.

So an open society needs the fluidity of speech as it strives to maintain a civil consensus. Yet while the landscape is large, those who test its boundaries by trading in hateful stereotyping need to take responsibility and face consequences in some form, even if only opprobrium. Let the informal punishment fit the informal crime, one could say, with a sense of proportion. An offhand remark in a moment of thoughtlessness need not be penalized as if the perpetrator were a child molester. Carelessness is not the same as cruelty and is not always a sudden sign of bad character.

Take Richard Cohen, a veteran columnist for *The Washington Post.* He is often insightful and thought provoking. Usually he writes from just left of center. But on matters of race he has a quirky lack of sophistication, and partly because he is moderately liberal, he periodically infuriates readers by sounding like an unreconstructed son of the Confederacy.

He has endorsed racial profiling at least since 1986, when he wrote sympathetically about jewelers who put security locks on their doors and refused to buzz in young black males for fear of being robbed. He supported the New York Police Department's controversial stop-and-frisk practice, in which black men were patted down on the street without the reasonable suspicion required by the courts' interpretation of the Fourth Amendment. In 2013, he half justified the shooting death of Trayvon Martin, an unarmed black teenager in Florida, by a self-appointed and unofficial neighborhood watchman named George Zimmerman, who was found not guilty of murder. Cohen said he could "understand why Zimmerman was suspicious and why he thought Martin was wearing a uniform we all recognize," a sweatshirt with a hood—a hoodie.

Cohen then wrote this: "People with conventional views must repress a gag reflex when considering the mayor-elect of New York—a white man married to a black woman and with two biracial children. (Should I mention that Bill de Blasio's wife, Chirlane McCray, used to be a lesbian?) This family represents the cultural changes that have enveloped parts—but not all—of America. To cultural conservatives, this doesn't look like their country at all."

The columnist was blasted from the left, where commentators cited polls showing that the vast majority of Americans now supported interracial marriage—87 percent in a Gallup survey. So the "gag reflex"—a strange choice of words—could hardly be considered "conventional." Perhaps he meant old-fashioned. Some demanded that he be dismissed. *Salon* ran a piece titled "Richard Cohen: Please Fire Me," and *The Huffington Post* posted his picture with the declaration "Dear Washington Post: Please Fire This Man."

But the seventy-two-year-old columnist didn't seem to be going anywhere, at least not right away. Besides, he'd just made a very public fool of himself. What more punishment was needed? "I think it's reprehensible to say that because you disagree with something that you should fire me," he said. "That's what totalitarians do." He claimed to be "expressing not my own views but those of extreme right-wing Republican tea party people. I don't have a problem with interracial marriage or same-sex marriage." If we take that at face value, his main offense was sloppy writing. His editor, Fred Hiatt, admitted, "I erred in not editing that one sentence more carefully to make sure it could not be misinterpreted."

People who are punished for offensive statements almost always make them in public. Donald Sterling, co-owner of the Los Angeles Clippers, made them in private and suffered after they became public without his consent. In the blaring outrage over his remarks, subtler questions were lost: Where are the boundaries of privacy? Does someone in the public eye possess any protected zone of indiscretion?

The occasion was a tense argument between Sterling, who was about to turn eighty, and a woman friend, identified as thirty-one-year-old V. Stiviano, in her apartment. According to her lawyer, she recorded the conversation on her phone, with Sterling's agreement, then sent snippets of it to a friend electronically. The friend or someone else distributed it to a website, where it went viral.

In the conversation, Sterling is clearly jealous. His voice breaks as he beseeches Stiviano not to be seen in public with black men. "Why are you taking pictures with minorities—why?" he asks her.

"What's wrong with minorities?" she replies, then adds a few minutes later, "People call you and tell you I have black people on my Instagram, and it bothers you."

STERLING: Yeah, it bothers me a lot that you want to promo—broadcast that you're associating with black people. Do you have to?

STIVIANO: You associate with black people.

STERLING: I'm not you, and you're not me. You're supposed to be a delicate white or a delicate Latina girl.

STIVIANO: I'm a mixed girl. [She explains that she is black and Mexican.] You want me to have hate towards black people?

STERLING: I don't want you to have hate. That's what people do—they turn things around. I want you to love them—privately. In your whole life, every day you can be with them. Every single day of your life.

STIVIANO: But not in public?

STERLING: But why publicize it on the Instagram and why bring it to my games?

STIVIANO: Why bring the black people to the games?

STERLING: I don't think we need to discuss anymore. It's over. I don't want to talk about it.

STIVIANO: I'm sorry that you feel that way.

STERLING: I feel that way so strongly, and it may cause our relationship to just break apart. And if it does, it does. [His voice breaks.] It's better to break apart now than to break apart later.

STIVIANO: I'm sorry that you still have people around you that are full of racism and hate in their heart. I'm sorry that you're still racist in your heart.

STERLING: . . . You can sleep with them, you can bring them in, you can do whatever you want. The little I ask you is not to promote it on that—and not to bring them to my games.

STIVIANO: . . . What would you like me to do? Remove the skin color out of my skin?

STERLING: There's nothing wrong with you or your skin color. Why are you saying these things? To upset me?

When she tells him she admires Magic Johnson, Sterling replies, "I know him well and he should be admired. And I'm just saying that it's too bad you can't admire him privately, and during your entire fucking life your whole life admire him, bring him here, feed him, fuck him, I don't care. You can do anything. But don't put him on an Instagram for the world to have to see so they have to call me. And don't bring him to my games, OK?"

STIVIANO: I don't, I've never brought, I don't know him personally.

STERLING: Please leave me alone. Please, please?

STIVIANO: I'm sorry. Is there anything that I can do to make you feel better?

STERLING: No, you can never make me feel better.

The rambling conversation, which reportedly lasted for an hour, was boiled down in the press to a couple of sentences: Sterling didn't want her seen with blacks, and he didn't want her to bring blacks, particularly Magic Johnson, to his team's games.

In a later, recorded conversation with someone else, broadcast by CNN, Sterling said he had been trying to have sex with her. "I know I'm wrong, what I said was wrong, but I never thought the private conversation would go anywhere, out to the public. I didn't want her to bring anybody to my game because I was jealous." He asked plaintively, "Am I a person? Do I have any freedom of speech?"

Not really, it seems, if you're something of a public figure who owns a professional basketball team—most of whose players, by the way, are black. The new commissioner of the National Basketball Association, Adam Silver, moved swiftly after verifying the authenticity of the recording. He expressed disgust, levied a $2.5 million fine, and banned Sterling for life from associating with his team or attending games. Silver also planned to try to mobilize other owners to force Sterling to sell the Clippers, which was held by a family trust. His wife moved successfully in court to have him declared mentally incompetent and replaced as trustee. Steve Ballmer, former CEO of Microsoft, then bought the team for $2 billion, said to be three times its worth—a windfall for Sterling's racist impulses.

Swift demands to silence offensive speakers are a feature of American polarization, but they don't raise the level of discourse. Those readying the muzzles and the duct tape could take a lesson from the Anti-Defamation League of B'nai B'rith.

The ADL is a tough defender of Jews and of Israel, but it has usually approached anti-Semitism as an educational problem and a teaching opportunity. It does not always denounce someone who makes a slip. In 1980, for example, the head of the Southern Baptist Convention, Bailey Smith, said that "God Almighty does not hear the prayer of a Jew." Instead of just condemning him, the ADL took him on a trip to Israel, where he was guided through the Holy Land on a tour of Jewish history and contemporary life.

I met him there during a breakfast discussion with several American correspondents. He asked about life in Jerusalem, and I mentioned that we'd been recently burglarized. A policeman had then arrived with a machine to etch numbers on our electronics so they could be identified if we had a future theft, and the cop seemed disappointed that we didn't have more gadgets to engrave.

Well, Smith said with a smile, he could etch numbers on your arm so you'd remember who you were! We sat in stunned silence. The two Jews at the table, both officials of the ADL, said nothing. Finally, another reporter explained that the Nazis had tattooed numbers on the arms of Jews in the concentration camps. Smith seemed embarrassed. Perhaps he really hadn't known.

The ADL might have been expected to jump at the chance to publicize such an instance of anti-Semitism, but the reaction was quite the opposite. Back in my office, I got a call from one of the ADL men, who pleaded with me not to write about the gaffe. It had come out of ignorance, not malice, the representative believed, and the ADL did not want a sour note to spoil the trip's purpose, which was to woo Smith into accommodation, not display his insensitivity. The effort fit into a broad campaign by Israel to garner support among American evangelicals, and it has worked. (I reported Smith's numbers remark anyway, but deep down in the story, and also mentioned that, according to the ADL, he had wept openly after visiting Yad Vashem, the museum devoted to the Holocaust.)

In 2013, however, the ADL did not denounce or seek to educate a Virginia Republican district committee chairman, John C. Whitbeck Jr., who warmed up the crowd at a Tea Party rally with an anti-Semitic joke he said he'd heard in a sermon by a Catholic priest, whom he later refused to name. The joke went like this:

During an ancient ritual that is held after a new pope is elected, the "head of the Jewish faith" (a position that does not exist) goes to the Vatican and ceremonially presents the pontiff with an old piece of paper. By tradition, the new pope ceremonially rejects the sealed document. Whitbeck continued, "Well, this time around, the pope said, 'I've got to find out what's on this piece of paper.' So he actually takes it from the head of the Jewish faith, and he opens it and looks at it . . . and his Jewish counterpart says, 'What was it?' He says, 'Well, that was the bill for the Last Supper.'"

A burst of complicit laughter erupted from the crowd. Did they recognize the old calumny?

The Jewish Daily Forward excoriated Whitbeck for the joke, which Ron Kampeas of the Jewish Telegraphic Agency noted "packs two of the most toxic anti-Jewish stereotypes into a single punch line: God-killers! Cheapskates!" The Republican gubernatorial candidate, Ken Cuccinelli (who narrowly lost the election two months later), emphasized that he hadn't been there but called the joke "inappropriate and certainly unfortunate." It didn't seem to bother Republican voters, though, 70 percent of whom picked Whitbeck in the primary for state senator. He then lost to a Democrat but remained Republican district chairman.

Not everyone gets a second chance, and the end sometimes carries a pang of sadness. So it was for Helen Thomas, the veteran White House correspondent for UPI and then Hearst Newspapers, who broke ground for female reporters in Washington and the National Press Club, where women were once relegated to the balcony. Thomas was known for her acerbic questioning of officials from the president on down, particularly about United States support for Israel.

In 2010, at the age of eighty-nine, she was approached by Rabbi David Nesenoff of www.rabbilive.com, who aimed a video camera at her and asked, "Any comments on Israel?"

"Tell them to get the hell out of Palestine," Thomas said. "Remember, these people are occupied, and it's their land. It's not German, it's not Poland."

"So where should they go? What should they do?" Nesenoff asked.

"They'd go home."

"Where's their home?"

"Poland. Germany."

"So you think the Jews should go back to Poland and Germany."

"And America and everywhere else."

Thomas was fired by Hearst, dropped by her speaker's bureau, and blasted by colleagues and officials. Walt Whitman High School in Bethesda, Maryland, canceled her invitation to speak at its commencement. She said later, "I deeply regret my comments," and insisted, "They do not reflect my heart-felt belief that peace will come to the Middle East only when all parties recognize the need for mutual respect and tolerance."

That wasn't enough for the Anti-Defamation League's director, Abraham H. Foxman, who said her statement was "bigoted" and "shows a profound ignorance of history." He urged "a more forceful and sincere apology for the pain her remarks have caused."

And so ended her illustrious career.

8

The Protocols of the Elders of Islam

Words matter in this war.
—JOHN GUANDOLO, Understanding the Threat

The obscure document lay with many others in the basement of a suburban house in Annandale, Virginia, just outside the Washington Beltway. It was about to be discovered, and once in the public eye one paragraph in particular would feed a rising movement of concern that the Muslim Brotherhood had designs on America.

Around this worry, spread rapidly by the Internet, an entire subculture of belief has been constructed, an alternative universe of thinking. It holds that radical Islam seeks to infiltrate, subvert, and conquer Western civilization and institutions, a view reminiscent of the fear of communism in the 1950s. With the document as a centerpiece, a cottage industry of bloggers, analysts, books, reports, journals, videos, conferences, and courses for police departments has been nourished by conservative funding. The movement has galvanized some legislators on the right to block the imagined spread of Sharia (Islamic law) and to press the FBI to end cooperative relationships with certain American Muslim groups. Its adherents have denounced, as dupes and enablers, those who preach tolerance of Islam and who oppose discriminating against Muslims.

The use of the document from the basement is a study in the balkanization of information in the digital age, when those who already agree garner evidence for what they already believe. The complexity of unfettered speech, its virtues and dangers, is dramatized by this move-ment of fear about Islam. In the robust liberty of the Internet, the like-minded gravitate to one another, explore and advocate at will, and propel unorthodox ideas into the public square. They get people thinking, but sometimes in hateful ways. Those are the risks that an open society takes to remain free.

The elaborate argument stemming from the document in question is largely ignored by mainstream media and dismissed as anti-Muslim big-otry. Yet it is not all crude and bigoted. Some research and writings are glazed with a patina of sophistication, drawn from studying the radical ambitions of the intolerant factions of Islam. So the claims have shown resilience.

The man in whose basement the document was found, a bookkeeper named Ismail Elbarasse, was driving his family home from a beach vaca-tion in the early afternoon of August 20, 2004. His silver Nissan SUV was heading west across Maryland's Chesapeake Bay Bridge as his wife took videos from the passenger seat. She was wearing a hijab, in the Muslim tradition.

Therefore, she was noticed by three off-duty Baltimore County police officers traveling in the same direction. Had she been a blonde, her hus-band's lawyer later remarked, nothing would have happened. But she was not a blonde. She was "a middle eastern subject" according to the subsequent police report, and the country was in no trifling mood when it came to Middle Eastern subjects.

The cops thought that she was aiming her lens upward at the cables and supports. She lowered the camera as their cruiser drew alongside, they said, and her husband slowed to let them pass. The officers then slowed too, and so did Elbarasse. They radioed ahead to transit police and pulled the vehicle over west of the bridge.

It was a difficult period of American history for photographers, espe-cially those who didn't have conventional wardrobes and creamy com-plexions. Tourists and professionals alike got hassled and detained for taking pictures near bridges, power lines, refineries, chemical plants, and federal buildings as cops nervously enforced nonexistent laws. The country was still caught in fevered anxiety after the attacks of Septem-ber 11, 2001.

The fever created years of delirium, widespread at first. Law enforcement and immigration agencies were energized by inchoate suspicion, which ebbed only gradually and left behind islands of alarmists clinging to apocalyptic fears.

Yet the SUV's passengers seemed to be what they claimed to be: a family innocently returning from a vacation on Maryland's Eastern Shore. With Elbarasse and his wife, Bushra Elmasri, were their daughters, aged nineteen and twenty-one, and their son, fourteen. The videotapes the police examined showed them leaving a beach condo and packing for the trip, the daughters sitting in the rear seat, and then the roadway across the bridge and—more ominously—shots of "the physical steel structure of the main span . . . the cables, running the span of how the cables ran up through the steel structure," in the words of the police report. Still, no evidence of a crime was seen. Bushra Elmasri was not arrested, and no charges were brought.

Elbarasse, however, came up in the national criminal database as "a person of interest" to the FBI, an alert that brought a canine unit to check for explosives. The dogs found nothing. The family was taken to a police station near the bridge.

Perhaps by uncanny coincidence, Elbarasse had just been named the day before as an unindicted co-conspirator in a major case the Justice Department was assembling against the Holy Land Foundation, a Texas-based charity accused of sending funds to Hamas, the Palestinian movement in Gaza that had been designated by the U.S. government as a terrorist organization. Cutting off the flow of money to terrorists had become a top priority after 9/11.

The FBI faxed a warrant to the police near the bridge to have Elbarasse detained as a material witness—meaning that he was not criminally charged but was considered at risk of flight to avoid testifying. (In 1998, he had spent eight months in jail for refusing to testify before a grand jury.) Seven hours after being pulled over, the family—minus Elbarasse—was allowed to continue home.

The following day, Saturday, August 21, the FBI executed a search warrant on Elbarasse's Virginia house, where agents found some fifty boxes of documents, old and new, in Arabic and English. They "were not even his," said his lawyer, Stanley L. Cohen, who has defended numerous terrorism suspects. "He had not even read them" and had merely agreed to store them for people who had closed businesses and moved away.

But the papers included bank statements showing that Elbarasse had shared an account with Mousa Mohammed Abu Marzook, deputy chief of the Political Bureau of Hamas, which had grown out of the Muslim Brotherhood.

Even more exciting to Islam watchers were fifteen pages in Arabic under the heading "An Explanatory Memorandum on the General Strategic Goal for the Group in North America." Its significance remains unclear, because it takes the form of proposals, not policies. Furthermore, its current relevance is questionable, since it is dated May 22, 1991. Nevertheless, having been translated by the government and introduced into evidence in the Holy Land trial of 2007, it has become the principal text in online efforts to build a terrifying specter of the Muslim Brotherhood in America. Some of the websites tell the story in their names: Discover the Networks, Now the End Begins, Understanding the Threat, Counterterrorism Blog, The Counter Jihad Report, Unmasking the Muslim Brotherhood in America, the Clarion Project (whose website is radicalislam.org), Jihad Watch, and the like.

Some purveyors of the material have lectured and conducted training courses for FBI agents, local police, and community leaders, although federal agencies stopped holding the sessions after their anti-Islam content became public. Again and again, when a county sheriff's department signs up for training, Muslim activists push back and sometimes succeed in getting the sessions canceled. The boundaries of acceptable speech are constantly drawn, erased, and redrawn.

The Explanatory Memorandum, whose entire text is easily available on the web, has been cited by the right-wing commentators Sean Hannity and Glenn Beck. It has bolstered the efforts of David Yerushalmi, an American who once lived in an Israeli settlement on the West Bank, to promote legislation prohibiting the use of Sharia in American courts.

The document can be found on the website of Steven Emerson, whose zealous research on radical Islam through his Investigative Project on Terrorism has made him a darling of the FBI and intelligence agencies, which seem to feed him selected information. The more respectable Anti-Defamation League posts references to the memo, without endorsing it, on its web pages covering the Brotherhood and the Holy Land Foundation.

The paragraph being portrayed as an undisputed, authoritative prescription for Western domination is this:

> The process of settlement is a "Civilization-Jihadist Process" with all the word means. The Ikhwan [Muslim Brotherhood] must understand that their work in America is a kind of grand Jihad in eliminating and destroying the Western civilization from within and "sabotaging" its miserable house by their hands and the hands of the believers so that it is eliminated and God's religion is made victorious over all other religions. Without this level of understanding, we are not up to this challenge and have not prepared ourselves for Jihad yet. It is a Muslim's destiny to perform Jihad and work wherever he is and wherever he lands until the final hour comes, and there is no escape from that destiny except for those who chose to slack.

Elsewhere in the memo, "settlement" is defined as meaning "that Islam and its Movement become a part of the homeland it lives in."

Vigorous use of the document's sinister implications has been made by Frank Gaffney Jr., a Pentagon official in the Reagan administration who now runs the Center for Security Policy, which reported nearly $4.5 million in contributions in 2011. The Explanatory Memorandum appears as the main basis of his ten-part video course titled "The Muslim Brotherhood in America: The Enemy Within." The videos are available in four DVDs at $12 each, and a bound copy of the memo with an introduction by Gaffney is $4.89 on Amazon.

In his written introduction, Gaffney calls the seized document a "Rosetta stone for the Muslim Brotherhood, its goals, modus operandi, and infrastructure in America. It is arguably the single most important vehicle for understanding a secretive organization." In his video, he declares, "It contains a mission statement for the Muslim Brotherhood in this country that should alarm every American. Put succinctly, the Muslim Brotherhood's purpose in our country is to destroy Western civilization from within by our own hands and the hands of Shariah's adherents."

Gaffney and those who share his alarm give great weight to the memo's appendix, in which twenty-nine Muslim organizations appear under the heading "A list of our organizations and the organizations of our friends. Imagine if they all march according to one plan!!!" More than two decades after the memo was written, Gaffney and others in his subculture take this far beyond where the document goes: as firm proof that all those groups are fronts controlled by the Muslim Brotherhood and are today, in fact, marching according to one plan!!!

Some of the listed organizations, plus CAIR, the Council on American-Islamic Relations, were named by the Justice Department as unindicted co-conspirators in the Holy Land Foundation case. CAIR is a leading advocate for the rights of Muslims against discrimination, stereotyping, and abusive immigration practices. It portrays Islam as peaceful, and its website features a series of moving videos of Muslims with American accents denouncing the 9/11 attacks and other acts of terrorism as offenses against their religious precepts. No proof was offered in the indictment that the organization had sent money to Hamas.

CAIR and two other groups moved to have themselves removed from the list of unindicted co-conspirators, but the effort backfired and gave Islam watchers more ammunition. Not only was their motion denied by Judge Jorge Solis, who presided over the retrial, conviction, and sentencing of the five Holy Land Foundation defendants (the first trial had ended in a hung jury). He also accepted the government's assertions by citing the seized Elbarasse documents, including the Explanatory Memorandum, without testing their accuracy in an adversarial proceeding. He did not distinguish between the memo's list of "our organizations" and "the organizations of our friends." He ruled, "The Government has produced ample evidence to establish the associations of CAIR, ISNA [Islamic Society of North America], and NAIT [North American Islamic Trust] with HLF [Holy Land Foundation], the Islamic Association for Palestine ('IAP'), and with Hamas."

Until the Holy Land indictment and subsequent pressure from conservative members of Congress, some FBI field offices had tried both to infiltrate Muslim communities and to cultivate overt cooperation with them, hoping to open lines of communication that might provide tips about suspicious individuals and incipient terrorist plots. After the co-conspirator label was attached, however, FBI headquarters instructed agents to restrict contact with CAIR—a policy that FBI field offices in

New Haven, Chicago, and Philadelphia tried to ignore as they continued relations with the organization.

To someone who is convinced that the Muslim Brotherhood strives to infiltrate American institutions by using large numbers of Muslim organizations as fronts, the threat resembles the darkest fantasies about communism during the early Cold War. The fears of insidious takeover were broader then; McCarthyism had a harder hold on the country than the anti-Muslim suspicions do. Discrimination against Muslims certainly exists, and the Islam watchers play to the anxieties and stereotypes. But no widespread movement has developed in society at large to blacklist individuals, brand them with rumors of association, and ruin their careers, despite the best efforts of some of the alarmists. ("I have direct sources," claims one of those watchers, John Guandolo, a former FBI agent, "[who say] that CIA director John O. Brennan converted to Islam while stationed in Saudi Arabia.")

Through his lucrative Center for Security Policy, Frank Gaffney is eager to revive the vigilance, drawing the explicit parallel in his video: "Stealth jihadists understand, *as did their communist mentors* [emphasis added], the importance of penetrating and subverting their enemy's educational system. School systems across the country are under pressure to accommodate Islamist demands for legitimation, preferential treatment, and opportunities for proselytization."

You may have to stretch your imagination to envision antireligious communists as "mentors" of fundamentalist Muslims, but the analogy is convenient. It discredits as subversive the most inclusive moves to combat prejudice against Islam. Gaffney names as offenders in this surreptitious strategy "interfaith seminars, panels, services . . . borrowing of Christian churches, Jewish synagogues for Muslim worship." His video displays a sign reading, "First Church of Chrislam." That is, ecumenical efforts toward tolerance, in the spirit of American pluralism, are vehicles of self-destruction.

The communist comparison also appears on Discover the Networks, established by David Horowitz to monitor the political left. Horowitz made his name by drawing up lists of the "most dangerous" liberal professors on various campuses and trying to mobilize alumni and students to have them ousted or censored.

His site carries an unsigned essay quoting from the Explanatory Memorandum's call for "a shift from the collision mentality to the absorption mentality." The posting interprets this as "meaning that they should abandon any tactics involving defiance or confrontation, and seek instead to implant into the larger society a host of seemingly benign Islamic groups with ostensibly unobjectionable motives; once those groups had gained a measure of public acceptance, they would be in a position to more effectively promote societal transformation by the old Communist technique of 'boring from within.'" The article accuses the Brotherhood of "emulating the Communist Party tactic of creating interlocking front groups during the Cold War in order to confuse its enemies and make it more difficult to combat."

The Explanatory Memorandum is also one of two principal sources for Guandolo, the former FBI agent, in a piece about the Brotherhood's "settlement process," posted by the online magazine *Guns & Patriots*. "How did the Brotherhood actually insinuate itself into the fabric of America?" he asks. "How is it possible that today the most prominent Islamic organizations in North America are controlled by the Brotherhood and actually seek to subordinate the individual liberties of Americans (and Canadians) to the slavery of Shariah (Islamic Law)?"

His answers are two and three decades old: the 1991 Explanatory Memorandum and a speech in the early 1980s by Zaid Naman, whom Guandolo identifies as the leader of the Brotherhood's executive office in the United States. Despite its age and its dubious relevance, the transcript of a recording of his talk was introduced by the government in the Holy Land Foundation trial.

Then a frightening report by the conservative Hudson Institute, based almost entirely on those two sources, lists among the Brotherhood's nefarious schemes the venerable American practice of "political action," which—the Hudson Institute warns—includes efforts to educate Muslim Americans about their voting rights. The convenience of this conspiratorial lens is that it renders civic responsibility as wily and dangerous. The most peaceful, democratic, and constitutional behavior becomes suspect.

Free speech includes the right to exaggerate, and no hyperbole about the document seems too grand. Douglas Farah on the Counterterrorism

Blog calls the memo "the smoking gun of the Ikhwan's [Brotherhood's] long-standing efforts to destroy the Western world as we know it."

The website Now the End Begins, whose home page is strewn with apocalyptic images and biblical slogans, repeats the "smoking gun" metaphor, citing the Northeast Intelligence Network.

The Counter Jihad Report issues a "call to purge Muslim Brotherhood influence from US government and civil life."

The Oak Initiative, describing itself as a grassroots movement of Christians, links to Gaffney's video course.

Citizens for National Security posts "Homegrown Jihad in the USA" with graphs and maps but no sourcing whatever.

Unmasking the Muslim Brotherhood in America quotes from the document as if it were brand-new.

The Clarion Project posts pieces urging that the spread of Sharia law be arrested, which several state legislatures have acted to do; Oklahoma even tried to bar Sharia by adopting a constitutional amendment, which was struck down by a federal appeals court as a violation of the First Amendment's prohibition against the establishment of religion. (The Republican presidential candidates Newt Gingrich and Michele Bachmann warned against Sharia as "totalitarian control," and Sarah Palin said that if Sharia "were to be adopted, allowed to govern in our country, it will be the downfall of America.")

Daniel Pipes's Middle East Forum contains a piece by an Anglican vicar, Mark Durie, citing the memo. And Pipes's *Middle East Quarterly*, in an article by Denis MacEoin, smears Keith Ellison, a black Democrat and one of two Muslims in Congress, under the headline "Keith Ellison's Stealth Jihad." MacEoin calls him "at best naïve in his associations, and at worst a fifth columnist, someone whose status within the House of Representatives provides cover for anti-American discourse and, possibly, anti-American actions."

This guilt by association is based on the document's twenty-year-old list of what its author considered "our organizations" or "our friends," which the Bush administration's Justice Department used to claim that the groups "are and/or were members of the US Muslim Brotherhood." Their designation as unindicted co-conspirators was a handy prosecutorial tool, because the federal rule barring hearsay doesn't apply to evidence from an alleged co-conspirator. The hearsay can be introduced, and some prosecutors love to drive through that loophole. The technique is controversial, because those named have no opportunity to rebut the label and the government has no obligation to prove its accuracy.

Those unproven allegations about organizations' ties to the Brotherhood, plus untested FBI reports, have been widely cited in the anti-Islam subculture. Robert Spencer, in Jihad Watch, attacked Tim Kaine, then a senatorial candidate from Virginia, for speaking at a 2011 dinner honoring Jamal Barzinji, whom Spencer labels a Muslim Brotherhood official. Follow the piece's sources and they trace back to the Explanatory Memorandum, posted at Emerson's Investigative Project on Terrorism, and to an article at *FrontPage* by Ryan Mauro accusing the honoree of holding offices in several of the friendly organizations listed in the document.

A raw, unverified FBI report from 1988, posted on the Investigative Project's site, includes Barzinji among several who "have been previously characterized as noted above by [source censored] as being members and leaders of the IKHWAN [Brotherhood]." But unfiltered FBI files collect all sorts of sketchy rumors and allegations. There is nothing automatically credible about them. And the use of the passive voice—"have been previously characterized"—is a standard technique of making unsourced allegations that cannot be checked for accuracy.

Without the documents from Elbarasse's basement, John Guandolo told me, "I think I'd have a very tough time doing what I'm doing," that is, making a persuasive case that Islam is bent on conquering America. Indeed, it was clear, from a three-and-a-half-hour presentation that the former FBI agent gave one afternoon, that while he dramatically flips pages and reads from scholarly volumes on Sharia law, analyzes the suras of the Quran, and quotes from a trove of legal and doctrinal documents, the Explanatory Memorandum is the linchpin. Its ambitious takeover scheme and its list of friendly organizations are pivotal to the argument that all those groups are surreptitiously mobilized to execute the plan.

Given the memorandum's central role, I decided to drill down into the document as far as possible and to ask various Islam watchers who cite it to provide evidence of its authenticity, importance, and continued pertinence more than two decades after being written. I asked them for information that would identify the role and responsibility of its author, named as Mohamed Akram; any evidence that his proposals were actually adopted by the Muslim Brotherhood; whether any copies of the memo had been found other than in Elbarasse's basement; and whether its concept of subverting America had been repeated in recent documents. I thought it was critical to know whether the fifteen pages had just been lying unread in a box or whether they remained alive as an animating set of ideas.

It goes without saying that the Internet's fluid transmission of information has enabled people to organize themselves easily into clusters of affinity and belief. Readers—including college students, much to the chagrin of their professors—rarely go back critically to the origins of what are presented as facts. Nuance and contradiction disappear; opposing viewpoints vanish. Assumptions are reinforced. The Internet, with its appealing graphics and hidden sources, offers a deceptive impression of authority. An assertion gains currency in the echo chamber of repetition and acquires credibility as like-minded analysts cite one another in circular reinforcement.

That is what happened in the case of the Explanatory Memorandum. The bottom line of what I learned was this: The writings of the watchdogs of Islam who depend on the memo would not get past the fact-checkers at *The New Yorker* or *The New York Times*.

I sent inquiries to seven leading authors, founders of websites, and others who have made recent careers of sounding the alarm about the Muslim Brotherhood's threats to American institutions, based mainly on the 1991 memo. Four of the seven replied, sometimes with extensive and interesting detail, but their answers did not quite hit the target of my search to justify the use of the document. The remaining three—Steven Emerson, Frank Gaffney, and Ryan Mauro—did not reply to my questions. This was unexpected, given their eagerness to promote warnings about Islam. Perhaps they were too busy. Perhaps they were suspicious of my motives, although I did not prejudge the issue and expressed no skepticism; I just sought facts as a neutral observer. Perhaps they were unable to provide answers because they didn't know much about the document they had publicized.

Gaffney scheduled a phone interview, then canceled and had his assistant refer me to Stephen Coughlin and John Guandolo, who spent considerable time and effort offering their views and sources, all stopping short of validating the memo. Denis MacEoin provided references to a rich variety of Muslim Brotherhood texts but nothing definitive about the Explanatory Memorandum.

Robert Spencer misstated when and where the document was found, exaggerated its "self-description as an explanation of the Brotherhood's strategic goals for North America," and assumed its veracity given "the total lack of any evidence suggesting that it was rejected, superseded, revised, or altered." But he cited no evidence that it had been adopted or approved in the first place.

Spencer admitted that he did not know whether any other copies had surfaced, and he had nothing to offer about the author, Mohamed Akram, although he remembered having read "a good deal about him." He suggested asking Steve Emerson, which I did, but Emerson never answered. Perhaps I'm making too much of these various silences, but my experience as a reporter tells me that when people are devoted to a line of argument, they'll spare no effort to drive home their point with the facts—if they have them.

In this case, we have a series of blurry facts. They exist, but like fuzzy dots on a page. If they represented positions on a nautical chart, you'd run aground.

The first item that's out of focus is the author, who is usually named as Mohamed Akram but sometimes as Mohamed Adlouni or Mohamed Akram Adlouni. "Akram was the head of the MB [Muslim Brotherhood] at the time the memo was written," said Stephen Coughlin, who made the same claim in a slick 2010 report he wrote for a security consulting firm where he worked, calling Akram "the General Masul [leader] of the Muslim Brotherhood in America." When I pointed out that Akram had addressed his memo to the general *masul* and therefore couldn't have been that person himself, Coughlin backtracked, telling me, "That information came from a F.B.I. CT [counterterrorism] Special Agent." Akram in 1992 "was a secretary which would have qualified him as a masul (but maybe not General at that time)."

There is no evidence, however, that Akram was ever the general *masul* of the Muslim Brotherhood in America. He appears in several documents seized in the Elbarasse raid, including an address book and an organization chart, as "committee secretary" for Palestinian Action, as a member of the executive committee, and as "office secretary." In the Holy Land indictment he was included among 306 unindicted co-conspirators in a list of those "who are and/or were members of the US Muslim Brotherhood's Palestine Committee." Wherever the Palestine Committee is mentioned elsewhere, it is assumed to mean the Muslim Brotherhood.

So there seems no doubt that Akram was a player in the Brotherhood. Whether that made him a figure of prominence and authority is an open question, however, not one the Islam watchers are inclined to ask critically. His Explanatory Memorandum is too crucial to their argument to call it into question.

"In the name of God, the Beneficent, the Merciful," the memo begins before addressing three audiences: "The beloved brother/The General Masul, may God keep him," the secretary of the Shura Council, and the members of the Shura Council. "God's peace, mercy, and blessings be upon you."

Within the flowery language that follows, the document's purpose emerges as more tentative than those who use it describe. Indeed, watchers have written that the Brotherhood "published" it or adopted it, when neither appears to be the case. It is actually to, not from, the governing Shura Council.

"I send this letter of mine to you hoping that it would seize your attention and receive your good care," Akram beseeches.

> What might have encouraged me to submit the memorandum in this time in particular is my feeling of a glimpse of hope and the beginning of good tidings which bring the good news that we have embarked on a new stage of Islamic activism stages in this continent.
>
> The papers which are between your hands are not abundant extravagance, imaginations, or hallucinations which passed in the mind of one of your brothers, but they are rather hopes, ambitions, and challenges that I hope that you share some or most of which with me. I do not claim their infallibility or absolute correctness, but they are an attempt which requires study.

He goes on to trace his ideas to "the long-term plan which we approved and adopted in our council and our conference in the year 1987. So, my honorable brother, do not rush to throw these papers away due to your many occupations and worries. All that I'm asking of you is to read them and to comment on them hoping that we might continue together the project of our plan and our Islamic work in this part of the world."

The watchers haven't produced the 1987 plan, but that doesn't prevent the right-wing site *Breitbart,* for example, from cleverly mixing it up with the 1991 Explanatory Memorandum to make Akram's proposals appear to have been adopted. "The strategic plan was written" by Akram, a posting declares, "and was approved by the Brotherhood's Shura Council and Organizational Conference in 1987." The article then quotes from Akram's memo, written four years later, as if it had been approved beforehand, in 1987.

So why should the suggestions of one Brotherhood activist, submitted to the Shura Council more than two decades ago, be taken as a serious statement of the Brotherhood's current policy? There are no convincing answers, even from those who went to considerable time and effort to reply.

One erroneous argument, spread by several watchers, is that the defense in the Holy Land trial did not object to the memo's being entered into evidence. The former FBI agent John Guandolo asserted, "The defense attorneys stipulated to the fact it is the MB's strategic plan for the US and North America. As a matter of legal fact, that is what this document is."

Not so. The defense team lodged vigorous objections to the introduction of this and other documents from the Elbarasse search, and two attorneys on the defense team, Nancy Hollander and Marlo Cadeddu, scoffed at Guandolo's statement. "There was no such stipulation by the defense," said Cadeddu. "Nor would we ever have stipulated to any such thing. Any claims to the contrary are simply untrue." Indeed, after the five Holy Land officials and fund-raisers were convicted, their lawyers argued specifically, in an unsuccessful appeal to the Fifth Circuit, that the trial judge had erred in admitting the documents, which the attorneys branded hearsay, irrelevant to the charge that the defendants had funneled money to Hamas.

Islam watchers have put in play a couple of other pieces of information that were not introduced in court, but fact-checking those turns up more conjecture than confirmation. For example, I asked for the source of Frank Gaffney's video statement that the "phases of the world underground movement plan" had been revealed by "another ominous bit of evidence." Neither Coughlin nor Guandolo could supply the answer, and Gaffney himself did not reply to my requests that he identify the "evidence."

This is important because it forms the basis of a dramatic online PowerPoint presentation by Gaffney of the supposed steps of the "stealth jihad" against America: the infiltration of government, then the use of mass media in the "escalation phase," which Gaffney calls "pre-violent." The goal, he says, is to encourage self-censorship by the press by condemning blasphemy and slander against Islam, by opposing the use of religious labels when describing terrorists. Then, in later stages, come proselytization; the promotion of Sharia-compliant financial activities (barring interest payments, pork, gambling, tobacco, alcohol, pornography); the infiltration of Sharia into American courts; and so on.

While Gaffney doesn't cite his "ominous bit of evidence," other watchers speculate. Several point to a 1982 document, "The Project," found by Swiss and Italian police during a search in November 2001 of the villa of Youssef Nada, an Egyptian-born Italian businessman suspected of helping to finance the 9/11 attacks. He belonged to the Egyptian Muslim Brotherhood and had some of Osama bin Laden's relatives as clients. But he denied funding terrorism, and he was never charged.

"The Project," nearly twenty years old when discovered, bears no signature. It makes no mention of the United States. It outlines "a global vision of a worldwide strategy for Islamic policy" in a dozen steps that are compatible with efforts to spread adherence to Islam as an evangelical religion—whether violent or peaceful depends on the interpretation of "jihad," a struggle defined by some Muslims as spiritual and by others, citing basic doctrine, as justifying military action and terrorism.

Its phases—called "points of departure"—do not coincide with those Gaffney mentions. They begin with the first, "know the terrain"; proceed through the fourth, "construct social, economic, scientific, and health institutions and penetrate the domain of the social services"; and go on to the fifth, "dedicate ourselves to the establishment of an Islamic state, in parallel with gradual efforts aimed at gaining control of local power centers through institutional action." The seventh phase calls for "temporary cooperation between Islamic movements and nationalist movements . . . against colonialism, preaching, and the Jewish state," and the eighth advises members "to avoid the Movement hurting itself with major confrontations, which could encourage its adversaries to give it a fatal blow."

The ninth phase ratchets up the action to "support movements engaged in jihad across the Muslim world . . . to protect the *dawa* [proselytizing] with the force necessary to guarantee its security." That feeds into the eleventh, "to nourish a sentiment of rancor with respect to the Jews and refuse all coexistence," and the twelfth, which sounds benign: "to conduct constructive self-criticism" and "to produce an official document on global Islamic policy."

Guandolo also sent me what he said was an FBI summary of a longer document, which he claimed was found in Elbarasse's basement but not submitted in evidence. Guandolo has only the summary, not the full document, and it bears no date and no author's name. Called "Phases of World Underground Movement Plan," it's addressed to "The Rulers" and lists five basic steps whose leading goal is "to become the third political power together with the U.S. and the former Soviet Union, and the third religious power together with the Jewish Agency and the World Council of Churches." Despite the fanciful tone, Guandolo takes it seriously.

The FBI summary describes the first phase as the "phase of discreet and secret establishment of elite leadership [which] has already been implemented in this country," but which country the document fails to say. It could have been written about Egypt, for example, the Muslim Brotherhood's birthplace.

Second is the "phase of gradual appearance on the public scene," which includes "establishing a shadow government (secret) within the Government." Third comes the "escalation phase, prior to conflict and confrontation with the rulers, through utilizing mass media." Fourth is "open public confrontation with the Government" through "political pressure" and "training on the use of weapons domestically and overseas in anticipation of zero-hour."

Finally comes "Phase Five: Seizing power to establish their Islamic Nation under which all parties and Islamic groups become united."

Neither of those documents—the undated "Phases" and the 1982 "Project"—matches Gaffney's scary stages of doom. And perhaps because they don't aim a stiletto precisely at the United States, they are quoted less widely than Akram's Explanatory Memorandum, which is more specific. But that memo also contains internal caveats, which are generally ignored.

Those tentative passages include the sentences in which Akram pleads with the Shura Council to take his ideas seriously and not to "rush to throw these papers away." If quoted, they would undermine the Islam watchers' selling of the document as a definitive prescription for a Brotherhood strategy. So you don't see those lines in the alarmist literature. You don't see any reference to the Explanatory Memorandum in other, current documents of Islamic organizations that have surfaced. Nor have those who give the memo weight produced any Muslim Brotherhood records of its having been adopted.

At a two-day training session for community activists, Guandolo projected a part of the document onto a screen, read excerpts, and then declared, "The strategic memorandum got the approval of the Shura Council. It got a note of approval from the general *masul*." He said the approvals were at the beginning of the document.

I hadn't seen them in the copy submitted into evidence, so I asked if he could point them out. He picked up a printed version, leafed through it, seemed a little embarrassed that he couldn't find what he'd just said was there, and promised to locate it for me. That was the last I heard about the elusive approvals. I asked him privately during a break if he could provide them, and I followed up by e-mail. No answer.

Even with the help of the advocates, then, I was unable to find independent evidence of the document's importance.

Instead, they argue for its significance by producing other fundamentalist writings that reflect the ambition of establishing global Islamic rule. There is no doubt about the extreme ideas contained in the most intolerant texts, which lay down a prescription that could be called totalitarian, in that the totality of society is to be placed within narrowly con-servative, religious parameters dominated by Islam.

But there is a long distance between the excessive aspirations and their practical application in a pluralistic democracy such as the United States. And in arguing the case for alarm, the watchers do not cross that distance successfully—at least not to my mind.

Their anxieties mirror those of Palestinian Arabs who read the most extreme Jewish texts and statements as Israeli doctrine, when they are actually endorsed by only a radical minority: the Arab as the biblical enemy Amalek, Genesis as the Jews' deed from God to all the land, the determination to destroy Islam's holiest structures in Jerusalem and build a third Jewish temple. These remain absolutist fantasies, as com-pelling as they are to that minority.

The same is surely the case in the United States, where Muslims make up just 0.9 percent of the population. But the alarmists attempt no assess-ment of American Muslims' religiosity in practice or their affinity for the concept of global jihad and the ultimate domination of Islam. If there is slippage from the doctrine to the personal belief, as in every other reli-gion, it is not explored. Instead, Muslim citizens, especially their leaders, are pictured in lockstep with the fundamentalist texts.

A panoply of such writings was offered by three authors to justify their regard for the Explanatory Memorandum, which Stephen Cough-lin called "part of a continuous stream of Brotherhood publications and other releases that speak to a common set of objectives predetermined by Islamic doctrines as universally understood by the Brotherhood."

He labeled the memo from Virginia and the 1982 document from Switzerland "seminal and enabling." But when I requested evidence to support his characterization, he replied with only a circular assertion: "The two documents are considered enabling because they reflect the strategic thinking of the Shura and its leadership and was [sic] written to enable activity." He did not offer substantiation.

One of the pleasures of free speech in America is the ability to draw from any source and statement to bolster your view. Nothing is placed off-limits by censorship. But unless the speech is heard with vigilance, unless the audience exercises critical listening, the result is not enlight-ening. So I tried to dissect the mechanism of argument here.

I found that following Coughlin and others into the weeds of fundamentalist texts does not make their case unless you accept their view that radical words uttered anywhere anytime are operative among virtually all Muslims here and today. Or, putting it as Coughlin does, "Brotherhood doctrines are premised on certain doctrines in Islamic law," and those doctrines are immutable and widely observed.

Denis MacEoin, editor of the *Middle East Quarterly*, goes back to the 1947 manifesto by the Muslim Brotherhood's founder, Hasan al-Banna, who writes of a Western civilization "now bankrupt and in decline. Its foundations are crumbling, and its institutions and guiding principles are falling apart . . . It only remained for a strong Eastern power to exert itself under the shadow of Allah's banner, with the standard of the Quran fluttering at its head, and backed up by the powerful, unyielding soldiery of the faith." MacEoin also quotes the founder of Hamas, Ahmad Yassin, on the wish for martyrdom, and others who stress the military and violent side of jihad.

That Islam has not conquered the West nearly seventy years later does not seem to dampen the alarmists' excitement, with MacEoin something of an exception. Unlike most other Islam watchers in this subculture, he is a scholar, having studied Persian and Arabic at the University of Edinburgh and taught Arabic and Islamic studies at Newcastle University. "The Brotherhood will never take over Europe or America," MacEoin e-mails me reassuringly, "but if you care to think back to [the] 1970s, I think you will recognize that great harm has been done since, and that much of it goes back to MB-affiliated organizations. They can and do continue to harm us."

Yes, but the question remains: Is the Muslim Brotherhood really working effectively to infiltrate and sabotage the United States, in accord with the 1991 Explanatory Memorandum?

Stephen Coughlin has read extensively. A reserve army major who worked as an intelligence officer for the Joint Chiefs of Staff, he reaches back to 1964 for what he calls "the true keystone document," *Milestones* by Said Qutb, an Egyptian fundamentalist whose months during 1949 at Colorado State College of Education convinced him of America's corruption and decay. Arrested with other Muslim Brothers by the Nasser government, he spent a decade in prison, was released for a few months, and was hanged in 1966.

Qutb's writings, regarded as a major influence on Osama bin Laden, rely on the expectation of Islam's ultimate conquest of the West. "The leadership of mankind by Western man is now on the decline," he writes in *Milestones,* "primarily because it is deprived of those life-giving values which enabled it to be the leaders of mankind . . . Islam is the only system which possesses these values." Victory "can take any form," he declares, "be it the victory of the freedom of spirit . . . or dominance in the world."

Coughlin mentions others' books published in 1984, 1985, and 1988, plus more recent textbooks and training guides for children. The most relevant are materials from the Tarbiyah Project, published by the Islamic Circle of North America, comprising lesson plans on the Quran, prayer, morals, and myriad rules and practices of Islam.

A 2001 booklet to guide curriculum in Islamic schools emphasizes "the belief that the mission of Islam is to positively effect [*sic*] and transform the world, and that the purpose of Islamic education is to prepare young men and women capable of carrying out this mission."

But that's the only suggestion that kids should be indoctrinated to work toward an Islamic takeover. Otherwise, there would be nothing askew if you took the entire volume and substituted the words "Christian" and "Christianity" for the words "Islamic" and "Islam" in the extensive sections on moral character, good manners, beliefs about war and violence and sin. "The Tarbiyah Project believes that Islamic education is concerned essentially with personality development, i.e., values, identity, self esteem, belonging, leadership, and other issues centering around developing a strong Muslim personality," the booklet explains. "To achieve this high level of moral maturity" requires "such skills as critical thinking, assertiveness, cooperative learning, conflict resolution, etc." I tried in vain to be scared by this.

A longer volume, the *Tarbiyah Guide* for training employees and members of the Islamic Circle, contains dense theology and esoteric history. It is cited by Coughlin and Guandolo as evidence of current conspiracy, but only a careful sifting through 321 pages reveals a few lines, in a section titled "Islamic Movement," that could be read as ominous— provided you view them through a lens of suspicion.

The guide does not mention the United States as a target and seems aimed primarily at the Islamic world. It calls for divine law in "the many so-called Muslim countries where governments now rule according to imported capitalist or communist constitutions." It declares that "in order to establish Islam functionally in the world the Islamic movement must strive against the thoughts and philosophies left over from colonialism, whether of European socialism or American capitalism," noting that "Islamic teachings and rules are comprehensive and designed by Allah to govern the affairs of man at all levels of community, from the family to the whole of the human race."

One lesson advocates "leadership at all levels of human community, in the family, neighborhood, national government and international institutions, in order to bring together Muslims everywhere so they can excel again in all endeavors, and recover the flag of jihad and call mankind to Allah and the good news of His Revelation."

In the interest of a "strategic orientation for long-range victory," stealth is recommended. The guide cites Hasan al-Banna, the founder of the Brotherhood, and the Prophet Muhammad's dictum "Seek secrecy in what you do." It urges "openness in work but secrecy of organization." It recommends keeping a "low profile" and promotes "gradualism in both thoughts and action" and "identifying good and reliable cadre to bear the burden of initiating and sustaining jihad." One phase, named "execution," is defined as "the stage of relentless combat and constant effort to achieve the goals," which include "securing power for an Islamic government."

If the United States is meant as the stage for this effort, it must be inferred, something the alarmists are eager to do. They do not quote this passage from the guide, which seems to argue against the takeover scenario: "The Islamic movement is designed to liberate man in dynamic change, not enslave him in efforts to stabilize and control the world, as do most utopian movements, including capitalism, in the West. [It] promotes science and technology not to gain power or to register new discoveries but to learn more about the greatness of Allah."

John Guandolo had placed a DVD and his book *Raising a Jihadi Generation* at each of our places around a polished table in a Virginia hotel. His afternoon session bore the discreet title, posted outside the room, "Media Awareness."

It drew only five of us, four of whom appeared to be zealous believers: a freelance writer for various right-wing websites whose computer lid was just big enough for a sticker declaring "Repeal Obamacare"; a beefy corrections officer from New Jersey who had spearheaded a petition opposing the state's plans to restrict solitary confinement in juvenile detention facilities; his colleague, who would identify himself only as "law enforcement"; and an editor from rural Virginia. She had written in praise of the local sheriff for defying the objections of CAIR and sending his deputies to a three-day training session by Guandolo, even after in-service credit was denied at the last minute by the Rappahannock Regional Criminal Justice Academy.

In person, Guandolo is not an imposing man. He is serious and friendly and seems to have found his footing after a checkered career at the FBI. "I'm not here to convince you of anything," he says disarmingly, and yet he is, of course, hoping to depend on pure facts, carefully selected. His patter is practiced, and he uses words economically, deftly integrating the spiel with slides projected on a screen. When he allows himself a smile, it usually comes at that moment when someone in his small audience displays a light of recognition that the threat is real.

This happened toward the end of his presentation. He had expertly connected the dots. The line ran from quotations by radicals, thrown up on the screen, to selected sentences from "Phases of World Underground Movement Plan"—that unverified summary of a document Guandolo didn't have—then on to words from al-Qaeda officials, including Osama bin Laden. He projected the Brotherhood's frightening symbol: a globe colored the green of Islam, crossed with two golden sabers and a Quran between their blades. "Their mission and objective have never changed since 1928," Guandolo asserted.

He cited the Explanatory Memorandum as proof, both in its grand plan and in its list of American Muslim organizations associated with the Brotherhood. The Brotherhood produced Hamas, so these American groups are Hamas, and their leaders are Hamas, and Guandolo could name names and follow the Muslim officers' careers from organization to organization, all stained with the label of the Brotherhood, conflated with Hamas. And so Hamas is abroad in the land, in student organizations, mosques, Islamic cultural centers.

He quoted various arrested terrorists. He raised the specter of Sharia. He analyzed suras of the Quran, arranging them chronologically to emphasize that those endorsing violence came later and therefore superseded the earlier verses that contained more peaceful teachings. He told a truncated history of Muhammad's flight from Mecca and the warfare against his followers as if Muhammad were the aggressor, operating from a mosque in Medina used as a fortress and arsenal.

Here was a dot to be connected to the present. When a mosque in America is built, Guandolo asked, "why is the ground floor concrete three feet thick? It looks like a fort, which is what it is if it's a Muslim Brotherhood center." Whatever the thickness of a building's walls, and whether designed for structural or security purposes, the statement clinched the argument among the four other people at the table. Guandolo saw the light of recognition switch on, and he smiled with satisfaction.

The Explanatory Memorandum contains a call to establish an "Islamic Center in every city." Indeed, the name Islamic Center is often given to a complex containing a mosque, community center, school, and other facilities. "The center we seek is the one which constitutes the 'axis' of our Movement," the memo declares, "the 'perimeter' of the circle of our work, our 'balance center,' the 'base' for our rise . . . a seed 'for a small Islamic society' which is a reflection and a mirror to our central organizations . . . a place for study, family, battalion, course, seminar, visit, sport, school, social club, women gathering, kindergarten . . . and the center for distributing our newspapers, magazines, books, and our audio and visual tapes." The memo likens the center's role to "the mosque's role during the time of God's prophet, God's prayers and peace be upon him . . . From the mosque, he drew the Islamic life and provided to the world the most magnificent and fabulous civilization humanity knew." Again, there is no evidence that this memo represents an approved plan.

Nevertheless, your everyday local Islamic center becomes Guandolo's target. At the end of his book he includes a boilerplate affidavit for law enforcement officers to submit to a judge to get a warrant to search any Islamic center or mosque. Its twenty-eight points begin with statements on the Brotherhood's creed of violence to establish Allah's law in the land. It then cites the Explanatory Memorandum's listing of American organizations and the unverified "World Underground Movement Plan." The affidavit includes a statement that whatever mosque or center is to be searched (fill in the blank) is owned by whatever Brotherhood organization is applicable.

The boilerplate concludes, "Your affiant believes that Probable Cause

exists that the Islamic Center of _____ is part of the Muslim Brotherhood's 'Islamic Movement' inside the United States whose stated objective
is the overthrow of the United States government and the establishment
of an Islamic State, including the use of violence in our local area. Your
affiant further believes that documents and instrumentalities to further
this movement, to include supporting criminal activity may be present
inside this location."

Toward the end of his presentation, Guandolo bent over a blank piece
of paper and drew two concentric circles, the inner one representing a
mosque, the outer one marking a three-mile radius in which property
was to be controlled. "They'll go with money from Saudi Arabia and buy
houses for more than the market price," he said, so that "right around
the mosque it's only Muslims living. This is sacred space. They're claim-
ing territory." Residents who hold out and refuse to sell are bribed with
excessive offers, then harassed and threatened, he insisted, without giving specific examples. The small audience was clearly impressed. The
stain would spread outward from the fortress.

Earlier, the New Jersey corrections officer had warned the editor that
while her rural county may have only 50 Muslims today, soon it would
have 150—and a mosque, he'd said with foreboding. Now, after seeing
the circles on the page, he held his head in his hands with an air of shock
and conviction, as if he had just been sent a revelation. I wondered how
he would treat Muslim juveniles in detention.

Two weeks later, in a slightly larger room in the same Virginia hotel,
Guandolo conducted a two-day training session for activists who displayed as little skepticism. They posed no probing questions about the
sources of his grand statements. They did not even follow up when he
was awkwardly unable to produce what he claimed were Muslim Brotherhood approvals of the Explanatory Memorandum. These folks came
across as intelligent, but when I asked them during a break toward the
end of the last day whether they doubted anything John had said, they
answered with a unanimous no.

Most of them were old enough to have been schooled in the archaic
tool of the library, where sources had to be painstakingly found and crit-

ical thinking was prized. So they weren't bred of the credulous Internet generation. But they had come with their minds made up, and their critical thinking was aimed not at researching the basis of Guandolo's argument but at honing their skills to combat the dastardly spread of Islam.

That made their curiosity highly selective, even on a point of much debate: the nature of jihad. To document his assertion that jihad means violence, Guandolo opened a dog-eared copy of a middle school textbook by Yahiya Emerick titled *What Islam Is All About* and read aloud: "If anyone dies in a Jihad, they automatically will go to paradise. A Shaheed, or Martyr, is described this way by Allah, 'Don't think that those who were killed in Allah's Cause are dead. No, they are alive, finding their bounty in the presence of their Lord.'"

If any of the trainees had bothered to pick up the book from the table in the front and read the context, as I did during a break, they would have discovered a counterargument earlier on the same page: "Now the word Jihad means to struggle or strive, or to work for something with determination. It does not mean war." Then, further on, the passage adds that the term "jihad" "can be applied to the act of fighting as well."

We have watched Islam enough since 9/11 to know that jihad means different things to different Muslims. Most of us who pay attention have absorbed competing information. Contradictions and ambiguities were wholly absent from this room, however, and the small group of activists had chosen categorical certainty.

They had invested some time and money for this. Three had flown in from Montreal, Denver, and Minneapolis and had paid for hotel rooms. Four had driven from elsewhere in Virginia and Maryland, not far from Washington, D.C., and all presumably had paid Guandolo's fee of $395 apiece. (The conference room, he told me, cost him $1,000 for the two days, and since the total he could have collected from the seven was under $2,800, he wasn't making a killing. He was waiting for tax-exempt status so he could receive deductible donations.)

What the attendees got was a course titled "A Civil Response to Civilization Jihad," condensed into "Civil Response" on the sign outside the door. Guandolo is security conscious—he calls it OPSEC, or Operations Security. As a condition of allowing me to observe, he asked me not to mention the precise location of the sessions and not to publish techniques that he would teach about how to gather information surreptitiously on local Muslims and their organizations. You can take the man out of the FBI, it seems, but you can't take the FBI out of the man.

The folks in the room seemed thrilled, sometimes spellbound, especially by the parts he didn't want reported. Without violating the ground rules I accepted, I can say that the investigative methods—all perfectly legal, he emphasized—closely tracked some used by criminal investigators where no warrant or subpoena is required. Being briefed on the techniques was exciting. The Minneapolis woman's eyes shone fervently.

Like most of the seven, she asked that she not be identified by name, but she spoke freely about her journey to this room. When a mosque was proposed for her neighborhood, she realized how little she knew about Islam. So she began reading—concentrating on the websites devoted to portraying the threat, apparently—and concluded that the mosque had to be stopped. She voiced her opposition at zoning hearings but was "shut down," she said, when she tried to quote from the Explanatory Memorandum. In the end, the board denied the zoning change that was required, but ostensibly for reasons of city planning, not because it feared a takeover by the Muslim Brotherhood.

The problem the activists face is the country's formal creed of religious tolerance. Even though they stress national security, their portrayal of Islam as a religio-political amalgam puts it in a box that doesn't exist for most Americans. A religion is a religion, and while religious establishments certainly have political positions on such issues as abortion, gay marriage, contraception, and aid to Israel, those are generally seen as corollaries to the main proposition of faith. If pro-choice liberals opposed the construction of an evangelical church to stop the spread of fundamentalist Christianity's political agenda, they would surely be denounced for religious bigotry.

And that is what had happened to most of the seven activists in this room. They seemed shocked and hurt by the accusations. "One of my fears is being destroyed before even being influential," said the woman from Minneapolis. She had suffered the charge "Islamophobe," as had a man who was willing to have his name reported: Dave Petteys of Colorado, a Tea Party activist and member of ACT for America, which agitates against Islamic centers and other Muslim organizations. A Maryland man, a retired air force officer active in the anti-immigration movement, was called a bigot and a vigilante after testifying before a state legislative committee.

A Virginia member of ACT worried that the extreme rhetoric of some of his colleagues made them easy to discredit. He saw the challenge as "how to get information out so we don't get labeled as right-wing extremists. There might be a way of talking about Islam to appeal to a broader swath of Americans, e.g., they abuse women, and things that a broad group of Americans, right and left, would find offensive."

Guandolo offered ideas on packaging their message and defusing the opposition. He put them through three-minute exercises in which he played the Muslim gadfly in the audience and threw arguments that required their brisk rebuttals. He coached them on approaching legislators with small doses of pure "facts" and thumb drives containing letters the lawmakers could just sign and send.

Yet in the safety of the like-minded circle in that room, he too employed incendiary vocabulary and startling assertions, referring repeatedly to "the enemy" who uses the "classic insurgent model" and characterizing the struggle as "a war we're losing, and we don't know it."

He asked rhetorically, "Why are most cab drivers at Reagan and Dulles [airports] Muslims? There is a reason." He gave no source for his statistic, and he left the reason to his trainees' imaginations until later in the session: "They're talking on their phones. Their network is like that." He likened them to Afghans who'd had little soda stands outside Soviet bases and would pass the word when a Soviet unit rolled out. "So when you see a hot dog stand outside FBI headquarters or the U.S. Attorney's offices, what do you think they're doing?" Some of the trainees nodded in understanding.

He went on. "Who owns a large number of gas stations and convenience stores? For twenty-three straight trips I took all over the country, the guy who was running the X-ray machine, et cetera, was an obvious Sharia-compliant Muslim." Guandolo had taught his cluster of trainees how to identify such a person: closely trimmed mustache but an unruly beard died red. (The trainees joked with me that I should come in the next day with my unruly gray beard died red.) If you see such a person in a strip club, Guandolo noted, beware: He can sin because he's about to go to heaven by way of a suicide bombing and thus be forgiven his transgressions. One more thing: "At least 80 percent of hotels have managers that are Muslims," he declared. "They are in. They have access to our systems." Again there were nods of agreement.

He urged the activists to speak not just of the Muslim Brotherhood but of Hamas and al-Qaeda, which trigger fear more acutely. Frequently, he used the terms interchangeably, as if they were all one and the same, applying the label "Hamas" to people in organizations allegedly associated with the Brotherhood.

He used the technique a few weeks later on his website under the headline "Kansas Sheriff Surrenders to Hamas." Guandolo had scheduled a two-day training session, which Sheriff Jeff Easter of Sedgwick County had canceled following objections by CAIR and local Muslim organizations. Guandolo wrote that Easter was "caving in to complaints by Hamas and local Muslim Brotherhood leaders in Wichita and other parts of Kansas. The loudest complaints came from Hamas spokesman Ibrahim Hooper. Hooper works for the Hamas organization called the Council on American Islamic Relations (CAIR)." A week earlier, Guandolo had accused a *Wichita Eagle* reporter of violating a federal prohibition against providing "material support" to a terrorist organization, because he wrote about CAIR's protests against Guandolo's training, an article Guandolo called "Hamas propaganda."

"Anywhere you can tie al-Qaeda in, tie al-Qaeda in," he recommended during his Virginia training, especially when approaching Christian ministers to urge their support. "Pastors are probably the most important. Right now the pulpits are silent."

Of course al-Qaeda is the red flag for Americans, and Guandolo waves it liberally. He claimed that Elbarasse was videotaping the Bay Bridge for al-Qaeda, for example, although there is no such evidence. If there were, you could be sure that Elbarasse, an American citizen, would be living in a federal prison instead of in cosmopolitan Beirut, where he was last seen by his lawyer.

Guandolo taught the group how to find and research Muslim organizations online, what websites to use, what IRS documents to call up through sites that list nonprofits, how to look at the groups' bylaws and boards of directors, and how to locate land records to demonstrate that many mosques and Islamic centers are actually owned by an organization with alleged ties to the Brotherhood. Because the Muslim Students Association was purportedly begun by the Brotherhood, he had the trainees proceed on the assumption that all chapters, on every campus, were merely fronts for the Brotherhood and Hamas.

Using their own computers, the activists trolled through the digital universe, and the results were about what you would expect if you stopped short of deep digging. Showing them a site for Kansas, Guandolo called up a list of universities, then zeroed in on Kansas State, went to a page titled "International Student Associations at Kansas State," and found the Muslim Students Association. One trainee, an elderly man from Virginia who said he'd been a newspaper reporter, fumed as he saw the associations come up in one place after another. "That's a great story about the infiltrations of our educational system!" he practically shouted.

Guandolo grinned and laughed. "Oh, we've got a fire going over there."

"I'm going to go out and shoot somebody," the Virginia man declared.

"Don't do that," Guandolo cautioned.

He suggested that when they find a Muslim Students Association, they look for the faculty sponsor. "You dig into that guy, you're gonna find a hard-core jihadist. Look at his Facebook page, look at who his friends are. You may find the black flag of jihad floating around there somewhere."

Guandolo, in his late forties, is a man of zealous stamina. Although he doesn't look as if he gets much exercise, he spoke for practically nine hours straight on each of the two days, with fewer breaks than the rest of us would have preferred. Lunch was served in the room while work continued, and only while he left trainees on their own to do a thirty-minute assignment on the Internet did he have time to sit down and talk about himself.

He grew up in a Maryland suburb of Washington, D.C., graduated from the U.S. Naval Academy, and served as a Marine Corps officer in the first Gulf War. After six and a half years in uniform, he joined the FBI, the first four and a half years on domestic and international narcotics cases, then a year as the FBI's liaison to the Capitol Police examining threats to members of Congress, the vice president, cabinet members, and Supreme Court justices.

Shortly after 9/11, he moved to one of two newly created FBI counterterrorism units, where he deepened his interest in Islam. He became convinced that the "extremist" doctrine of global jihad is not extremist at all, but squarely in the mainstream, codified by every major Muslim scholar. His answer to anyone who tells him there are moderate versions of Islam is to offer $1,000 to the person who can cite any such book by an authoritative Muslim figure. "They can't, because it doesn't exist," he tells the trainees. "When al-Qaeda cites Islamic law, they are accurately citing Islamic law." He gives his students a line to use when confronted in a public forum: "I am open to the idea that there is another version of Islam out there, but what you're telling me is that all these grand muftis out there, all the schools, are teaching the wrong versions of Islam."

When his challengers cite American academics such as John Esposito who paint a picture of Islam as benign, Guandolo can hardly contain himself. "Crackpots," he calls such professors. He derides Esposito, founding director of the Prince Alwaleed Bin Talal Center for Muslim-Christian Understanding at Georgetown University, for getting a bouquet of roses every week from the Saudi embassy, figuratively speaking. Esposito engages in "intentional deceptions," Guandolo told the trainees, "which makes it enemy propaganda. If you're doing it wittingly, I think there's a criminal charge there." (My multiple requests failed to persuade Esposito to talk to me about Islam in America.)

Guandolo said he'd worked on the investigation of James Yee, the Muslim army chaplain who was locked up for seventy-six days in 2003 and charged with "wrongfully transporting classified documents" after he came under suspicion for his behavior at Guantánamo Bay. Yee had organized translators in prayers, had given explanatory lectures on Islam to the prison staff, and had intervened to stop the abuse of prisoners and the desecration of Qurans by guards.

The case unfolded in the press as an example of retribution combined with anti-Islam anxiety. The Army then determined that the documents were unclassified and changed the charge to adultery but finally, facing bad publicity, just let Yee leave the service. Guandolo remains convinced that the chaplain was illegally conveying information to and from inmates and that he could have been charged with espionage.

No such proof has come to light, however, and the conclusion is thrown into doubt by Guandolo's own deep suspicions of Islam, which he expressed so vehemently inside the FBI that senior officials were rankled. "I created a lot of friction," he said to me, and he admitted to his trainees, as a cautionary tale, that he had been too insistent and confrontational.

The FBI put obstacles in his way as he tried to instruct agents in the perfidies of the Brotherhood. A two-week course that he finally won permission to conduct at the counterintelligence training center in Maryland drew thirty FBI and other law enforcement and intelligence officials, he said, and it got favorable reviews. Afterward, he recalled, his supervisor gave him a pat on the back but then told him his administrative reports were overdue. In other words, forget the trainings and get back to your normal duties. Again and again he was stymied, able to do nothing more than two-day training sessions for the Park Police.

Senior officials "were saying, No, Islam isn't like that," he recalled. "They said I was generalizing. I had the head of CT [counterterrorism] for the FBI say, You're right. Is that what you want to hear? Now shut up." So after twelve and a half years, his frustrations at a boiling point, he left the FBI, went briefly to the Pentagon as a contractor doing strategic analysis, then moved into the private subculture of Islam watchers to continue sounding the alarm.

A small scandal taints Guandolo's career. Seven months after he resigned from the FBI, officials learned from a female informant that while she was passing information to Guandolo, who was working undercover on a corruption investigation, the two had had an affair. The criminal case wasn't jeopardized. The target, Representative William Jefferson of Louisiana, was sentenced to thirteen years after cash from a bribery scheme was found in his freezer. But Guandolo, married at the time and now divorced, admits that "it was improper under FBI rules."

In the realm of free speech, as in physics, every action has a reaction. Some of the alarmists have earned condemnation from the Southern Poverty Law Center, which tracks hate groups, usually concentrating on racists, neo-Nazis, and white militias. It has pointed to Frank Gaffney, Steve Emerson, Daniel Pipes, Robert Spencer, and others, implying that their anti-Muslim rhetoric might have sparked a surge in attacks on Muslims and mosques. It blasts the Republican representative Peter King of New York for hearings he conducted in 2011 on the radicalization of American Muslims, sessions the center denounced as resembling the Cold War anticommunist witch hunts of the House Un-American Activities Committee.

The center names John Guandolo in its Hatewatch blog and has turned a glaring spotlight on local law enforcement agencies that contract for his training. The organization also calls Spencer "one of America's most prolific and vociferous anti-Muslim propagandists" and reports that he "was banned from the United Kingdom as an extremist in July 2013."

The Center for American Progress, a liberal think tank, produced a 138-page report in 2011, *Fear, Inc.*, exploring "the roots of the Islamophobia Network," its funders, and adherents. Guandolo dismissed the center as a creature of George Soros, the liberal donor whom conservatives love to picture as a world-government conspirator, and as a "merger of liberal socialist-Marxist groups and Hamas." Then he added, "Well, maybe not Marxist." He told the activists that there was "no point reaching out to left-wing groups, because they're not gonna hear us." He blamed "multiculturalism, relativity," for dictating equal regard for all cultures and religions, a concept that makes anxiety about Islam look like prejudice.

The most frequent epithet directed at the phenomenon of alarm about Islam's supposed designs is "Islamophobia." There's even a website called Americans Against Islamophobia (www.islamophobiatoday .com). It likens the tracts of the anti-Islam movement to the *Protocols of the Elders of Zion,* which has endured for more than a century, feeding bigotry against Jews as conspiratorial manipulators with hidden power.

The *Protocols* was a hoax, a forgery purporting to be the minutes of a meeting in Basel of wealthy Jews scheming to control the world. First published in 1905, the slim volume has been reproduced ever since by the purveyors of classic anti-Semitic stereotypes that portray Jews as rich plotters wielding great influence in banking, industry, politics, and the media.

Soviet files indicate that it was concocted in 1898 by a Russian living in France, Mathieu Golovinski, possibly for the Russian secret police. He appears to have drawn from two works of fiction: Maurice Joly's satirical 1864 attack on Napoleon III, *The Dialogue in Hell Between Machiavelli and Montesquieu,* and Hermann Goedsche's 1868 novel, *Biarritz. The*

Times of London discovered in 1921 that the author of the *Protocols* had copied verbatim from the Joly *Dialogue*, attributing Machiavelli's lines to the Jews. And he apparently took as inspiration a scene from Goedsche's novel in which rabbis meet at night in a Prague cemetery to lay plans for world domination.

The Islamic documents cited by the alarmists are not forgeries, as far as we know. But they are not authoritative blueprints, either. No doubt Muslims exist in the United States aspiring to the ultimate goal of rule by Islam. But the watchers present no convincing evidence that they stand anywhere except at the margins.

To receive the alarms as convincing, you have to ignore all the accommodating statements by Muslims who do not call for jihad against America, for the infiltration of its institutions, or for the totalitarian result that the fundamentalist doctrine envisions. So Guandolo tried to inoculate trainees against Muslims' expressions of moderation and nonviolence by showing a BBC interview broadcast after two Muslim men hacked a British soldier to death on a London street. There are three Muslim guests on the program, two moderates and a militant. The host is pressing a radical cleric to denounce the attack, but the cleric denounces British foreign policy instead, rejects free expression and democracy, and calls for Sharia to replace the monarchy in the United Kingdom.

This appalls the two other Muslims, a man and a woman, who condemn the killing passionately and turn their anger on the radical imam, the woman saying, "This kind of rhetoric really has no place whatever in this country."

Guandolo paused the video and told the activists, "This is all a show." The supposed moderates, he said, were playing a role. When one trainee called the cleric a schmuck, Guandolo countered, "He is not a schmuck. He's squared away." He is not an extremist. His position is in tune with Islam. So, in Guandolo's formula, the hateful and aggressive statements from Muslims are real, and the moderate statements are phony.

After two long days, I felt trapped in an intellectual ghetto whose barriers were impervious to contradictory facts. From inside, every gesture by Muslims on behalf of the American tapestry of tolerance seemed like a wily subterfuge; peace, Guandolo explained, is a tenet of Islam meaning peace after an Islamic victory. So CAIR's repeated denunciation of violence is done in a kind of code; one has to know the key to read the truth.

That means that even the beauty of pluralistic America—the regard for religious diversity, the distaste for prejudice and discrimination—is being manipulated by those who yearn for Islam's domination. Seen through that prism, the beauty is made to look naive and ugly.

"They've adopted our language," the Minneapolis woman declared with distress. "They've put on a cloak; they've deceived us."

Since Guandolo had spoken of being at war, I asked him at the end, "What does victory look like?"

Dave Petteys jumped in: "We still have a democracy in five years."

Guandolo answered, "The Muslim Brotherhood is decimated. They are designated by the U.S. government as a terrorist organization, we have shut down all MB Islamic centers, all Iranian centers, and we have locked up all the MB officials in the United States. That's a good start. And all those who have aided and abetted them are locked up after being tried in federal courts."

PART IV

Politics

9

Money Is Speech, Poverty Is Silence

My father used to say, "No peso, no say-so."
—HENRY R. MUÑOZ III, National Finance Committee chair,
Democratic National Committee

In 2013 and 2014, a debate occurred over two of the federal government's most significant programs to provide food and health care to millions of poor Americans. But the poor were not heard from. The affluent conducted the discussion among themselves.

When they disagreed with one another, they did so in abstractions, not as real people affected by the policies they espoused. The real people whose children felt the gnaw of hunger every month as food stamps ran out, the real people who lacked insurance for medical treatment, the real people with the greatest stake in the outcome, were silenced by the very same problem that afflicted them: their poverty. They lacked money to buy into the public square of political debate.

So they depended on the moneyed classes to speak on their behalf: Democratic legislators, liberal lobbyists, charitable organizations, and the press when it chose to report down at the grassroots. The voices of the poor were "mediated," in the jargon, because they did not have the wherewithal to speak directly for themselves. That is, the voices of the poor were muffled, drained of the raw, personal anguish that could turn the voting public to their cause.

This happened during Republicans' efforts in Congress to slash food stamps and in the twenty-six Republican-led states that initially rejected an expansion of Medicaid. It's reasonable to suppose that if the poor could make themselves heard directly in such discussions, they might make a difference. Some polling supports that conclusion, and in Texas in 2004 it got a Democrat elected to Congress from President George W. Bush's heavily Republican district.

The political landscape, marked by the hierarchy of class, cannot be navigated by citizens of modest means without guides and groups drawn from the elite. The poor cannot truly exercise their freedom of speech without forming alliances higher in the scale of affluence, and they cannot count on the formerly poor to migrate into levels of influence, since upward mobility has practically disappeared. Most Americans who begin near the bottom stay there, and while they get sympathy from certain figures at the top, they cannot muster the financial and organizational power to outshout the rich. The political culture runs on dollars.

That seems ironic in an age of Twitter and Facebook, smart phones and instant texting. Technology should decentralize the power to speak effectively, making mobilization easy to organize from below. But we've seen the phenomenon more vividly in precarious dictatorships than in established democracies. Reformers in Cairo and Tunis, Kiev and Tripoli, may use social media to gather tens of thousands on a tide of angry grievances—but not in Washington, where anger doesn't have the bitter edge, at least not now. The regime is not despotic, at least for the long future. The goal is not revolution but revision. Periodic marches and demonstrations end with everyone going home to see if they made it onto the nightly news. These days in America, the street is not the stage for politics.

Moreover, pluralistic democracy is methodical and glacial in its pace of change, which is all to the good unless you are a victim of the status quo. Then your voice may be heard less clearly on the National Mall than in Tahrir Square. Stability in Washington has a comforting but dampening effect. Volatility in Cairo, when it arrives like a summer storm, opens a fleeting space for speech—yet with unpredictable results, as Egyptians and others learned tragically after the Arab Spring: The alternative to a dictatorship may be another dictatorship.

It is precisely the ease of communication that can make democracy movements ephemeral. "Before the Internet," wrote Zeynep Tufekci, "the tedious work of organizing that was required to circumvent censorship or to organize a protest also helped build infrastructure for decision making and strategies for sustaining momentum. Now movements can rush past that step, often to their own detriment." She noted how much work it took students and a professor at Alabama State College to organize the 1955 bus boycott in Montgomery: an all-nighter secreted in the copying room spent mimeographing 52,000 flyers for distribution by churches, unions, and other local organizations. "Even mundane tasks like coordinating car pools," she said, "required endless hours of collaborative work."

It would be best if American democracy could somehow have it both ways. It would be advantageous for the country to have both stability and fluidity, to hear more clearly from those of lesser means and incorporate their views into the political debates that determine elections and policies. But the institutions that naturally organize the poor and the working class are decimated. Membership in labor unions has plummeted to just 6.7 percent of those employed in the private sector. Community action agencies, through which the government essentially subsidized speech by poor people, have become mostly toothless or extinct since the War on Poverty ended. Those neighborhood organizations had found the pressure points of government to agitate for improved antipoverty programs.

For all the lamentations about "income inequality," the Americans suffering from it haven't coalesced into an effective movement. Occupy Wall Street, composed mostly of the young and the middle class, indulged in symbols, rhetoric, and feel-good campouts but intentionally avoided promoting program or policy agendas.

The conflict over Medicaid, the health insurance program for low-income families, brought the problem into bold relief. President Obama's Affordable Care Act mandated that states broaden coverage to all adults with incomes up to 138 percent of the federal poverty line, with the federal government paying 100 percent of the cost until 2016 and 90 percent thereafter. But then the Supreme Court overturned the requirement, leaving the expansion as an option, which the states could either pick up or turn down.

It was hard to see why anyone would turn it down. With Washington covering practically the entire cost, millions of state residents would be healthier and less vulnerable to financial ruin, and hospitals that were treating the uninsured without reimbursement would see their balance sheets improved. But rational calculations were no match for the partisan animus toward Obama and "Obamacare," so while a few conservative-run states finally gave in and accepted Washington's largesse, most Republican governors and legislatures held firm and rejected the offer. The political clashes that followed made no significant room for the voices of the low-income citizens who had the most to gain or lose.

Many are low-wage workers caught between subsidies: They earn too much to be eligible for standard Medicaid and too little to benefit from a tax credit if they buy private insurance on a government exchange. "These are the people the GOP purports to represent," a *Washington Post* reader wrote regarding Virginia, where Republicans in the legislature were blocking Democratic governor Terry McAuliffe's push to expand Medicaid. "The GOP is alienating their constituents in southside and southwest," the reader argued, "and it will cost them in 2015 and 2016."

Perhaps, but only if the policy choices are driven home pointedly and if low-income voters go to the polls in larger numbers than they usually do. The wealthy vote at much higher rates than the poor; 80 percent of citizens with annual incomes over $150,000, and only 46 percent of those under $20,000, cast ballots in the presidential election of 2012. In the tight election of 2000, Al Gore would have beaten Bush if the poor had turned out in the same percentage as the affluent, given what exit polls show as the tendency of lower-income voters to support Democrats over Republicans.

There are many reasons for lower voting rates among impoverished citizens: inconvenient hours on the job and family stresses endured by the working poor, deep alienation from a system that looks unresponsive, and the confusion of ads and biased news that emphasize "the middle class" but almost never speak the word "poverty" or address policies relevant to people at the bottom. One researcher estimates that half of all Americans fall beneath the poverty line for at least a year of their adult lives before reaching age sixty-five, and nearly 40 percent do so before the age of forty-five. If that's accurate, a huge potential constituency exists on behalf of government assistance.

Conservatives in the courts have exacerbated the problem by tilting the playing field of speech—effective speech—in favor of the affluent. The Supreme Court has defanged the 1965 Voting Rights Act by throwing out its requirement that jurisdictions with a record of racial discrimination get clearance from the Justice Department before changing election procedures.

That has unleashed a wave of voter ID laws enacted by conservative state legislatures, disfavoring minorities and the poor who may not have driver's licenses or other government-issued identification to show at the polls. Because the disenfranchised are not heard, their predicament is not sufficiently grasped: If you need a birth certificate to get such credentials, you need to pay a fee—a modest fee if you're financially secure, a crippling fee if every dollar expended is a dollar less for food. The costs are tantamount to the insidious poll taxes that were once used to discourage voting by the impoverished.

Since voting is the citizen's ultimate freedom to speak, everyone's speech on Election Day carries the same weight, whatever the distortions that money has created during campaigns. Therefore, "the most effective way to change policy is to change who wins elections," says Sandy Newman, once an organizer of voter registration drives and now head of Voices for Progress, an advocacy group of liberal campaign contributors.

"I'd start with expanding the electorate. The single most cost-effective way to do that is through voter registration. This is an area where there is gross underinvestment." Plus, to register a voter is "cheaper than to persuade a voter, by a factor of ten, at least," he says. It costs only a few dollars to register each voter, Newman estimates, but about $300 per voter in campaign spending to increase a candidate's base of support.

In at least one case—the Texas district where George W. Bush's Crawford ranch is located—spending a little money to give the poor a voice generated enough compassion in the larger electorate to upset political calculations.

The Seventeenth Congressional District had just been gerrymandered to make it heavily Republican and fundamentally conservative, so Bush was expected to trounce his opponent, Senator John Kerry, and he did so by thirty-six percentage points. A powerful Republican state legislator running for the House of Representatives was also poised for victory until the incumbent Democrat, Representative Chet Edwards, tried an unusual tactic: He made government health insurance for children and pregnant women an issue of family values.

Edwards was helped by a small organization called Every Child Matters, which raises a couple of million dollars a year to inject children's issues into a few races. Its president, Michael Petit, believes that steps to improve the lives of low-income children "in the end are political decisions," which have "everything to do with who is in control of the microphone."

In late summer, Petit commissioned a clever poll in Bush's district. The first phase of each interview showed a four-point lead for the Republican, Arlene Wohlgemuth, who had run a blizzard of television spots decrying partial-birth abortion, opposing child adoptions by gays, and bragging that her leadership had cut $1 billion from the state budget.

The questioners then went on to ask, in the same poll, whether Wohlgemuth would still get the respondents' support if they knew that her $1 billion savings had come from dropping 17,000 pregnant women from Medicaid and 150,000 children from CHIP, the state's Children's Health Insurance Program. Having been given that information, 13 percent fewer white Republican women said they favored Wohlgemuth, and Edwards jumped to a three-point lead overall.

The Democratic candidate took note. "He was moved by our poll," Petit said. His campaign produced a simple, eloquent television ad allowing a white working mother to speak directly from the edge of poverty. She was twenty-eight, with a rich Texas accent. Her husband had died in a fire, she told viewers. Her adorable little girl of three was pushed off CHIP. "I don't want welfare," she said in a voice-over. "I just want good insurance for my child."

The ad makers interspersed touching photographs of the mother and daughter with lines of text announcing Wohlgemuth's cuts to CHIP and her devastating quote "CHIP has never been one of my top priorities." At the end of the spot, the mother said, "Look at my little girl, look into her eyes, and tell her why she's not good enough to be taken care of."

Edwards won by four points, thanks largely to Republican women crossing over. According to Petit's postelection poll, 87 percent of the district's voters believed in government's "moral responsibility to make sure every child has the opportunity to succeed." Edwards gained reelection twice more in the heavily Republican district, until he lost to the Republican Bill Flores in the 2010 off-year sweep that brought Republicans control of the House.

By the run-up to the 2014 congressional elections, a slight concern about the sentiments reflected in that poll crept into conservative ranks. "If the presidential election told us anything, it's that Americans place a great importance on taking care of those in need and avoiding harm to the weak," said an internal memo, obtained by *Politico,* circulated inside Americans for Prosperity, the super PAC funded largely by David and Charles Koch. "We consistently see that Americans in general are concerned that free-market policy—and its advocates—benefit the rich and powerful more than the most vulnerable of society," the memo continued. "We must correct this misconception." Whether that meant anything more substantial than a public relations effort to burnish the image of capitalism, the memo did not say.

Amid the resistance to expanding Medicaid, another threat to the poor arose in early 2014, when House Republicans called for severe cuts in food stamps, now known as the Supplemental Nutrition Assistance Program (SNAP), whose benefits come no longer on stamps but on debit cards. Here again, little was heard from the 49 million Americans deemed by the Agriculture Department to be suffering from "food insecurity."

In their stead, two respected organizations—a nationwide network of food banks called Feeding America and a nonprofit antihunger group, the Food Research and Action Center—spoke for the low-income Americans who depend on the assistance. Hundreds of antipoverty practitioners from throughout the country gathered in Washington in early March for their annual conference of panels, discussions, and training on the techniques of approaching legislators. Then they put their lessons into practice on Capitol Hill by appealing to representatives from their districts.

"I went on a number of visits with food bankers," said a conference participant, and while they were articulate and persuasive, "they'd kind of choke up at the ask." The "ask," for those unfamiliar with the vernacular of fund-raising and lobbying, is the ultimate request at which all schmoozing is aimed: Will you give? Will we get your vote?

But "food bankers" are more comfortable giving members of Congress and their staffs the policy arguments, it seems, than in zeroing in on the final plea for support. They were supposed to ask both for greater SNAP funding and for the annual renewal of the charitable deduction available for donations of food, a tax break that motivates restaurants and supermarkets. "People weren't as comfortable talking about that," said the participant.

Thanks to their efforts nonetheless—and especially to the Democrats in the White House and the Senate—the cuts were much less disastrous than the Republicans proposed: $8 billion rather than $40 billion over ten years.

But what if the antipoverty organizations had the millions that are available to political candidates to advertise as Chet Edwards did in Texas? What if the airwaves were flooded with desperate mothers and hungry kids? What if voters understood the lifelong handicaps that children will suffer if malnutrition occurs during critical periods of brain development? What if the myths about food stamps—that they create dependency, laziness, and corruption—could be rebutted decisively? What if millions could be spent on raising the emotional conscience of the electorate?

When I put the questions to activists, I got surprising answers. The public and the press have been mesmerized by television political advertising, the most visible effect of the huge sums released into elections by the Supreme Court's eagerness to strike down campaign finance laws. So I naturally wanted to know what kinds of ads the antipoverty folks would like to run.

But they didn't want to run ads. Their imaginations ran in another direction: Any miraculous influx of dollars would better be aimed at grassroots advocacy, the way the National Rifle Association (NRA) and the American Israel Public Affairs Committee, the pro-Israel lobby known as AIPAC, blanket congressional districts with organizers who hold elected officials tightly accountable. This is political speech in another form.

For Feeding America, the ideal mechanism would rely on food banks, according to Lisa Davis, the organization's senior vice president of government relations. She developed an ambitious plan to raise enough, from a few big donors, to fund staff and training so that food banks across the country could mobilize local support, invite legislators in their own districts to visit the facilities, and press them for more generous policies. "We call it 'educating' members of Congress rather than 'lobbying,' " she says.

Food banks have no allies with the passion of those who support the NRA or AIPAC. What they do have is admiration from both sides of the aisle. "Whether they are superconservative Republicans or liberal Democrats, everybody loves the food banks," Davis notes. Many are faith based, which appeals to Republicans, and since they're private, they don't violate conservative ideology against big government. "Those members of Congress not sympathetic to low-income people or programs to help them," Davis explains, "are supportive of food banks. They love private charity. We say charity can't fill the gap."

The gap is obvious to anyone who listens to the poor themselves. They will tell you that their family's declining balance on a SNAP card usually runs out by the third week of the month. They will explain that the local food bank is a limited backstop, with lots of empty shelves; the supplies of government surplus and privately donated food are inadequate to the need. So even with subsidies, many low-income households are left without proper nutrition. This elementary fact of poverty has been slow to penetrate the halls of Congress.

In surveying food banks in 2012, Feeding America found only 27 percent engaged in a range of activities that could be considered "strong" or "very strong" advocacy. Almost all—94 percent—wanted to do more advocacy alongside their main purpose of feeding people, but they had too few staff, limited funds, lack of training, and inadequate technical support. In response, Davis proposed multiyear grants to food banks, initially as a pilot project of five awards of $50,000 each for two years. Pending substantial donations, Feeding America was providing "webinar trainings, tool kits, and individual consulting to help them build capacity and mobilize," she reports. If money came in, she hoped to hire a staffer in Washington to bring food banks to a high level of grassroots organizing and legislative "education." That would work better than

TV commercials, she believes. The effectiveness of ads "really gets over-stated," she says. "Grassroots mobilization can top money in politics every time."

Quite right, agrees Joan Claybrook, president emeritus and a board member of Public Citizen, the country's premier advocate for consumer safety and good government, founded by Ralph Nader. "Grassroots orga-nizing is really the best thing," she says, "the last resort of those who are poor." Public Citizen can be credited with getting seat belts and air bags in cars, pressing for government transparency, and holding regulatory agencies accountable for monitoring safety issues. So, it represents the little guy, but not with political advertising. That wouldn't change even if it had extra millions.

Involvement in election campaigns is "not our business," Claybrook explains. "We lobby, we litigate, we research, we're very thoughtful and tight-fisted about the stuff we put out." Only "an occasional, unique, original ad" would be considered. Public Citizen ran one against Newt Gingrich of Georgia during his close reelection campaign in the early 1990s. It didn't work.

Two cases illustrate the limited effect of campaign money when it runs up against voters' deeply held beliefs. One is the former New York mayor Michael Bloomberg's Mayors Against Illegal Guns, which has taken aim at pro-gun members of Congress. But the "outside money" has been denounced locally, and the NRA's grassroots movement has proved unbeatable in certain districts. The NRA has the advantage of constituents' personal ideology of gun ownership, just as AIPAC's posi-tions are integrated into its constituency's support of Israel.

The second case is the surprising 2014 primary loss by the Republican House majority leader, Eric Cantor of Virginia, whose big money was overwhelmed by the foot soldiers energized by conservative broadcasters on behalf of an obscure economics professor, David Brat. The Tea Party considered him a lost cause, until his candidacy was touted by the right-wing pundit Laura Ingraham, who promoted his ultraconservatism and hosted him on her show. When she joined him at a rally, *The New York Times* reported, the crowd was so huge "that the overflow parking nearly reached" Cantor's driveway, half a mile away. The parking index proved a better indicator than polls, which failed to predict Brat's victory with 55.5 percent of the vote.

An alternative to grassroots is "grasstops" organizing. It means mobilizing local leaders who, because of their prominent positions in a community, can get access to legislators. A leading example is Fight Crime: Invest in Kids, comprising some 5,000 sheriffs, police chiefs, prosecutors, and victims of violence. The organization has established chapters throughout the country to press for early childhood education, after-school mentoring, home visiting programs to prevent child abuse, and enhanced grants for efforts to keep kids out of gangs.

If there were enough money for people on the margins to have their say, no choice would have to be made between organizing and advertising. They aren't mutually exclusive. Both could be employed in tandem, with good results, notes an antihunger activist who is so carefully schooled in politics that he doesn't want to be named. He counts fifty to seventy-five congressional districts where Democrats and Republicans are evenly split and where the rates of poverty and hunger are significant. Candidates are "totally unaware," he says, that 15 to 20 percent of their constituents are skipping meals. "I would consider advertising in Republican districts" with such conditions and targeting Democratic congressmen who cut deals to slash antipoverty programs. He would get the media and voters to confront the politicians during candidate forums "with information about how members are just pushing their constituents off the cliff" and "to ask members, Why do you consistently vote against food stamps when x percent of residents are dependent on them?"

One difficulty in raising funds to generate speech about poverty lies in the priorities of liberals themselves. On the left, where such support is most likely, "progressive" organizations with money aren't very interested in poverty—mainly they want to get Democrats elected—and issue-oriented groups with antipoverty agendas don't have much funding. Election-oriented groups have made "a politically correct judgment not to engage with issues of poverty," one activist observed. "They may run ads against Republicans on the minimum wage, but they certainly don't touch food stamps or welfare." Furthermore, even the left is highly dependent on corporate contributions.

When it comes to political speech, then, the agenda is set by elites. Even the press, which can be an accessible megaphone for the disenfranchised, rarely reports adequately the viewpoints of the poor. The failing is built into the structure of news coverage, which concentrates on government first of all. This makes sense in a democracy where the people need to know what their government is up to. But it also gives government major influence in defining news. During the War on Poverty, covering government meant covering poverty, for government then was heavily involved in antipoverty efforts. In New York City, for example, hardly a city council or planning commission meeting went by without some housing, welfare, or urban renewal issues in play, which led to turnouts of impoverished citizens who became skilled in the tactics of debate and advocacy. As government gave less attention to the problems of poverty, so did the press, and so did the people.

News organizations are complicated laboratories of class distinctions, owned by the affluent and staffed by reporters and editors from an array of backgrounds. Dean Baquet, the first African-American executive editor of *The New York Times,* is a working-class college dropout (Columbia University). But he is an exception to the trend toward socioeconomic homogeneity. Newsrooms contain little of the class diversity of decades past, when college diplomas were not required and graduate degrees were scarce. The staffs were not diverse by race or gender, but the white men who gathered and edited the news had broader histories. Some were streetwise characters who knew what a dime meant to a family on the edge. The Great Depression had been the great leveler of life experience, and its aftermath left a long memory of deprivation, a memory now mostly expired.

It is a truism that those in authority are privileged, removed from the poor: judges who uphold institutions against individuals, lawyers and legislators who fail to consider housing and food as human rights. High legal barriers to class action lawsuits have been erected by the courts, depriving labor unions, consumers, and ordinary workers of an important means of aggregating the power of the middle class. As one activist noted, nobody on the House Agriculture Committee is getting food stamps.

10

True Believers

All speakers, including individuals and the media, use money
amassed from the economic marketplace to fund their speech.

—JUSTICE ANTHONY KENNEDY for the majority in
Citizens United v. Federal Election Commission

D id you ever wonder why Americans started talking about "global
warming" and then shifted gradually to "climate change"? How did
the "estate tax" become the "death tax"? And why did "drilling for oil"
change to "exploring for energy"?

Frank Luntz takes credit for manipulating the terminology, which
he does professionally, usually in favor of Republicans who hire him to
advise on campaign ads and rhetoric. He is a wordsmith, and the words
he carefully chooses by testing them in focus groups seem to work their
way magically from TV spots to politicians' speeches and finally into
mainstream news reporting, which ought to be immune from the lazy
influence of partisan vocabulary.

He pays ordinary citizens to gather in front of TV screens and twist
little dials to register their instant reactions to slogans, videos, advertising copy, and language in various forms. His resulting analysis of broadcast and Internet spots is acute and unambiguous:

Start with a story, not a political statement. Use the same phrases
an angry voter would use. Employ memorable rhymes and alliterations.
Shoot close-ups of your candidate's face. Use videos, rather than stills, of

an opponent you're targeting. "The moving visuals make everything you say more authentic and credible than photos alone."

Avoid excessive text, but use a chalkboard—"the single best visual technique we've tested"—because it takes people back to school and makes them "feel like they're *learning* something *accurate,* a very tough sell in this cynical political environment." Use facts, sourced by newspaper headlines. Report numbers, not generalities. Summon up small-business owners and people in the military, who appeal to voters across the spectrum.

Don't talk down to voters. In a negative ad, end positively. Avoid words and editing that seem fake. "Don't use actors to stand in for real people. Ever." Instead of "promise" or "pledge," say "commitment."

As increasing sums pour into politics, the ad-men gain ground, because producing and broadcasting commercials is an easy way to spend lots of new money. All you have to do is hire a company to do focus groups, shoot and edit video, and make the buy on local stations—or put the ads up for free on your own website. As local news reporting declines, the vacuum for voters' attention is quickly filled, especially by negative ads.

They're entertaining. How effective they are is a question, however, especially against a sophisticated computerized system that targets likely voters by their demographics. Obama's campaign ran an extensive operation in both 2008 and 2012 to solicit small contributions and get his supporters to the polls. The system overwhelmed the $400 million spent by the conservative Koch brothers, David and Charles, and the $150 million given by the casino magnate Sheldon Adelson, to Republican candidates in the primaries through the general election.

There is no question, though, that big money drowns out the smaller, quieter voices, and so deafens the public to the less boisterous speech of the less affluent. This has been true for many decades and is now enhanced by the conservative justices on the Supreme Court as they throw out various restrictions on political contributions as unconstitutional.

There has always been a First Amendment issue shadowing the attempts by Congress to place ceilings on campaign donations. Although liberals generally see no problem in such restrictions to reduce the prospect of corruption and to re-tilt the political playing field, conservatives see violations of free speech. That's no accident, since there is more corporate money on the conservative side than on the liberal. But the

American Civil Liberties Union also had a problem on First Amendment grounds, especially with the first law that was struck down, which denied corporations and unions the right to advocate the election or defeat of candidates within thirty days of a primary and sixty days of a general election.

This is not as simple an issue as it appears. In fact, it is a dilemma in the true sense of the word: a choice between two undesirable alternatives. One is the unfettered flood of riches from hidden contributors to buy dominance of the public debate, to spread propaganda, and thereby to influence elections. The other is the government regulation of speech in a democracy's most critical arena. Campaign financing restrictions are, in essence, government limits on political expression. Even limits designed for the common good—to reduce the influence of money in political campaigns—carry dangers of censorship.

Congress had restricted corporate electioneering for a century, since the Tillman Act of 1907, so the case began not as a grand constitutional challenge but as a dispute over a statutory interpretation and whether the law was constitutional as specifically applied. The conservatives on the Court took the unusual step of requesting reargument so they could expand the case into a sweeping ruling on the law's constitutionality as a whole.

The issue was a video. As Hillary Clinton prepared a run in the 2008 Democratic presidential primaries, a small group of well-heeled conservatives, under the corporate name Citizens United, made a slick propaganda film, *Hillary: The Movie,* impugning her character, her policies, and her fitness for the Oval Office. The film, to be distributed through cable by pay-per-view, was successfully blocked in court by the Federal Election Commission, the FEC, which has the authority to bring criminal charges for violations. Citizens United contended that the law did not apply, because the film did not qualify, under the statute's definition, as "electioneering communication" that was "publicly distributed."

The Supreme Court could have freed Citizens United by interpreting the law narrowly, or Citizens United could have funded the film legally through a political action committee rather than out of its own treasury. Instead, the 5–4 majority threw out the entire statute as an abridgment of the right to free speech enshrined in the First Amendment. In doing so, the Court appeared to equate corporations with people.

Under the law, Justice Anthony Kennedy wrote for the majority, "If parties want to avoid litigation and the possibility of civil and criminal penalties, they must either refrain from speaking or ask the FEC to issue an advisory opinion approving of the political speech in question. Government officials pore over each word of a text to see if, in their judgment, it accords with the . . . test they have promulgated. This is an unprecedented governmental intervention into the realm of speech."

But while the majority found ample precedent for protecting corporations' speech rights, it did so mostly by citing dissents in prior cases, rather than majority opinions, noted Justice John Paul Stevens for the minority. "The majority blazes through our precedents," Stevens wrote, "overruling or disavowing a body of case law."

That made the ruling one of the most activist opinions in the Court's current history. It gave corporations human qualities in a novel sort of anthropomorphism, which Stevens handily rejected:

> In the context of election to public office, the distinction between corporate and human speakers is significant. Although they make enormous contributions to our society, corporations are not actually members of it. They cannot vote or run for office. Because they may be managed and controlled by nonresidents, their interests may conflict in fundamental respects with the interests of eligible voters. The financial resources, legal structure, and instrumental orientation of corporations raise legitimate concerns about their role in the electoral process. Our lawmakers have a compelling constitutional basis, if not also a democratic duty, to take measures designed to guard against the potentially deleterious effects of corporate spending in local and national races.

The results of *Citizens United* were dramatically felt in the next presidential election.

Heavily funded political action committees, "super PACs," sprang up during the nasty Republican presidential primaries of 2012, with the Koch brothers, Adelson, and other billionaires tossing money into a cockfight that probably damaged the eventual Republican nominee, Mitt Romney.

The clearest example came in an ad slashing Romney for immoral, exploitative practices of his holding company, Bain Capital. Long before the Democrats had to say a word, the commercial defined Romney as a coldhearted businessman. It was paid for by the super PAC Winning Our Future, which supported Newt Gingrich and depended on $5 million from Adelson.

The ad opens with a brief paean to capitalism, then shifts to greedy bankers and corporate raiders, then names Romney as one of those raiders. "His mission? To reap massive rewards for himself and his investors," the announcer declares. A stocky, bearded worker appears on the screen and complains, "Mitt Romney and them guys, they don't care who I am." An elderly woman says, "He's for small businesses? No, he isn't. He's not."

Another elderly woman, trembling and looking exhausted, comes on camera: "They fire people, they cut benefits, they sell assets . . . I feel that is the man that destroyed us." And a third, middle-aged woman: "That hurt so bad, to leave my home, because of one man that's got fifteen homes."

Then come a couple of clips of Romney bragging jauntily in front of an audience, "I am intimately familiar with how our economy works." He adds, "Everything that corporations earn ultimately goes to people." Laughter from the crowd interrupts him. He asks, "Where do you think it goes?"

"In your pocket!" people yell.

On the screen appear a fist of money and a towering skyscraper, while the announcer calls Romney and his corporate raiders "more ruthless than Wall Street." The spot concludes with close-ups of workers' faces and the somber intonations of the narrator: "For tens of thousands of Americans, the suffering began when Mitt Romney came to town."

It was the first such caricature of Romney—by a fellow Republican, no less—and it stuck, right through the general election. Free political speech can be a loose cannon, wounding like friendly fire.

During that primary season, the flow of money into the Republican super PACs created a library of brutal commercials that tore down all the candidates. Republicans had generally hailed the *Citizens United* decision, but in this case, at least, it benefited Democrats who had decried it.

Dave Heller dislikes super PACs as a citizen and loves them as a media consultant, as head of Main Street Communications, which makes TV and radio ads. Because their donors don't have to be named publicly, super PACs provide "a financial incentive to avoid accountability," he says. "If you sat down the smartest people in the world to devise a campaign finance system, you couldn't come up with one that's more screwy."

He adds, however, "Anybody in my business would prefer to work for a super PAC than work for a candidate." The consultant gets more money, a percentage of everything spent on electronic media, and broadcasters charge higher rates for super PACs than for congressional candidates. Then, too, "You don't have to talk to a campaign manager five times a day," Heller notes. "You don't have to talk to a candidate four times a day; you don't have to deal with a candidate's spouse or brother or sister or family. That saves a tremendous amount of time and headache."

In reaction to *Citizens United* and the Court's obvious hostility to other limits on campaign financing, liberals began to cast about for some mechanism that might level the playing field without running afoul of the First Amendment. A constitutional amendment was proposed to permit Congress to limit the amounts spent by or given to candidates. Support in both houses appeared to be far below the two-thirds needed to send it to the states, where ratification by three-quarters would be required.

A more realistic proposal consistent with the First Amendment would allow government to give campaigns $5 or $6 for every dollar raised from small contributors, those who donated $150 or less. This would subsidize and amplify the voices of the less affluent rather than curtail the speech of the rich; that is, it would result in more speech, not less. The concept has a certain appeal, even to some Republicans who raise money from big givers but are weary of spending huge amounts of time soliciting donations.

"There's a common hatred of the current system," said David Donnelly, executive director of the Public Campaign Action Fund, which is pressing for reform. Legislators who agree include "those members who have been around so long that they've seen how awful the system has gotten, or those who are new and just realized that their job is a telemarketer." A bill proposed by John Sarbanes, a Democrat from Maryland, didn't pick up much immediate support from Republicans in the House, however.

"These are transformative policies, and they can work if we can figure out the politics," Donnelly said. Several states, including Maine, Connecticut, and Arizona, enacted various mechanisms of matching grants and public funding, and New York City's system, he noted, enabled the liberal Democrat Bill de Blasio to fund his successful mayoral campaign with small contributions. It's a way for "everyday people to be heard," Donnelly said.

"It's really important to shift the debate from getting money out [of politics] to getting people back in. I don't think we're going to regulate our way out of this problem. I think we need to participate our way out of it." At the federal level, the expense wouldn't be huge—less than $1 billion a year for all congressional races, he estimated, compared with the nearly $7 billion of American taxpayers' money that went missing in Iraq.

Alongside the super PAC, which is a purely political animal, a strange hybrid has developed: a cross between a political action committee and a tax-exempt "social welfare" organization. It contorts itself to fit awkwardly into a legal box that avoids taxes even as it does politics. The most visible example is that irreverent, recalcitrant, quasi-libertarian phenomenon, the Tea Party, spawned by Republican gadflies who hate Obama's health-care law and find traction on the public's general distaste for big government.

Local Tea Party chapters fashioning themselves into nonprofits raised a storm of protest when the IRS was caught using the terms "Tea Party," "patriot," "9/12," and others to flag them for special scrutiny when they applied for tax-exempt status. The date 9/12 is the name of the right-wing commentator Glenn Beck's web-based movement. Republicans howled that the IRS was being politicized (a flashback to the days when it actually was, under President Richard Nixon), although it later emerged that political-seeming applicants on the left were facing similar screening and delays.

As they should have been, equally on both sides, because they were stretching the law, section 501(c)(4) of the Internal Revenue Code. It grants exemptions to organizations "operated exclusively for the promotion of social welfare," defined not by the statute but by IRS rules, which require the organization to be "primarily engaged in promoting in some way the common good and general welfare of the community."

According to past examples cited by the IRS, groups receiving approval may rehabilitate and place the unemployed, provide a school district with a stadium, "develop methods of achieving simplicity and dignity in funeral and memorial services," give youth leadership training through a junior chamber of commerce, help financially strapped individuals solve budgeting problems and pay their debts, run a roller-skating rink for all residents of a particular locale, provide a shooting range and safety instruction, and so on.

You may be convinced that you're promoting the common good by campaigning for one side in an election, but the IRS regulations allow such an organization only "some political activities, so long as that is not its primary activity." This has been interpreted to mean that no more than half the group's money may be spent in elections. Therefore, it wasn't unreasonable for the IRS staff to receive BOLO (Be on the Lookout) warnings for such applicants. The problem, according to the Treasury Department's inspector general, lay in using the shortcut of "their names or policy positions instead of indications of potential political campaign intervention."

Rich folks like the Koch brothers have created an army of 501(c)(4)s. Their big advantage over political action committees is that they can keep secret the names of their donors. And although the donations are not tax deductible, the organizations pay no taxes on income. They face no restriction on lobbying, only on electioneering, whose limits are not spelled out in the statute, only in squishy language in the regulations.

The vagueness of the law and the confused landscape of freewheeling political organizing lend themselves to inconsistent and inadequate enforcement. The IRS officials might have had a political agenda, as Republicans insist, or they might have been just struggling bureaucrats who happened on an unacceptable way of coping. They faced a sudden flood of applications from groups—largely from the right—that skated very close to the ill-defined edge of what the law permits in exchange for being exempt from taxes.

Given the sordid history of the Nixon administration, which targeted political "enemies" for audit, it's healthy to be sensitive to any whiff of politicization in tax enforcement. To avoid the suspicions, the rules have to be unambiguous, and that's not the case. Congress could revise and clarify the law to minimize the wiggle room for IRS employees. They and the public need transparent, precise definitions of electioneering and how much is too much. There should be no mystery, as there is now. One salient feature of the rule of law is transparency. Another is predictability.

If blatantly political activities are to be formally accepted under the law's "social welfare" rubric, it will be a legal shift, and political pressure seems to have pushed the IRS in that direction. Large numbers of Tea Party chapters were approved for tax exemption after the uproar, with no attempt to codify the degree of acceptable political involvement.

Ironically, amid the din of outrage over the delays and scrutiny of Tea Party chapters applying under section 501(c)(4), there was virtually no attention paid to politically active churches that do electioneering in clear violation of the absolute ban in the section of the law, 501(c)(3), that applies to religious and secular charities.

Only 110 of the purported 3,000 parishioners were at the Sunday morning service of the Hope Christian Church in Maryland, despite the daring occasion. Along with 1,500 other ministers across the country, Bishop Harry Jackson was "gonna push the envelope a little bit" on politics, the choir director said.

The members of the congregation, carrying their own Bibles, drifted gradually into the odd-shaped sanctuary, wider than it was long, located in a low, sprawling office building once an IBM regional headquarters. Almost all the worshippers were women, almost all were African-American, and because they were so thinly distributed among the blue chairs, the place looked practically empty to the two cameras facing the pulpit, one from Christian television, the other for a documentary by the Public Broadcasting Service. A crew member said something to an assistant pastor, who asked people to move to the center. They dutifully obeyed for the sake of appearances.

A Bible lay open on a clear plastic lectern. An all-female choir, dressed in their own blue dresses of various styles, sang modern hymns vigorously and often off-key. An electric keyboard emitted piano sounds. A set of drums, positioned behind Plexiglas to soften the volume, kept time. Two young women in black clothing improvised dance steps while an older woman twirled two lavender flags on polls.

It was Pulpit Freedom Sunday in early October, when preachers who've signed up to trespass into electoral politics go well beyond the limits their churches have agreed upon when accepting tax-exempt status. Organized by the conservative movement Alliance Defending Freedom, they praise or condemn candidates. They urge parishioners to avoid this politician or that one; Barack Obama was a regular target, even in a few black churches such as Hope Christian, because of his support for gay marriage and abortion rights. Occasionally, favored politicians are even invited to a service to be anointed by the minister's endorsement.

Some pastors tread nervously onto this forbidden ground, because they don't want to lose their churches' tax exemptions. But others zealously hope for just that. They are trying to provoke the Internal Revenue Service into an adverse ruling so they can challenge the constitutionality of the law, which they believe violates the First Amendment. For many years, the IRS has refrained from taking the bait, and citizen complaints against churches' electioneering have disappeared into the agency's bureaucratic abyss.

Bishop Jackson's parish is located in a Maryland suburb of Washington, D.C., but his true constituency is nationwide, thanks to Republican donors who adore the anomaly of a black conservative. He does not mince words, and he delivers dramatic hyperbole. He wears glasses and a black beard cropped short. His uniform is simple but elegant: a white collar and a gold chain draped diagonally across his chest, from his right shoulder to his left side.

His roots are tangled and intriguing. His grandfather's father was white, he explains, and his grandfather's mother was "a very dark-skinned black woman." His grandfather was a Gullah from coastal South Carolina, and his father was the first in the family to go to college. Jackson's maternal grandmother was part black, part Cherokee. And he, Jackson, went to excellent schools: Williams as an undergraduate, then Harvard Business School for his MBA. For a while, he worked for Corning glass in upstate New York, then turned to religion and founded a church. He sees religion as an agent of change and of moral preservation.

"If it had not been for a free pulpit," he declared on Pulpit Freedom Sunday a month before the 2012 presidential election, "there would not have been an abolitionist movement . . . It was a free pulpit in the civil rights movement that called for justice."

And, as he might have added but did not, none of that would violate the law under the Faustian bargain that church and state have entered. In exchange for the generous public subsidy of avoiding all income and property taxes, and for its donors' ability to deduct their contributions from their taxable income, the church limits its speech by staying out of electoral politics. That doesn't mean it can't take positions on issues such as abortion, gay marriage, civil rights, and poverty, unless the matter "has been raised as an issue distinguishing candidates for a given office," according to the IRS explanation. When they apply for, and receive, tax-exempt status under section 501(c)(3), religious and secular organizations alike may not "participate in, or intervene in (including the publishing or distributing of statements), any political campaign on behalf of any candidate for public office."

Jackson understands that perfectly well, as he told me in his study after the service. "If you just advocate the issue, that's OK." But as soon as you speak for or against a candidate, "evidently it's against the law." Getting involved in a campaign is prohibited. "That's the boundary. And don't even mention if you're gonna try to do ads. So we're just putting our toe across the line."

But pretty far across the line. Aided by a PowerPoint slide show, which livened up Sunday worship, Jackson gave the congregation four reasons to oppose Obama. First, a health-care program that pays for abortion, which does not value human life. "I cannot vote for someone like this." Second, lack of support for marriage only between a man and a woman. After a long citation of scripture decrying homosexuality, Jackson denounced same-sex marriage as a profound violation of biblical teaching.

Third, "You're not for Israel," an odd and erroneous notion that haunted Obama throughout his presidency. "If we are against Israel, there comes attached to that the vengeance of God," Jackson declared ominously. "So now you want to put my nation under a divine vengeance, and you think our economics are gonna get better?" He continued, "You've got the black community that has been the most faithful Christian community, has the highest unemployment rate of any subculture in the land, and they are foolish enough—listen to me, black Christians— you are foolish enough to vote against the God that brought you out of slavery . . . Just because somebody's skin is black you're going to support an anti-God, anti-gospel offender. No wonder you can't get a job."

Cheers and applause arose, mostly from the choir—yes, he was preaching to the choir.

Then to the fourth reason to oppose the president at the polls the following month: religious liberty. "Four more years of Barack Obama will ensure an aggressive anti-Christian spirit that has currently grabbed hold of the administration and this country. Beware, my Christian friends, you should not vote for Barack Obama. We're gonna pray now."

"We endorse Faith Loudon for Congress in the Fourth District of Maryland," and he gestured to her in the front row, "and we do not endorse Barack Obama for president of the United States. Would you bow your heads with me in prayer."

With soft piano music in the background, Jackson prayed: "Our Father, our God, we thank you today, and we ask that this word, this message, especially the last five minutes, will go out as a trumpet to the nation. I thank you that cameras from several networks are here. Lord, let it go forth on the Internet, and, Lord, let it go forth on the CD."

Jackson tries for an amalgam of what he calls righteousness and justice, by which he means religious gospel and social policies that address the plight of the less powerful. "Something is wrong in America," he announced in his sermon, when immigrant families can be separated by deportation, when Obama creates "pressure on Hispanics and first-generation African immigrants so he can look like a hero when he lifts the pressure that he created. Something ain't right in America."

He did not go quite as far as to endorse Romney. Was it Romney's Mormonism or the justice issue? "It's the justice issue," he told me later. "If we keep going down that road that we only vote righteous, righteous, righteous, then we're like a bird trying to fly with one wing. You never get to a true—in my view, humble opinion—representation of the Christian ethos in our generation."

His congressional candidate, who was white, was trounced by the black incumbent, Donna Edwards. His nemesis, Obama, rode easily to victory for the second time. And in the end, Jackson endorsed Romney, but not in church: in a television studio, where the First Amendment protected him.

The ban on electioneering by tax-exempt charities may seem high-minded, but it was enacted for crass political reasons. It may be a principle of good government to protect taxpayers from subsidizing candidates' supporters, but the prohibition was added to the law to protect one candidate, Lyndon B. Johnson, who faced extreme right-wing opposition in his reelection bid for the Senate. On July 2, 1954, he rose on the Senate floor to propose amending section 501(c)(3), which already restricted lobbying. Now he asked that the ban be extended to political campaigning. "The whole thing was over in a matter of minutes," writes the sociologist James D. Davidson. "There was no discussion, and the amendment was passed on voice vote."

Johnson faced a tough race against a Dixiecrat, from the segregationist wing of the Democratic Party, who was supported by two rabid anticommunist, tax-exempt organizations: the Committee for Constitutional Government, founded by the publisher Frank E. Gannett, and Facts Forum, funded by the oil magnate H. L. Hunt, a friend of Senator Joseph McCarthy's. Facts Forum published a monthly newsletter and produced programs that were broadcast without charge by numerous radio and television stations.

The country was in the grip of McCarthyism, a fervor of anticommunist fears and witch hunts for supposed communist sympathizers. Johnson needed Dixiecrat support but dared not attack the organizations directly, lest he strike his own death knell in Texas by appearing soft on communism. His larger goals, "to end McCarthyism [and] protect the loyalist wing of the Texas Democratic Party," Davidson writes, would also be served by his amendment. It was not aimed at churches, but its broad wording applied to religious and secular institutions alike, awarding tax-exempt status under 501(c)(3) on the condition that the organizations steer clear of political campaigns.

Religious groups in America made forays into specific elections before and after the 1954 Johnson amendment. In 1928, the first Catholic presidential nominee, Al Smith, was explicitly opposed by some Protestant churches, particularly Lutherans and Southern Baptists. In 1960, just six years after the law was passed, opposition to John F. Kennedy, the second Catholic nominee, came from some evangelical churches and a group of Protestant clergymen who formed the National Conference of Citizens for Religious Freedom.

Since the change in the law, IRS enforcement has been erratic and unpredictable. Secular nonprofits have been watched a little more closely than religious organizations, but only egregious violations trigger action. In February 2014, after years of blatant politicking, the Patrick Henry Center for Individual Liberty of Manassas, Virginia, lost its tax-exempt status for what the IRS called "a pattern of deliberate and consistent intervention in political campaigns" and "repeated statements supporting or opposing various candidates by expressing its opinion of the respective candidate's character and qualifications."

The center was led by Gary Aldrich, a former FBI agent who had written a book in 1996 assailing Bill and Hillary Clinton—a book full of lies, according to White House officials at the time. His group had represented Linda Tripp, whose recorded conversations with Monica Lewinsky exposed Bill Clinton's sexual relations in the Oval Office. But the center's trouble with the IRS originated later, in attacks it made on John Kerry when he ran for president in 2004. Aldrich claimed that the investigators had concentrated on just 1 percent of its activities. "A few of our fund-raising letters had inflammatory teasers on the envelopes," he said, and he'd written "a few op-eds that were not purged from the archives, which they were supposed to have been." And, he noted, he'd been involved more recently with the Tea Party.

On its website, three months after the IRS action, the center still claimed to have "a 501(c)(3) classification from the Internal Revenue Service" and said that donations "are tax-deductible to the fullest extent of the law." After my inquiry, the notation was changed to read that the center "has applied for renewed recognition" by the IRS as a charity, but in fact that hadn't happened yet, Aldrich said in an interview. "Our attorneys are still working the issue."

Under his interpretation of the statute and its enforcement, the IRS was being pressed by Democrats in Congress to target conservative groups. "Anybody who's saying things aren't running well, they should be suspected. We want lower taxes, less intrusions in our lives, less NSA snooping, and all of that, so we're suspected by our government. The IRS is our agency. Our representatives formed it. They do what we ask them to do. We send them our money."

Enforcement is as selective as it is on the highways, Aldrich said. "There are thousands of organizations, and many, many are active in the area of political opinion, and they're motoring along. When the IRS decides they want to give you a speeding ticket, when everybody else is moving along at high speed, they can."

Without the tax exemption, his center is hobbled. Donations can still be received, but the donors won't get tax deductions. The organization would have to pay taxes on its income. But the larger result will not be silence, he promises. "The thing about a political movement is that people who are in it for the long haul like me do the best to adhere to the rules and regulations," he said. "The government can't take away our right to free speech by denying us a forum . . . If they say we can't assemble under this umbrella, then we're going to assemble under another. They're not going to stop the true believers."

Lately, churches have been treated with kid gloves. Only in the distant past has the IRS issued warnings and occasionally revoked or suspended tax exemption: a couple of religious publications for endorsing Lyndon Johnson in 1964, Pat Robertson's Christian Broadcasting Network in 1986 and 1987, the Church at Pierce Creek in New York for an ad against Bill Clinton in 1995. More often, however, complaints to the IRS go nowhere.

This is partly because of a lower court ruling that was never appealed. In 2009, a federal district judge in Minneapolis decided that the IRS had failed to comply with the Church Audit Procedures Act of 1984, under which the Treasury Department had issued regulations requiring that no official lower than a regional commissioner authorize the audit of a religious institution. A less senior employee had requested information from the Living Word Christian Center, whose pastor had allegedly endorsed Representative Michele Bachmann for Congress. The church refused to comply, won that point in court, and was never further challenged by the IRS.

The agency has dithered ever since. Just before the presidential election of 2012, for example, Americans United for Separation of Church and State filed a complaint with the IRS against the Church in the Valley in Leakey, Texas, which posted on its front-yard marquee "VOTE FOR THE MORMON, NOT THE MUSLIM! THE CAPITALIST, NOT THE COMMUNIST!" There is no indication that the IRS investigated.

Nor was tax-exempt status removed from Bishop Jackson's church or any of the supposed 1,500 participants in Pulpit Freedom Sunday. One of them, Abundant Life Church in Altoona, Pennsylvania, has a Pentecostal pastor who has been nervous nonetheless.

He is Walter Smith, a friendly guy with a sandy brush cut and a short beard. His modern church building, with a thin spire, stands in a fairly poor district. "Our heartbeat's been about trying to get outside our four walls," he says. "We've really been trying to just love all the people in the neighborhood." His senior parishioners run a food bank on Wednesdays, to which the local hospital has contributed Thanksgiving turkeys. Another group in the congregation started a soup kitchen, which has served 100 people. The church does a ministry at a federal prison, has helped a few ex-cons get jobs, throws a summer block party, has added a part-time children's pastor, and wants to start after-school tutoring programs. Since moving into the building—formerly owned by a Lutheran congregation—"our white church is finding that we're becoming a multicultural church, which thrills my heart," says Smith, who is also white.

He grew up in Pennsylvania's coal country. His father "got in trouble with the law, robbed a bank in Pittsburgh, did ten years of a twenty-five-year sentence. But this was even before I was born . . . I had a sister who committed suicide, and I've got two younger brothers. Both were in the military," and both are doing fine; one works for the post office in Oregon, the other at a spa and resort in Pennsylvania. "I got in some trouble when I was a teen—a little bit of drugs, experimented with some drugs, that type of thing." He laughed. At some point, "The Lord really got ahold of my heart," and Smith went to Valley Forge Christian College, then took online divinity courses, earning a master's in biblical studies.

He seems a more nuanced man than his sermon on the day of defiance, which ran for one hour and five minutes, a ranting, rambling speech in front of a big projected slide reading, "Pulpit Freedom Sunday." He declared then, "I truly believe that it should be the pastors and the church leaders that decide what is preached in the pulpit, not the IRS. OK?" He waved a Bible. He preached against abortion. Two members of his congregation had told him they wouldn't attend, "because they felt I was going to talk politics. I'm not doing that . . . What we're facing in our country right now is not Republican, Democrat, Independent. It's none of that. It's good or it's evil. It's righteousness and unrighteousness."

But he only danced close to the line, not across it. He stuck to issues and didn't name candidates. "Churches and church leaders have to speak up," he said. "We are in an election year. We are going to go down a very, very steep cliff that's going to destroy ourselves and our country." Then he declared, melodramatically, "I'm not supposed to preach against same-sex marriages according to the law from Washington, D.C. But this boy will do that. You may have to visit me in jail, and I hope that maybe some of you will be with me there."

He left the brown wooden lectern and pranced around on the steps of the sanctuary. "I beg you, please vote. I'm not telling you who to vote for. I won't do that. But I will tell you, vote for the candidate that's closest to this book." He held up the Bible. "On a local level, state level, national level. Let's vote candidates in that are closest to this." When he put the Bible in his left hand and put his right hand on the book as if being sworn in and said, "Do they uphold this? Will they sign in, putting their hand on the name of the Bible?" the congregation applauded. "I don't vote parties," he declared. "I vote what the candidate says about God's word."

Pastor Smith prayed that someday we would go past empty Planned Parenthood buildings and see them as relics of evil, "like the places where they burned up the Jews." Then he added, "I'm not supposed to preach that, according to the federal government."

A couple of weeks later, when I quoted back to him his line "You may have to visit me in jail," he laughed out loud and put on a sheepish smile. Could he please explain? Did he think that was the penalty for speaking against same-sex marriage?

"It could be. It could be. It could be. I mean it could get to that. And again, that's kind of the evangelistically—you know, you know." He smiled broadly. "Pulpits throughout history have done those kinds of things." He stopped, and I prodded him to finish the thought.

"That we sometimes, you know, we stretch things to try to—get across a point," he finally admitted. "We push the envelope so far so we can at least bring someone midway. Almost like the pendulum thing." So this was a kind of poetic license? "Poetic license, yeah. But I do believe that we as a country are losing our freedom of speech, and I believe at one point it might very well come to that. I believe that."

He did not endorse a candidate, because, frankly, he did not want to risk his church's tax-exempt status. "I don't want to be a test case, no sir . . . Let's let somebody else—yes, I'm that much of a coward." And he laughed, as he likes to do.

PART V

Plays

11

Red Lines and Black Lists

Theater will be able to speak the unspeakable.
—HANNA EADY

Ten blocks north of the White House is an unpretentious theater that has become the pet peeve of several self-appointed censors. It goes by the name Theater J, and its location in Washington's Jewish Community Center (JCC) makes it vulnerable to donors for whom Israel is a sacred cause.

The auditorium has a worn humility. The stage has none of the whistles and toys of fancy theaters—no hydraulics with sinking floors, no fly space and towering equipment to lift whole sets out of sight. An audience of just 242 can be seated, about the same as in a typical off-Broadway house. Along each side runs a one-row balcony, and the orchestra's eleven rows rise from the stage as steeply as an amphitheater's. There's not much legroom, but it's discomfort of another kind that is most memorable. Many of the plays open difficult subjects. Often, following the curtain calls, panelists lead searching discussions onto controversial ground.

While the performances are highly artistic ends in themselves, Theater J is known in Washington as more than a place to watch passively, then simply leave and carry away whatever private awakenings the drama has stirred. The stage is a launching pad for discourse, debate, and disagreement. When they succeed, the conversations begin immediately, not merely on the drive home. The production reverberates. Once the panels end, some members of the audience linger in the lobby, still talking, as midnight approaches.

This vision—that a performance of fiction should infiltrate people's sense of reality—is kept alive stubbornly through 2014 by Theater J's artistic director, the playwright Ari Roth, an impresario of dialogue as well as stagecraft. "There's no conversation without the art," he says, and so the play's the thing for him. Yet no production exists in a vacuum, either. "We do feel that our sweet spot is in a slightly different place than what some other highly respected theaters might look at," he explains. In that place, "the art is intersecting with society."

So in late winter, with the political tempest brewing, he and his staff do "what I would call scripting a season," he says. A dozen gather on Tuesday mornings at a long table in the JCC's book-lined library to brainstorm on how this play will interact with the next or the one before, whom to invite to comment afterward, what additional readings and panels and discussions to arrange for the season that starts in the fall.

Titles of possible plays are written on yellow Post-it notes and stuck to the walls, and pragmatic questions prevail. Will this director or that actor be available? Can the rights be obtained for a reasonable price? How many in the cast? (The answer may be decisive; fewer actors cost less.) How can an audience be drawn by advertising or outreach? Then an occasional stray question comes about the critics—both drama and political. How might they react? Roth bravely dismisses the concern, although he is aware of his own worries. A bad review in *The Washington Post* can damage the bottom line. And political risks hover in the background: If the play is by an Israeli, will Israel's embassy be sought as a sponsor, and if not, what Jewish organization might lend its name as a partner to provide some cover?

Roth sits at the head of the table. Born in 1961 on Chicago's South Side, he keeps in shape by playing tennis, but he looks like a man who doesn't get outside much, even after a short vacation in the Bahamas. His black hair, unruly and thinning, frames a soft smile and a calmness that conceals the professional anxieties he will freely reveal over a meal. He seems respectful toward his staff, yet he can be seen as unyielding and not always accommodating to subordinates' aspirations. He insists that he tries to broaden their responsibilities, "but I don't heed their concerns or trepidations always," he concedes. "I'm too often the most aggressively ecstatic/experimentally minded in the room. My younger staff is more reserved and conservative."

On subjects dear to him, Roth speaks in quiet, even tones but with strong words, which he often chooses carefully with his eyes closed when he wants to find the most precise way of capturing his idea; in short, he is a writer. He is tough-minded in such a gentle way that it is hard to imagine his having a knock-down, drag-out fight with anyone. In fact, he is so ingenuous and trusting that it would seem impossible not to trust him in return, yet his eagerness to take risks triggers anxiety in his superiors, who try to keep him on a short leash.

He sketches out the next season with themes of intellectual engagement in mind. And while he and his staff are inevitably consumed with the mundane issues of budgets and ticket sales, and are perpetually haunted by the specter of losing money on a production, he also manages to keep focused on the greater mission of cultural and political inquiry, especially into the anguish of the Middle East.

This has brought Roth both admiration and vilification, and he has struggled to keep his footing. He is a persistent navigator among the riptides of principle, art, business, and institutional politics. He is also the son of Holocaust survivors, and his caring for Israel is embedded in his personal and professional life. That means listening to Jewish Israelis themselves, and to Arabs inside and outside Israel, and seeing with the X-ray vision of an artist. So he has opened his stage to edgy plays by Israeli playwrights who anchor their human stories in Israel's psychological landscape. He brings to American audiences the conflicts between the religious and the secular, between the Jew and the Arab, between the righteous and the self-righteous. And as he invites into discussions an array of pro-Palestinian Arabs, American Jews and Christians and Muslims, rabbis, civil rights activists, and liberal Israeli critics of their own country, he opens a window onto a very close view of Israel's predicament—to some, an unwelcome window.

Theater J's self-definition is broad enough to encompass a diverse literature, "entertaining plays and musicals that celebrate the distinctive urban voice and social vision that are part of the Jewish cultural legacy," its mission statement declares. In practice, that means "looking for the Jewish hook," Roth explains, a preference for Jewish characters, stories relevant to Jews, or at least Jewish playwrights where topics are not specifically Jewish: *After the Fall* by Arthur Miller, for example, and *Race* by David Mamet, a play that drew a good number of African-Americans into the Jewish Community Center. Even a "discreet Jewish angle," as he puts it, has been enough for him to stage plays by non-Jewish authors: *Yellow Face* by David Henry Hwang, for example, and *The Tattooed Girl* by Joyce Carol Oates. Comedy, tragedy, and music explore racial and ethnic tensions, anti-Semitism and the Holocaust, religious identity and intolerance. In addition, Roth likes to do a couple of full productions a season by or about Israelis and Arabs, with others in dramatic readings. These offer Washington theatergoers considerable insight into the Middle East, which they do not get elsewhere.

Not everyone applauds the enlightenment. Roth is faced with a political spectrum among American Jews that roughly reflects that among Israeli Jews. At one end are those who support extensive Jewish settlement in the mostly Palestinian West Bank, occupied by Israel since the 1967 war. They are certain that Palestinians would obliterate the Jewish state if they were able—a conviction reinforced by the rocketing from Palestinian militants that Israel has periodically endured since withdrawing from Gaza in 2005.

At the other extreme, standing against the militant right, are the remnants of an Israeli peace movement yearning for a conciliatory Israel to end settlements, to bargain generously, and to cede the West Bank for a Palestinian state. Across this continuum run concerns for Israel's humaneness and morality, as well as its safety. To an extent, Israel's self-doubt and incessant introspection are mirrored among American Jews devoted to the country's survival.

The largest American Jewish organizations, sensitive to Israel's utter dependence on the United States, have never been comfortable criticizing the policies of whatever Israeli government happens to be in office. So while some leaders of those organizations may personally disagree now and then, they usually refrain from saying so. The main pro-Israel lobby, the American Israel Public Affairs Committee, does not question West Bank settlements. Neither the Zionist Organization of America nor the Jewish federations that raise money for Israel urge more conciliatory approaches toward the Palestinians. Supporting Israel is taken to mean supporting the current government.

This habit rankles some American Jews on the left who have organized countermovements, sending the establishment into spasms of worry that criticizing Israel risks eroding America's commitment. One group is J Street, a liberal campaign against AIPAC's slavish reverence for Israel's policies. (In a split vote in 2014, the heads of major Jewish organizations rejected J Street for membership in their association.) Another is the New Israel Fund, which raises millions in American contributions for programs in Israel supporting Arab-Jewish dialogue, civil liberties, antipoverty efforts, religious tolerance, women's rights, environmental protection, and opposition to discrimination against Arab citizens of Israel. That left side of the spectrum is also home to some prominent writers, inside and outside Israel.

For several years, Theater J's dissection of the Israeli-Palestinian conflict examined Israel's claim to moral virtue. In 2009, it staged two readings of *Seven Jewish Children: A Play for Gaza,* a biting, ten-minute work created by the British playwright Caryl Churchill after Israel assaulted heavily populated areas of Gaza following Palestinian rocket attacks. Seven actors were used to deliver the competing, contradictory fragments of advice and instruction.

Churchill called her piece "a political event, not just a theatre event," when it was first performed at the Royal Court in London. It begins, as she explained in an e-mail to Roth, at an unspecified time of persecution, "which could be nineteenth century Russia (as I think I was inclining towards when I wrote it) or (as we chose at the Royal Court) in thirties Germany."

> Tell her it's a game
> Tell her it's serious
> But don't frighten her
> Don't tell her they'll kill her
> Tell her it's important to be quiet . . .
> Tell her not to come out even if she hears shouting
> Don't frighten her . . .

Then, after the Holocaust:

> Tell her this is a photograph of her grandmother, her uncles, and me
> Tell her her uncles died

Don't tell her they were killed
Tell her they were killed . . .

The dialogue foresees a migration to Israel:

Tell her it's sunny there
Tell her we're going home
Tell her it's the land God gave us . . .

And after arrival, amid the anxieties of settling in:

Don't tell her who used to live in this house
No but don't tell her her great great grandfather used to live in this
    house
No but don't tell her Arabs used to sleep in her bedroom.
Tell her not to be rude to them
Tell her not to be frightened
Don't tell her she can't play with the children
Don't tell her she can have them in the house . . .

Then, in modern Israel and the settlements:

Don't tell her the trouble about the swimming pool
Tell her it's our water, we have the right
Tell her it's not the water for their fields
Don't tell her anything about water . . .
Don't tell her they set off bombs in cafés
Tell her, tell her they set off bombs in cafés . . .

And after the long history of conflicting, knife-sharp desires—
wanting the child to know and not to know, to protect the child from
seeing and to help her see clearly, to sweeten the reality and to expose it,
to cushion her from fears and to make her afraid, to give her vision and
to shape her myopia—the play ends at the war in Gaza:

Tell her we killed the babies by mistake
Don't tell her anything about the army

Tell her, tell her about the army, tell her to be proud of the army . . .

Tell her we won't stop killing them till we're safe, tell her I laughed
    when I saw the dead policeman, tell her they're animals living in
    rubble now . . . tell her I look at one of their children covered in
    blood and what do I feel? Tell her all I feel is happy it's not her.

Don't tell her that.

Tell her we love her.

Don't frighten her.

Some saw Churchill having "demonized Israel," in the words of Jeffrey Goldberg, a former Israeli army prison guard and American journalist who called the work "polemical and agitprop" and urged Roth not to do the readings. "You're the useful Jew," he told Roth cruelly. "You've made yourself into the useful Jew."

Goldberg heard implications of the ancient blood libel, the old anti-Semitic myth of Jews' killing Gentile children to make matzo from their blood. Yet the play was not about Jews alone, even if Churchill meant it to be. Who, close to violence, is not relieved to learn that the victim is not her own and is not then ashamed to be relieved? This miniature piece of theater did what art must do: transcend the particular and speak to the universal, where the veneer of civilized restraint is stripped away.

Roth saw Goldberg's point, he told me later. "I can understand how it plays with the blood libel ultimately," he said, "reveling in Jewish vengeance over goyish blood of goyish children. It's kind of a terrible allegory."

Nevertheless, this was just the kind of debate that Roth cherished onstage. "I don't sanction this work. I'm critical of this work," he said. "I want to take our space as a venue for discourse and investigation: What are the achievements of this play, and what's egregious about this play?" So he insistently invited Goldberg to explain and discuss his views at Theater J. Goldberg insistently refused, imagining that his appearance would somehow confer legitimacy on the play. Instead, he posted a transcript of their conversation on his blog at *The Atlantic*.

Roth tried to get him to recognize that Churchill was an acute listener, a shrewd recorder of Jewish anxiety. "So many of the lines resonate not with the language of hate but with the language of perception," Roth told him. "She has captured the language that Jews speak to each other," which rides on crosscurrents of contradiction and ambivalence.

Audiences reacted with as much sympathy as antipathy for "people who are aggressive because they not surprisingly feel defensive," Churchill wrote in her e-mail to Roth. "It's perhaps relevant," she said, "that I was told of one audience member who said she came to the theatre feeling angry with Israel but left feeling more understanding towards it."

The Holocaust is a dangerous analogy. It is too close to the core of Jewish identity and suffering to use in speaking of Israeli behavior toward Palestinians—except to explain Israel's resolve to survive in strength. Breaking the flow of historical weakness and persecution, yes, that is the essence of the Jewish state, to build an antithesis of Jewish victimhood. But some politicians, journalists, and dramatists who draw an implicit parallel between what was done to Jews and what is done to Palestinians cheapen the Holocaust and trigger charges of anti-Semitism. They harbor a "pornographic interest in proving Jewish immorality. It makes them feel better," Goldberg declared. "It makes them feel less immoral if they can prove that Jews are immoral too—that the ultimate victims are just like everybody else. Or worse than everybody else!"

One can debate whether that's what Churchill was doing, but there is no debate that writers touch that nerve at some peril. An Israeli playwright, Boaz Gaon, did so in *Return to Haifa,* his adaptation of a novella by the late Ghassan Kanafani, spokesman of the Popular Front for the Liberation of Palestine. After the play was performed in Tel Aviv's Cameri Theatre, Roth brought it to Theater J, the cast of Jewish and Palestinian Israelis speaking in Hebrew and Arabic and illuminated by projected English translations above the stage. It fueled the movement to censor Theater J.

The story puts the Holocaust and Israel's 1948 war of independence on the same platform, in a sense, which is enough to raise infuriated objections from the passionately pro-Israel. The 1948 war remains a great divide. What Israel joyously names Independence Day, Palestinian Arabs call *al-Naqba,* the Catastrophe. So severely do the two sides' historical narratives define the conflict that not until the early 1980s did Israeli censors permit officials to describe the expulsion of numerous Arabs during the war. Even the former prime minister Yitzhak Rabin was not allowed to do so in 1979, when his personal account of having ousted the residents of Lydda and Ramle, two Arab towns near Tel Aviv, was deleted from his memoirs by the censorship committee headed by the justice minister.

Theater, on the other hand, is not literal. It is not true, unless you understand fiction as an aesthetic truth beyond the archives and documents and data, reaching a level of reality that nonfiction cannot quite approach. Those who object to plays and books for political reasons may reside in a more political world than regular theatergoers or seasoned readers of fine literature. The universe of art depends on what Coleridge called the "willing suspension of disbelief," where the metaphor is not a fact but has the power to elicit feeling and reflection, which induce introspection. When judged only on the flat plane of politics, the art loses that imaginative fluidity, and a play such as *Return to Haifa* looks like a polemic, nothing more.

The narrative is haunting, for both Israeli Jews and Arabs. During the tumult of fighting in 1948, an Arab woman goes outside for a moment and cannot get back to her house—and to her baby boy. The house, and the infant within, are given to a Jewish couple who have lost their child in the Holocaust. They raise the Arab boy as an Israeli Jew. He knows nothing of his origins. And after the 1967 war, when the Arab parents are able to return to Haifa, they find their house and their son, both now Israeli, uniting and dividing the two families in a symbolic confrontation with history.

The play, first performed in Israel in 2008, was produced in 2011 during Theater J's annual festival called Voices from a Changing Middle East, which included other productions and readings that challenged audiences' fixed ideas. After-curtain panels were electric mixtures of opinion about Israel's behavior.

In reaction, five Americans active in the Washington area's Jewish community—led by a Maryland lawyer named Robert G. Samet—printed up letterhead declaring themselves Citizens Opposed to Propaganda Masquerading as Art (COPMA), and they used it for a complaint to the Jewish Federation of Greater Washington, a tiny part of whose fund-raising goes through the Jewish Community Center to support Theater J.

At first, there was no indication that COPMA had an office, a phone, or an e-mail address of its own—or much of a following beyond the five who signed the complaint and gave themselves the titles of chairman, vice-chairman, general counsel, treasurer, and secretary. But they aimed at the pressure point of money, and so they created enough nervousness to make some impact on Theater J's productions, at least for a time, providing a lesson in both the fragility and the durability of free expression in the theater.

"We are not disputing the right to free speech," they wrote. "We are disputing the appropriateness of federation funds' being used to support activities by its partner agencies that undermine Israel's legitimacy and security." They would not grant interviews to explain how a play or a panel discussion could undermine Israel's legitimacy and security.

At first they rattled the federation and the JCC. Plays that portrayed Israel harshly or Palestinians sympathetically came under fire. For one season, the theater pulled back from performing any plays about Israel at all and the next year only tiptoed toward where Roth wanted to be, by staging two productions on purely internal Israeli issues—religion and corruption—nothing on the Palestinian conflict. Two plays about Israeli-Palestinian relations, one each year, were done only in dramatic readings and not on Theater J premises. (Roth also arranged a reading at the JCC of *The Big Blue Tent and Jewish Dissent* by an Israeli, Robbie Gringras, about a Jewish federation's CEO caught between a donor and a Jewish community center's artistic director who wants to stage a play highly critical of Israel.)

Plays weren't the only complaint. According to COPMA's bill of particulars, Roth was guilty of associating with the wrong people and being endorsed by the wrong associations. Theater J was condemned for being a "friend" of liberal J Street because its president had been invited to a Theater J panel (actually, J Street representatives had been on multiple panels beginning in 2009) and because Roth had participated in workshops, held at a 2008 J Street conference, on culture as a tool for change. The schedule for a 2011 conference had recommended, as an optional session, a reading at Theater J of *The Admission* by the Israeli playwright Motti Lerner, the story of an Arab-Jewish friendship tested by unearthed memories of a massacre at an Arab village during Israel's 1948 war of independence. So the close interactions between J Street and Theater J became a rallying point for conservative critics.

J Street calls itself "the political home for pro-peace, pro-Israel Americans." But in COPMA's view, J Street itself was responsible for numerous offenses: taking contributions from George Soros, the bête noire of conservatives; promoting a Washington visit by Richard Goldstone, the author of a United Nations report critical of Israel's attacks in Gaza; urging the United States not to veto a bid for recognition of Palestinian statehood by the UN Security Council; and on through a cascading litany of connections and affiliations with individuals and groups whose liberal positions, anathema to the hard right, were presented as if they somehow spoke for the theater.

Ari Roth's views did not appear explicitly in the fifteen-page COPMA complaint. Instead, he was excoriated for the opinions of others, especially speakers at Theater J events who elsewhere had advocated "BDS," shorthand for the weapons of boycott, divestment, and sanctions against Israel. As the peace process stalled, Secretary of State John Kerry warned that BDS was gathering support internationally, posing a danger.

Sanctions are a red flag to advocates of Israel, and if COPMA had found pro-BDS quotations from Theater J discussions, the damage would have been severe. But nothing of the sort was reported. Instead, all the citations impugning the speakers were collected online, and some relied on the assertion that a speaker's group—such as the respected Israeli human rights organization B'Tselem—had links on its website to other groups that supported sanctions. The stain was then smeared from one group or person to another and another in an effort to taint Theater J.

In fact, according to Roth, "The word 'boycott' has never been uttered on a Theater J stage (as of yet). None of our speakers have ever brought up the subject." But so what if they had? As unjustified as sanctions may be, they are very much part of a global debate about Israel's behavior in the conflict, and they can be opposed handily in any discussion. Theater J has earned tributes for being a large umbrella permitting an expansive range of ideas. That idea, however, was put off-limits during the din of attacks. The JCC's director, Carole Zawatsky, canceled a scheduled speech by the author David Harris-Gershon, who had endorsed the tactic, and potential speakers were checked to be sure they had never supported boycotts or sanctions. Roth detested the vetting as "limiting personal expression and political affiliation while impinging on a private citizen's history." So when he had to ask the Pulitzer Prize–winning playwright Tony Kushner, before a play of his could be scheduled for the 2014–15 season, whether he had ever expressed such support, Roth protested the demand by couching it in the formulation used by McCarthyites to interrogate Americans about membership in the Communist Party: "On behalf of the Jewish people, are you now or have you ever been a signatory to a boycott of Israel?" Kushner was stunned and saddened by the question. "What has happened to our Jewish community?" he asked Roth in return. "No, I'm opposed to cultural boycotts of any kind. But what kind of question is that? You know, you go from redlines to blacklisting in a heartbeat."

The one place where Roth could recall BDS having been mentioned was not in Theater J but in a restaurant at sessions of the Peace Café, a forum he helped found, where attendees, not invited speakers, had occasionally raised the issue.

The Peace Café was also anathema to COPMA, whose protests provoked the JCC to sever Theater J's ties with the forum, despite its noble design as a remedy for silence. Struck by the dearth of conversation between American Arabs and Jews, Roth in 2000 had teamed up with the Iraqi American restaurateur Anas "Andy" Shallal and the writer Mimi Conway to create a roving, movable feast of dialogue, usually held in one of Shallal's restaurants, now a chain called Busboys and Poets. Occasionally, the Peace Café was conducted in the JCC under the auspices of Theater J, and once—during his tussle with COPMA—Roth worriedly admonished an attendee who questioned Israel's right to exist, telling her that such comments did not belong in the Jewish Community Center.

"It was alien rhetoric in those halls," Roth told me later. "People had been agitating for the cancellation of our relationship with the Peace Café as a place for anti-Israeli rhetoric. Nobody was taking notes or recording, but the walls had ears." Two JCC board members were present.

Roth's disavowal did not immunize him. In fact, he firmly supports Israel's existence and opposes BDS as a tactic; his own productions of Israeli plays could be affected by a boycott. But no matter. COPMA made much of his appearance at a meeting of Sabeel, a Palestinian Christian movement of liberation theology that advocates "nonviolent resistance to the Israeli occupation," in part through BDS. At the gathering, held in a Baptist church, Roth introduced a reading of a play written by Najla Said, who was condemned in the COPMA complaint as "the daughter of the notorious Edward Said," the late Columbia University English professor who served on the Palestine National Council of the Palestine Liberation Organization.

In his introduction, Roth speculated that he had been invited perhaps as a fellow playwright, perhaps as a fellow second-generation American, perhaps "as co-founder of the Peace Café—a forum bringing together Muslims, Christians, and Jews to reflect on the nexus of art and politics in candid but-always-civil discourse." This was an accurate description of the gatherings I attended, where advocates on both sides of the Israeli-Palestinian divide felt free to speak forcefully. "Learning to listen is the biggest thing in the Peace Café," said Conway. And good listening occurred as a cardinal characteristic of useful free speech.

Although COPMA members had been seen taking notes copiously at Theater J discussions, they provided no evidence that they had witnessed more than a single Peace Café event, which two of them attended at Busboys and Poets in Hyattsville, Maryland. More often, they culled online references to participants, pulling out quotes that branded speakers pro-Palestinian or anti-Israel. The Peace Café was skewered for arranging a bus to take forty-five people to the Contemporary American Theater Festival in West Virginia to see *My Name Is Rachel Corrie,* a one-woman performance stitched together awkwardly from the diary and e-mails of a twenty-three-year-old American protester who was crushed as she stood in passive resistance before an Israeli army bulldozer moving to demolish a house in Gaza. Theater J had nothing to do with the excursion or the production.

"We didn't produce it," Roth said. "It wasn't a good enough play." It provoked outrage because "it co-opted the Holocaust with the diary of a young girl, a life cut short," he explained. "It generated a lethal argument that Rachel Corrie would shove Anne Frank aside as a raison d'être of Israel."

Roth's recognition of these sensitivities enhances his commitment to conversation, because he likes to see people challenged, politely. So does Andy Shallal, the Baghdad-born restaurateur, and that challenge extends to himself. "I remember telling my mother I was going to speak at this Jewish community center," Shallal said, "and she was, You're going where? Why are you putting yourself in this situation? Be careful. I remember walking through the door to the JCC—I'd never been to a JCC before, inside of one—feeling a sense of taking a deep breath: This is a new experience."

The occasion was a Peace Café discussion of the British playwright David Hare's one-man show *Via Dolorosa*, a dramatized monologue of vignettes and impressions from a journey he made to Israel and Palestinian territory.

"Ari was lovely, and I had a wonderful time with him," Shallal remembered. "I think a lot of dialogues after *Via Dolorosa* were game changing for a lot of people. We did them very intentionally and carefully. We had so much time and effort we spent on putting them together, being very specific about who we were going to invite, where they were going to sit, what kind of questions we were going to ask them."

But discussions cannot always be managed. Once at Shallal's restaurant, after Israel invaded southern Lebanon, several Arabs were moved to tell of their families' experiences during the attacks. "A Jewish woman, one of the regulars, she said, This is really awful . . . but I want to share that my brother lives in a kibbutz in northern Israel and they had to evacuate the kibbutz because of the shelling by Hezbollah. And people were, Really, you had to bring that up? All the shelling of Lebanon, and you're worried about your brother being alone in the kibbutz? She was kind of intimidated about the barrage . . . I had to step in," Shallal recalled, and urge them to listen to her. "The following day her brother was killed by one of those rockets. It was so shocking and upsetting that we actually convened another Peace Café the following week, and everybody ended up sitting shiva for her brother."

Nevertheless, COPMA put a hostile label on the Peace Café. As the controversy developed, Shallal made clear that he had no ambition to control programming. "If you guys at Theater J want to have a Peace Café and have the most ardent Zionists," he told them, "that's OK with me, that's a Peace Café as well. I don't want to have anything off the table, as long as it's respectful." If you start putting topics or viewpoints off-limits, he warned, "you're going to lose the purpose."

Losing the purpose seemed just fine with COPMA. In its effort to conflate the theater and the Peace Café, it declared inaccurately that Shallal and the third co-founder, Conway, also "serve in a governing role at Theater J." In fact, they merely sat on a thirty-member advisory council, with no governing authority, and Shallal stepped down at the end of the 2011 season. "Peace Café is a convenient way for Theater J to far exceed its artistic mandate," COPMA charged. "It is a front for the political activism of its founders." Such activism "by the recipients of community charitable contributions is a violation of trust," the COPMA activists complained. "It should be stopped."

And it was. The decision was made by the JCC board, supported by the chief executive officer at the time, Arna Meyer Mickelson. "We believe in a stable and secure Israel," she explained shortly after retiring. "That's what brought us to where we said we had to separate from the Peace Café." But wide-ranging discussions would continue, in effect. "I said we shouldn't be co-sponsoring anymore but would be doing them in our own space under a different name." The board also wanted to create a mechanism to vet all plays and panel discussions, to do unseemly background checks on participants, to build "a firewall for renegade productions like mine," Roth said, "to send a signal that I don't have free rein." It didn't happen. The hierarchy of oversight was never created, but previous statements of speakers and playwrights were scrutinized.

So COPMA won a mixed victory initially: a few small battles, but not the war. At first, its protests failed to strike a chord in Washington's Jewish community, where Theater J had many supporters. Only conservatives such as those at *Commentary* magazine briefly joined the outcry, and they were crowded out by audiences who flocked to the theater.

COPMA's campaign was undermined by several defects. First, Americans who spent time in Israel could see that the spectrum of ideas acceptable to the right-wing group was so narrow that it wouldn't be recognized by Israelis themselves, whose politics embraced acerbic debate. Second, hardly anyone wanted the internecine warfare among American Jews that was being promoted by a COPMA activist, Carol Greenwald, when she attacked two respected Jewish institutions. She blasted the Union for Reform Judaism for choosing a president supportive of J Street and the New Israel Fund, and she excoriated the United States Holocaust Memorial Museum for mounting exhibitions that soft-pedaled "the genocidal ideology of radical Islam and the threat to world Jewry."

Finally, COPMA's vocabulary and tactics were crude. The word "front" came from an earlier, ugly era in American history. And while the Jewish Federation was clearly anxious about donors "who believe anything they see in e-mail," as one insider put it, the fund-disbursing hierarchy was too sophisticated for COPMA's methods. When the attacks included an allegation that "Ari Roth was seen in the company of so-and-so," an official reported, "that was McCarthyite."

Roth calls it typical politics. "You cherry-pick an offending moment, turn everything into a cliché. The downfall of a politician has always been the misstep, not the body of his legislative work. It's a game of gotcha. Oppositional research is trying to find evidence that will blacklist you, will censure you. Are you now or have you ever been in contact with a BDS group?"

Because of squeezed finances, not politics, the federation has provided declining single-digit percentages of the JCC's budget, down to about 4 percent in 2013. The JCC gives Theater J free utilities and facilities, in effect. Ticket sales in 2013–14 earned 53 percent of the theater's $1.7 million budget, Roth reports, and the rest has come from family foundations, other charitable contributions, the D.C. Humanities Council, and the National Endowment for the Arts. So the Jewish Federation would have only limited, indirect financial leverage over Theater J, should it try to exercise such influence.

Yet the federation is the JCC's largest single donor, and it grants a kind of community imprimatur, one that the JCC would not want withheld. "The influence of the federation is formidable and exceeds its relatively modest contribution," Roth said. "It's very respected within the board and the senior leadership of the JCC."

This political weight has not been exercised. In response to COPMA, the federation merely issued a declaration stating the obvious: its steadfast commitment to Israel, its endorsement of "robust dialogue and diversity of opinion," limited by one red line—no funding "any organization that encourages boycott of, divestment from, or sanctions against the State of Israel." Because the JCC and Theater J did not support BDS, contrary to COPMA's charge, their money was not curtailed. Still, the political environment required careful tending, and it affected what audiences saw in the nation's capital.

Wherever there are censors, there are writers who learn how to evade them. In an earlier age, freethinking Soviet playwrights, filmmakers, and novelists wove their ways through the underbrush of official restrictions rather deftly, using history and allegory to sneak past taboos against exposing the foibles of contemporary society. Either the censors were too dense to get it, or they chose to look the other way, which Russians call "looking through your fingers."

Of course Roth did not face Soviet-style censors after the COPMA assault, but he did operate within a jittery bureaucracy. So during the 2011–12 season when he pulled back from explicit Israel themes, he found in history an analogy to the present. He addressed the topic of heresy and denunciation by staging *New Jerusalem: The Interrogation of Baruch de Spinoza* by David Ives and then convening a daylong symposium on intolerance, censorship, and the risks of dissent.

Born into Amsterdam's vulnerable community of Jewish exiles from Portugal in 1632, Spinoza eloquently preached heresies. In his treatises he denied that the soul was immortal, that God was providential, and that the Torah was literally the divine word; he saw it as literature written by humans. He did not elevate organized religion; he regarded it as an outcome of superstitions and rituals promoted by clergy. He believed that one did not need religion to be good and that it should be separated from the state.

In 1656 he was excommunicated in a writ of *herem* by Amsterdam's Jewish leaders. For his "evil opinions and acts," for "the abominable heresies which he practiced and taught," the governing body proclaimed,

> By the decree of the angels and by the command of the holy men, we excommunicate, expel, curse, and damn Baruch de Espinoza, with the consent of God, Blessed be He . . . Cursed be he by day and cursed be he by night; cursed be he when he lies down and cursed be he when he rises up. Cursed be he when he goes out and cursed be he when he comes in. The Lord will not spare him, but then the anger and wrath the Lord will rage against this man, and bring upon him all the curses that are written in this book, and the Lord will blot out his name from under heaven. And the Lord shall separate him to his injury from all the tribes of Israel, with all the curses of the covenant, which are written in this book of the law.

In conclusion, the writ warns "that no one should communicate with him orally or in writing, or show him any favor, or stay with him under the same roof, or within four ells of him, or read any treatise composed or written by him."

His treatises survive nonetheless. The admonition was ignored in the wider world. Several years later, Spinoza left Amsterdam—and Judaism, apparently—and wrote the words that have been read through the centuries and have placed him in the pantheon of great philosophers. He is still fascinating because his offense and punishment were extreme variations of the unwelcome speech and retaliation that can occur today.

Ives's play imagines his interrogation. Theater J's accompanying all-day symposium (called a Spinozium) took the form of a moot court, held in the theater with the federal judge Patricia Wald presiding, which heard from a range of historians, philosophers, theologians, lawyers, and rabbis. The audience served as the jury.

During *Spinoza*'s run, Roth gave a talk titled "Red Lines and Black Lists: Spinoza as Metaphor in Jewish and Israeli Drama." Speaking at a conference by J Street—that bastion of political heresy—Roth hailed the dramatists who portray "the individual of conscience struggling to utter something that our community doesn't want to hear." He described the red lines "in the world of Jewish culture that trigger a banishing and blacklisting of artists and organizations."

The campaign for boycotts, disinvestment, and sanctions had produced a backlash, "a community-initiated red line which makes associating with anyone connected to or espousing BDS as untouchable, unhireable," he said. "My theater has been in the blacklisting cross-hairs of Jewish community agitators, but we've managed to avoid being blacklisted." Still, he noted, "We have been telling stories about characters who do become blacklisted . . . These characters become traitors. Apostates. Heretics. Enemies of the people. In an earlier time we put such people in *herem*. People like Baruch de Spinoza."

"Today our authors walk the red tightrope, have yet to fall into *herem*, but are teetering." He called his theater "provocative and careful at one and the same time; we balance our choices. We sing out and then pull back. We dodge and weave. Baruch de Spinoza was less compromising. He was rigorous in his adherence to reason."

David Ben-Gurion, the first prime minister of Israel, had asked the chief rabbinate to lift the excommunication of Spinoza three centuries later, but the request was denied. Now, more than five decades on, a day of erudite discussion and argument was ending, and the jurors (the audience) of the moot court in Theater J were submitting their written ballots. The count was complete, the jury reported. The vote was not unanimous, even in this gathering of twenty-first-century Americans: Including viewers of the simulcast who voted online, those for lifting the writ numbered 702 and those against, 92. The black candle of excommunication onstage was extinguished, new candles lit.

In the end, three rabbis took the podium to confirm the new verdict. "We have learned," said Rabbi Bruce Lustig, "through the brilliance of playwright David Ives and the genius of Theater J and its director, Ari Roth—" at the mention of Roth's name, a long outburst of cheers and applause erupted. Lustig continued with the moral of the story: "to embrace all Jews—Reform, Orthodox, anywhere in between, straight Jews, gay Jews, believers, seekers, AIPAC or J Street [cheers, applause]. Our tent is big enough for diversity, and such diversity will only strengthen us."

No complaints came in about the Spinoza play or the discussions. Perhaps the aspirational censors didn't get it. But in the following season of 2012–13 when Roth repeated the allegory in a story set in modern Israel, one COPMA activist objected.

It was the year in which Theater J reintroduced Israeli plays to its Washington audience, albeit without any reference to Palestinian Arabs—a safer route than taking on the Arab-Israeli conflict.

The first, *Apples from the Desert* by Savyon Liebrecht, the daughter of Holocaust survivors, is a tightly written portrait of an orthodox Sephardi family. The imperious father chains his daughter to narrow tradition so unyielding that she finally breaks the bonds and runs off to a secular kibbutz to be with the Ashkenazi man she loves. Her aunt gives her support, and, at last, so does her mother. Confronting the newly assertive women in his family, the father, played with complexity by Michael Tolaydo, shifts reluctantly until, as the lights darken at the end, he is inching toward accommodation with a permissive, diverse modernity. The script might have been criticized for presenting a caricature of the strictly religious, but perhaps the strictly religious didn't see the show.

The sequel to *Spinoza* came next, and it was performed at George-town University instead of at the Jewish Community Center, whose auditorium was conveniently occupied with the annual Jewish film fes-tival. Roth sometimes moves controversial events off the JCC's prem-ises to blunt attacks that the center is being used to defame Israel. This time, though, the change of venue was turned against him by COPMA's then general counsel, a retired administrative law judge named Herbert Grossman, who, Roth said, accused Theater J of going to a Christian institution to air Israel's dirty laundry in public.

The play, *Boged (Traitor): An Enemy of the People,* is an adaptation by the Israeli writers Boaz Gaon and Nir Erez of Henrik Ibsen's *Enemy of the People,* written in 1882. *Boged* closely follows Ibsen's plot through a struggle between integrity and hypocrisy, relocating the action from Norway to an Israeli town in the Negev, where economic dependence trumps health and safety. In Ibsen, it's a resort's famous baths that are poisoned; in Gaon and Erez, it's a town's drinking water that is contami-nated by toxins from factories deemed economically essential.

A doctor, hired by the city council to test the water, sounds the alarm. The doctor's brother—who happens to be the mayor, up for reelection—suppresses the test results and mobilizes townspeople against the bearer of bad news. As the doctor grows more outspoken and aggressive in try-ing to get the truth heard, he becomes a threat to the town's livelihood. "Traitor" is scrawled on his house, his daughter loses her teaching job, his wife fears for her university position. And so even his family turns against him—less for his principles than for his confrontational manner. His daughter, venturing out to talk to a mob of angry demonstrators, is beaten and hospitalized. News reporters are bought off and corrupted. It is not a pretty picture of modern Israel.

In the closing scene, the chastened doctor faces the audience. He begins with an obsequious apology to the town and a paean to his brother, the mayor. But gradually his monologue is touched by sarcasm and then rises to a full-throated appeal to those in front of him—the theatergoers, the public, all of us—to seize our responsibility for the environment to protect our children and their children. In transferring his defeat and guilt to all of us, he gains some measure of redemption.

One Friday, a matinee was attended by Thomas Drake and Jesselyn Radack, the two persecuted whistleblowers, who saw something of their own experiences onstage. As a ranking official of the National Security Agency, Drake had complained about huge financial waste and constitutional violations in the NSA's illegal electronic eavesdropping program; he was indicted under the Espionage Act before the government's case against him collapsed. Radack, as a Justice Department lawyer, had complained about the illegal FBI interrogation and abuse of an American captured in Afghanistan, John Walker Lindh; she was hounded out of the Justice Department and became the subject of an abortive criminal investigation that practically destroyed her legal career.

Both were struck hard by *Boged*. Both used the word "eerily" to describe how they thought it resembled the American experience. Radack e-mailed Roth that she was "profoundly moved" and thought it was "prophetic." Drake told Roth that he was riveted emotionally. "It eerily parallels what is happening in the United States today for those who dare speak truth to power," he wrote. "Thank you so much for your phenomenally gripping play and bringing it to the stage for audiences to experience."

Roth forwarded the e-mail to Boaz Gaon, who replied effusively: "Thank you for your words, thank you for your fight, thank you for standing up for Truth. And know that you are not alone. But a member of a proud community, without whom all of us would be poorer."

Herbert Grossman did not see the play, but he did not like it. He knew the Ibsen story, he told me (when he called to cancel an interview we had arranged), and he would not watch it now, because he did not want to pay anything to Theater J for tickets. It may seem odd that such a fierce critic would not bother to read or witness what he is attacking, but it's not unusual, as we've seen; it happens frequently when people try to get books removed from classrooms and libraries or paintings removed from museums.

Grossman did attend a talk by Gaon at the JCC, Roth said, and there is a revealing picture of Roth, Gaon, and Grossman sitting together with the relatively new CEO of the JCC, Carole Zawatsky. The three men look as if they are all talking at once. Zawatsky might have been as well, but you can't tell, because her back is to the camera.

She seems more inclined to trim sails so the theater can advance into the wind without major confrontation. As Roth ventured back into Israeli topics, he and some of his staff saw her as more supportive than her predecessor. After taking office in 2011, she sat down with Robert Samet and his COPMA colleagues to listen, but in 2012, according to Roth, she decided not to reply either to Grossman's written complaint about *Boged* or to Samet, who objected to including J Street representatives in panels. All this she told Roth without bothering him with copies of COPMA's e-mails. When I asked her whether COPMA had lodged complaints about anything in the season (knowing that it had), she replied quickly with one word: "No."

Her lack of candor may be designed to muffle the sound of protest, rather than amplify it, possibly to insulate Theater J. She favors deflections and abstractions. She knows to launch major projects by greasing the skids with minor compromises.

When asked how she assesses the COPMA controversy, she slides away from the question by reframing it. "The word 'controversy' to me is a loaded term," she says. Her preference is to inquire "how wide the margins of a conversation can be. How does one hold the respectful dimension of a hard dialogue?" She does not define the limits herself but notes, "If those margins are too wide, it's difficult for both ends of the spectrum to hear each other."

At Theater J staff meetings, which Zawatsky hardly ever attends, an occasional question is put to Roth about her opinion on doing a play that is bound to spark objections. She is the CEO, after all, and while she appears to respect Roth's artistic freedom, to a point, she is entitled to nudge and urge and even veto if she sees him running into a buzz saw—and taking the JCC with him. As planning for the 2013–14 season was nearing conclusion, Roth scheduled a meeting with Zawatsky to see if she would sign off on some dicey ingredients, primarily Motti Lerner's searing play, *The Admission*.

12

Post-traumatic Syndrome of Another Kind

Don't teach me what to remember or what to forget.
—AZMI, in *The Admission*

Aaron Roth, called Ari since his birth in Chicago in 1961, regards his work as an amalgam of his parents' professions. "My father's an attorney; my mother's a psychologist," he explains. "I always thought that marrying behavioral science and jurisprudence was the perfect way of seeing the theater as a forum for argumentation, disputation, and behavior."

He is also the product of his parents' childhoods. "They were child survivors, child refugees, child orphans." The legacy has infused his writing and his professional values. It informs his loosely autobiographical play, *Andy and the Shadows,* except that his fictional family searches through silences. His real family talks openly. He is deeply rooted, and his parents' stories explain a good deal about why he has made Theater J into such a significant Washington institution.

His father, Walter, born in Roth, Germany, outside Marburg, lost his mother to influenza in 1934, when he was six. He remembers "so vividly an incident" in school soon after the oppressive Nuremberg Laws were enacted in 1935. "The teacher gave a math problem, and the one who got the answer first would raise his hand, come up, and would get a prize," he recalls. "So I raised my hand, and the teacher said, No, you cannot come up. You're a Jew. You have no right to anything."

After his mother's death, Walter's father remarried. He owned a prosperous farm, but his business selling grain collapsed under prohibitions against commercial dealings with Jews. With the walls closing in, his new wife found an exit: She had relatives in America, enough to qualify the family for visas to the United States. The American consul general in Stuttgart, "an anti-Semite to the nth degree," Walter recalls, "treated us rudely" and looked for any excuse to refuse. "If there was any kind of illness, you wouldn't get a visa. If you were elderly." But they were healthy and young and in 1938 sailed from Bremen to New York on a ship festooned with Nazi flags. They went immediately on to Chicago, where his father, Marcus, spent years as a boner in the Chicago stockyards, working "all day long in a freezing room cutting up beef."

"The tragedy of my mother was that [her death] probably saved our lives," Walter observes. Without his stepmother's relatives, the story would have ended differently. "If my mother had lived, I don't think we would have gotten out."

Ari's mother, Chaya, had a more tortuous journey. Born in Berlin, she was five in 1939, on the eve of Rosh Hashanah, when her father was deported to Sachsenhausen concentration camp and beaten to death; his cousin saw the murder and survived. Chaya's mother, Hannah, spent the next five years using her diamonds to buy forged papers and pay smugglers and honing an instinct to detect danger in time to hide and move with her two daughters just ahead of the Germans. "Mother Courage," Ari Roth calls his grandmother.

In 1939, "my mother engaged a smuggler," Chaya says, "and he smuggled my sister and me out of Berlin to Belgium," to her father's family in Antwerp, with Hannah spirited out the following year. And what strong, conscious memory was left with the little girl, then five and a half? It was a proxy for the real trauma. "My mother put woolen socks on me, because it was going to be cold," she now recalls. "When you study trauma in children, which I have, it is extremely interesting what a child will remember. My trauma was I had to wear these woolen socks, and they really hurt. I just couldn't stand those socks. Was it that I missed my father? No. My father was up in the sky behind the clouds, and I was told he was looking down on me. He was not gone. He was always there."

The next year the Germans invaded the Netherlands, then Belgium. As the British were withdrawing to England, "we made our way to Dunkirk, and we stood by the big boats and my mother begged one of those soldiers to take us along." The British did not, but they "gave us packets of biscuits and cans of boiled beef. And then they left." A couple of ships, perhaps including one they would have been aboard, were sunk by mines in the North Sea.

Then back to Antwerp, where her mother sensed the next roundup of Jews was coming. "And so we went to Brussels, and we stayed in Brussels for over a year, until 1942."

Sometimes Chaya Roth speaks of herself in the third person. It puts her a step away. "A traumatized child is put into first grade and cannot learn to read or write," she says. "All she can do is to sing songs and tell poems."

Again with forged documents, Hannah, by then remarried to a friend of her deceased husband's, managed to get the family smuggled from Belgium into France, where they went into hiding in Nice, then fled to Vence, in the hills nearby.

Needing cash, Hannah traveled one day from Vence to Nice to sell diamonds to a cousin. She took her older daughter, Gitta, leaving her husband and daughter Chaya behind in Vence, which quickly deteriorated into a danger zone. Roundups began. As Chaya played outside, a passing French gendarme asked where she lived, and she naively "pointed to the pension where we were supposed to register." The policeman entered, the receptionist showed him upstairs, where he found Chaya's stepfather, "and we were both taken." Chaya told this to a Theater J audience after seeing Ari's play and confessed, "I remember the guilt."

The police separated Chaya from her stepfather, who later died on the way to Auschwitz. She was crammed into police barracks with hundreds of other Jews. "I proceeded to scream and yell and had a panic attack," Chaya recalls. "I said that I wasn't Jewish, they made a big mistake, I've got to get home to my mother. And here I'm speaking fluent French . . . I'm screaming my head off, and one of the gendarmes came up to me and said, 'You have to stop screaming right now,' and I said, 'Why? I'm not Jewish.' He said, 'You have to stop screaming right now, and when my work is done, I'll take you home.'"

And he did, although she did not direct him to the hideout. She gave the address of her aunt's family instead. When the policeman dropped her off, she insisted on going upstairs without him. "And guess what: The door was sealed. They had already been taken." Little Chaya was alone and adrift.

Her mother, Hannah, had been warned by her cousin in Nice not to return that day to Vence, now suddenly unsafe. "My mother nearly went crazy that her little girl was lost and gone," Chaya says, "so she sent my sister to go find me. She had no way of knowing where I was." Yet at the intersection of timing and coincidence, Gitta came looking at their aunt's. "She really did save me, because I don't know where I would have ended up."

Gitta took her to Nice, where they went into hiding until 1943, after Italy capitulated to the Allies. Then they made their way to the village of St.-Martin-Vésubie, from which they were guided over the Alps, heading for Italy, hundreds of Jews trudging among the peaks and across the high ground.

"If you want to know something about where our love for Jewish music comes from," Chaya says, "the second night we were lying on a plateau in the mountains, and there must have been about 500 people lying on the grass, September 9 and 10. We're lying, looking at this beautiful sky, all Jews, and this little boy starts to sing in Yiddish . . . and suddenly the entire group sings along. It is unbelievable. It is unbelievable. What's unbelievable about it is the Germans are at our tail, but somehow the Jews came to forget that, that they're at our tail, because after all you have to rest, and if you have to rest, you have to sing."

One night, while they were sleeping on straw mats, their mother awakened the girls and the family they were traveling with. It was one or two o'clock in the morning. "We must go," Hannah said. "We must leave right now. You know that the Germans are right behind us and we must leave." Chaya cannot imagine how her mother smelled danger, "but she had a sense that this was the wrong place to be. She took us up to the mountains, back the way we came from, and we walked five or six hours. And by the time it's six o'clock in the morning, we are nowhere except we made a circle way up the mountain. We can look down and we can see the road, and the Germans are coming in.

"And so they picked up 350 Jews and shot a few, and some committed suicide, and the rest ran into the mountains. The ones they picked up they put into a small concentration camp. They stayed there. Many of them were saved; most of them were killed."

With help along the road from a man who might have belonged to the Italian resistance, they were led to a woman who gave them shelter in her *cava,* a stone structure for cowherds. It had no windows, and near the ceiling it filled with so much smoke from their cooking fire that "if you stand up, you start to cough." They remained there, and in a barn, for six months, until in 1944 "the Germans are losing the war, and they're up in the mountains, just absolutely rabidly looking for Jews, for people in hiding. The person lending us the *cava* was very scared," so Hannah asked for her help getting papers.

The next day an Italian priest arrived: Francesco Brondello, whose name the family later urged be listed among righteous gentiles at Yad Vashem, the Holocaust memorial and archives in Jerusalem. He "brought them clothes, shoes and photographed them to forge identity papers," according to Yad Vashem's records, then gave Hannah names of people in Rome who would help.

Hannah was "a very beautiful woman," Chaya says of her mother, and "she had this black hat that she pulled out for occasions when she had to be dressed up. She started to hitchhike," with her daughters waiting off the road, out of sight. Along came an army caravan with "a jeep and a German driver." Her mother talked to him in German and showed her fake papers identifying them as Hungarians—allies of the Third Reich. So into the jeep they all climbed for a ride to the outskirts of Rome, courtesy of the German army. There, through the Swedish ambassador, who was one of Father Brondello's contacts, they ended up in a convent right outside Vatican City for three months.

As the Allies liberated Rome in June 1944, another chance encounter turned their lives once again. Chaya's mother had moved them out of the convent into an apartment and one day noticed Stars of David on the uniforms of a group of soldiers. "Are you Jewish?" she asked one of them. They were in the Jewish Brigade. "So she keeps walking next to them," Chaya says, "and she wants them to come to her house for Friday night dinner," which six or seven of them did, bringing food along. "They became such really warm friends. One of them was from the youth aliyah [immigration] movement in Palestine, the Jewish Agency, and he said, Listen, you've got to get these kids out of here. The war isn't over, and we don't know how long we can stay."

Now Hannah stood at a cruel crossroads. She wished to return to Antwerp, where she had family and where she had hidden her possessions with non-Jews. But she could not do so safely with her children, for no solid peace had yet settled across Europe and the girls would have been at risk on such a journey. So Hannah sent her daughters to Palestine aboard the *Princess Katelin*, which arrived March 26, 1945, with its illegal immigrants. They were held in a camp called Atlit until transferred to Ben Shemen Youth Village, a boarding school also attended by Israel's former president Shimon Peres. In 1947, shortly before Israel's statehood was declared, they returned to their mother in Belgium; in the early 1950s they immigrated to the United States.

In 1982, Chaya took Ari and the rest of her family to Europe to find the hiding places, and even some of the people, along her escape route. In the small French village of St.-Martin-Vésubie from which she had begun the march across the Alps, she went into a bar to ask about anyone who remembered 1943. A man came up and stood by her at the bar. Yes, he said. His name was Cergier. He was fifteen when he helped guide a group of Jews up into the mountains. A little more conversation determined that it was he who had helped lead Chaya and her family.

So she was rediscovering her past, but not alone. "The kids helped me find it," she says. "It was necessary to me for them to help me in this chase." That was her way of transmitting her journey to the next generation.

When I thanked her for taking so much time to speak in such detail, she replied graciously, "The listener is everything in telling a story." And so her son enlists listeners for the stories on his stage.

If you remember Chaya's and Walter's childhoods, you will more deeply understand Ari Roth and his play *Andy and the Shadows*, performed at Theater J in the spring of 2013, seven decades after his mother was fleeing through the Alps. It is part comedy, but like all serious comedies its wit bites and its laughter tightens, and the yearning it portrays is scarred by family wounds.

The play is true and false, autobiographical and imaginary. It "fuses elements of non-fiction and fantasy," Roth writes in a preface to the script, "drawn from experience, transformed by invention, filtered through the lens of memory." The main character, Andy, is not a playwright but an aspiring maker of documentaries. He is a young man searching for himself by searching for his parents' history in the Holocaust, a more complete account than they have given. As the play swings back and forth through his life, runs of humor are punctuated by dark scenes, the shadows. Andy's father emerges as oblique and taciturn, deflecting questions about his story; Andy's mother is angry and combative when engaging hers.

The ships from Dunkirk are there, but with a more definitive ending than in reality: The mother actually sees the one they would have boarded explode.

Her screams "I am not a Jew!" are there, but Roth gives the incident a grievous ache of guilt. Not only does the mother shriek, "I am a good Christian girl!"; she also disavows her stepfather: "Get this Jew away from me! Guard!" And he jumps from the train to Auschwitz and is shot and bleeds to death in the snow, while she is allowed to go home. "Is this what you wanted to hear?" she asks Andy, her inquisitive son, trying to liberate him from her suffering by punishing him for wanting to know. Roth's play pivots on the need to pass the torch of memory and the difficulty of doing so without getting burned.

Israel runs as a minor theme through *Andy and the Shadows*. The parents lived there. The sister goes off to the Israeli army, offering flip caricatures of the country when she returns. Andy—unlike Ari, his creator—is exasperated with all the questions about the place. "I have seen the future and it is an endless conversation about Israel," Andy says impatiently. Ari Roth, watching a rehearsal, laughs mightily at his own line.

But Ari is not annoyed by conversation about Israel. Contrary to what his naysayers on the right seem to believe, "We grew up with a very, very strong Zionist identity," Roth explains. After college his father spent a year in Israel, on kibbutz Maaleh HaHamisha. "Israel factored deeply in our family culture. We went there frequently. Both my sisters have lived in Israel for long periods of time. We're all living here, but we all have deep attachments, and, you know, the Labor Zionist gestalt."

So neither Israel nor the Holocaust is an abstraction. "I'm certainly hip to everyone who thinks that the Holocaust has been overused and misused as a political instrument within Israeli society," Roth says. "It just so happens that when you come by it rather authentically, being the child of survivors, the child of refugees, informs everything about my identity and my siblings' identity as well. It's a touchstone. I mean, we're all in the healing professions, whether those be endemic or therapeutic or cultural."

Here lies the key to understanding Ari Roth and, by extension, the theater he leads. Among the elements of his mother's survival that she transmitted was this, in her words: "I knew that many Christians had a part in saving me, and that is why I never lost faith or hope in people . . . If one goes through difficult times, but comes out of these alive, it is because in the last analysis there was someone who provided help."

This is post-traumatic syndrome of a different kind, and Ari took it into himself. "My parents survived," he says, "because good people existed during the war as well. You sort of look for that righteousness in the other. That's what compels you forward. That's what compels you into these cross-cultural dialogues."

Then there was Roth's America. "Growing up on the South Side of Chicago, the whole racial drama of white flight and our decision to stay and be in an integrated neighborhood was always woven into this family narrative of coming from Germany and making a new home in Chicago. We weren't leaving out of fear of black people. That was going to be part of our values, to make meaning in a changing city. And those have formed what I do as a programmer here."

What he was about to program would expose him to extreme vilification. He planned to stage *The Admission* by the Israeli playwright Motti Lerner. The reverberations would echo long after the last curtain call.

13

The Drama Behind the Drama

Is only the truth important to you?
What about the fires it will ignite?
—AVIGDOR, in a line deleted from *The Admission*

The Admission is a fictional story based on a fact—or on a lie, depending on the lenses you wear. The fact or the lie is that on May 23, 1948, during Israel's war of independence, Jewish troops massacred Arab residents of Tantura, a village three miles from where the play's author, Motti Lerner, grew up hearing tales of the atrocity. Israeli scholars disagree about what happened there.

On that disputed piece of history Lerner invents an Arab family and a Jewish family, living as friends in Haifa four decades after the war. The Jewish family's son and the Arab family's daughter are lovers semi-secretly across the divide. Their fathers are closer than is common in Israel, but they carry the hidden burden of having both been in Tantur (the name Lerner gives the town) on the fateful day—one as a young regiment commander, the other as a village youth who saw with his own eyes, or thinks he did.

The past is not past, not for Lerner and not for the characters he creates. It is searched and revealed through layers of truth by the next generation, as in Arthur Miller's *All My Sons*, a model of a larger story told through a family drama. When the big story is still alive and raw, as in *The Admission*, the family silences are magnified into buried history and manipulated memories—allegories of the clashing historical narratives that drive the Israeli-Palestinian dispute. And that is why conservative American Jews fought mightily to keep *The Admission* off the stage of Theater J.

No worthwhile piece of fiction is purely fictional. Writers steal from reality, select and combine the elements, and rearrange interactions and character traits into composites derived from life experience both imagined and actual. To think otherwise is like arguing that water doesn't resemble its elements of hydrogen or oxygen—accurate but misleading.

Lerner makes no such pretense. "I knew all my life there was a massacre," he says. In that sense, the play began to germinate decades before he sat down to write it. The seed was sown at age seventeen as he worked one summer in his father's vineyard.

A Jewish truck driver came to load grapes, and Lerner overheard snatches of an argument with Arab workers, some of them former residents of Tantura or their descendants. "What do you want of me?" the driver asked them. "I only buried the dead."

The remark sent Lerner to question his father, "who sent me to a neighbor" who had been one of the company commanders, a man the teenager knew as "a wonderful human being, very warm." What Lerner heard was startling. "He said, Yes, there was killing." Then Lerner questioned his aunt, who at age fourteen had been taken by the local doctor to help as his assistant in Tantura. "She said, Yes, I was there; it was all true," Lerner recalls. "She was shocked. She saw the piles of dead, and she'd never seen a dead person before."

Other conversations with local Arabs and Jews left no doubt in his mind, even without the kind of documentation that historians treasure. "This is oral testimony," he concedes. "Nobody wrote it down." Hence the historians' dispute. "As I became older, I understood that this was an important moment in our history with the Palestinians." So while Lerner wrote many other stage plays and screenplays, the incident at Tantura remained close to his core.

For years he worked on constructing the family narratives as fiction around fact, and he believes his play faithfully gives voice, through its various conflicted characters, to the competing versions of events in the real village. "Every word in the play is correct," he declares. "I challenge the person who said the play is a lie to find one line in the play that is a lie. And I will change it."

The most difficult role to write, the most complex and painful, was the Jewish father, Avigdor, based on the company commander Lerner so admired, now deceased. "I called him uncle, although he was not my uncle," Lerner remembers. "When I discovered he was one of the company commanders in that battle, I was shocked. He was a good man, and I wanted to understand how a good man was involved in such a thing. Part of my struggle in writing the play was to understand Avigdor."

And part of the struggle in seeing the play is to understand Avigdor. At the time the action takes place, forty years after the war, the old Israeli soldier is a prosperous housing developer who gives money for Arab schools; makes a loan to his longtime Arab friend, Ibrahim, to start a restaurant; and arranges a research grant for Ibrahim's daughter. At first, Avigdor's generosity looks like simple altruism, but gradually, as your eyes adjust to the dark secret, you perceive the faint outline of guilt and of a search for solace.

In the very first scene, an outburst of memory by Ibrahim sets in motion an anguished quest for history. Ibrahim has noticed something while visiting the site of his old village to pick herbs after the spring rain: surveyors. They work for Avigdor, who plans to dispatch bulldozers to begin a development.

All these years, not wanting to visit fear upon his children, Ibrahim has been silent about what he witnessed there. He has grievously avoided confronting the man he has long recognized as the commander. But now, with construction planned for the place where Ibrahim believes the lost bones of the massacre lie scattered, there looms a wanton exhumation of buried pain, an act of desecration. The bones could be unearthed and washed by the rains into the sea. "It's forbidden to build there!" shouts Ibrahim in pleading agony, facing the Jew who has been his friend and benefactor. "The stones are screaming 'forbidden.' The skies are crying 'forbidden.' And you are not listening." He grabs a knife, lunges at Avigdor, and inflicts a wound. The attack sends Avigdor's son Giora on an angry search for the truth.

Lerner does not write gingerly, and his metaphors are hardly mysterious. But neither is the struggle that surrounds him. The history can be buried and concealed, or it can be excavated with care and clarity, as he believes it must be so that each side's story of displacement can be heard and understood by the other.

The play's Israeli director, Sinai Peter, explains this to a small gathering in a Maryland synagogue, noting that Palestinians "will always be a part of my future. They will always be part of my tribe. We will always live together. My Israel includes Jews and Palestinians side by side . . . You should be much more curious to know their dreams," their views of what has gone before and what should come after.

There used to be an old joke in Moscow: What's the definition of a Soviet historian?

Answer: A person who can predict the past.

History is in the hands of those with the power to write it, and as fair and factual as it should be, it is easily distorted and mobilized. It has been especially useful to both sides of the Israeli-Palestinian conflict—a conflict between two nationalisms, and two victims, whose mainstreams still, after all these decades, try to delegitimize the other. One side's story touches the nerve of the other side's righteousness. Israelis and Palestinians cannot talk about today without talking about yesterday.

The 1948 war exploded after surrounding Arab countries rejected the United Nations partition plan of 1947, which would have divided the sliver of land between the Jordan River and the Mediterranean Sea into two states, one Jewish, one Arab. The Jews accepted, but a crescent of Arab armies attacked, and a fledgling Israel, newly independent but sparsely armed, fought through olive groves, stony hills, and local Arab villages to repel the invaders and establish the national boundaries of the new nation.

In the course of the war, Arabs inside what is now Israel picked up rudimentary weapons and fought as well. They did not see the deep Jewish roots of ancient Israel, and they did not appreciate the need for a Jewish refuge. To many Arabs, the influx of European Jews was the latest rendition of colonial rule, usurping their grazing lands and their comfortable homogeneity. Along with noncombatant women and children, some Arab fighters died, some fled, some remained, some were intentionally driven out by Israeli forces, and some were massacred. All those things happened, but that mixture of chance, circumstance, and strategy doesn't make it into the absolutist narrative of either side.

The simplistic Palestinian story holds that all Arabs who left were deliberately expelled; they and their descendants are now refugees, many scattered in a diaspora from Ohio to Oman, and many others mired in permanent slums called "refugee camps" in Gaza, the West Bank, Lebanon, Jordan, and Syria.

On the other side, the unyielding Israeli version holds that all Arabs who left did so either of their own accord or because their leaders urged them out until they could return after an expected Arab victory. To acknowledge that some were ousted was officially forbidden until the mid-1980s, when the gradual declassification of Israeli government archives documented the expulsions. That's why Yitzhak Rabin's memoirs were censored in 1979 and he was not allowed to describe his role in removing Arab civilians from two towns near Tel Aviv.

Several years later, Benny Morris, a careful Israeli journalist who became a respected historian, delved into the Foreign Ministry's newly opened archives and assiduously cataloged the official evidence of expulsions from many parts of the country—the northern Negev, the coastal plain, the southern front, and a few villages in the Galilee. Thereafter, the fact of expulsion began to find its way into college-level histories, high school textbooks, and television documentaries, over objections from politicians on the right.

Later still, Morris also documented about two dozen massacres—far beyond the famous case at Deir Yassin, where Jewish guerrillas slaughtered 116 to 250 Arabs, according to various tallies. But Tantura eluded Morris's probing research. He was unable to nail down reports of a massacre there. Pending declassification of relevant military archives, Morris found oral histories that gave him "a deep sense of unease" but little documentary evidence except for one soldier's inexplicit diary entry, Morris concluded, "that gives off the rancid smell of atrocity."

As competing beliefs about expulsions and massacres still reverberate through the continuing conflict, Palestinians hold on to their abject victimhood and nostalgia for picturesque villages and olive groves no longer theirs. Israeli Jews cling to their celebration of a heroic golden time of rebirth, noble and untainted. To admit otherwise, an Israeli professor once explained, would be to see an Israel "born in a sin."

It does not seem to be sin that Lerner seeks in *The Admission,* but rather reconciliation. He doubts that Israeli Jews and Palestinian Arabs can coexist, as they must, without at least hearing each other's stories and facing the past. He also means for his play to ask, "How do we create our memory? What are the elements of our memory that we use to create our identity?"

Those questions define his characters with nuance and introspection—even Avigdor, who rationalizes and explains, justifies and agonizes with all the familiar arguments about his youth and inexperience in the chaos and brutality of war. Ibrahim, spent by his own rage, recoils from the vengeance of truth and ultimately withdraws from seeking it or wielding it. At the height of his angry clarity, he tells his daughter that he saw Israeli troops line people up and shoot them. Then, after a time, he bargains with himself: He won't remember if Avigdor doesn't dig.

"I don't even remember if there are bones," Ibrahim tells Giora, Avigdor's son, the next generation digging for the truth. "And if there are, I don't remember whose. Maybe there was a village. Maybe not. Maybe soldiers came and killed. Maybe not. Maybe it was someone who only looked like your father. Who can remember such things today?" And minutes later, a message to Avigdor: "Tell him to come here tomorrow. We'll sit. We'll talk. We're old men. We don't want more blood on the ground. Even the bones lying there want to rest. If someone digs there, a fire will come out from the stones and burn him."

But it's not a memory easy to extinguish, not in the play and not in reality. In the 1982 Lebanon war, Avigdor's son lost the use of his legs from wounds that he now believes, in a moment of despair, were a punishment for his father's crime. On crutches, Giora twists and wrenches himself through his insistence on the truth. He demands a monument and proper burial for the bones. Avigdor resists and denies and begins to lose his son to the whirlwind of discord and disbelief until, reaching more and more deeply through the layers of excuse, Avigdor finally admits in an upsurge of grief, "Perhaps we were too quick to shoot. Perhaps we shot too much."

"Perhaps?" asks his son.

"Yes. I shot too much," Avigdor replies. "Yes. In rage. In revenge. In madness. Yes. We stormed their streets. Yes. I got swept away by the other soldiers. I couldn't control them. Yes. I couldn't stop."

Every "yes" hits the audience like a gunshot.

Roth had been wanting to do *The Admission* for several years, but the play had to ripen. It needed revision and "workshopping," in theater jargon. Lerner worked on it; Roth edited it, knowing full well that a portrait of Israel's birth as tainted by sin, and of Israel as muzzled by historical silence, would not bring unanimous applause.

The play is of a genre designed "to leave an audience deeply unsettled and unresolved and in a way to break somebody open so that they can pick up the pieces outside the theater," Roth says, "and ultimately effect change in society by leaving the theatergoer devastated, pulverized, opened up, and agitated." He takes a breath. "The movement towards effecting positive change comes only after the theater closes." In other words, the play never ends.

But how it ends is crucial to Roth, and he pushed Lerner to avoid demolishing his protagonist. Instead of leaving Giora lying prone onstage, as in an early draft, Roth wanted him standing at the conclusion, leaning on his crutches but upright.

Why? "The dramatist has a responsibility to remake the broken world—to point toward redemption within the context of having put the audience and characters through a sacrificial tragedy," Roth explains. "I learned the hard way, in 1998, when I didn't seek to forge a redemptive ending" onto Motti Lerner's *Exile in Jerusalem,* which finishes with an exiled German poet being stoned to death by children in Jerusalem. "The play did poorly with our Washington audience—utterly depressing, not uplifting, affirming nothing.

"Motti's play, *The Admission,* did not end with a pulverized protagonist. I wouldn't abide that artistically. I insisted on some resilience. I insisted that the drama would be for naught if Giora had been pulverized (like the audience) and had been vanquished, defeated, and unable to rise again." Instead, Roth wanted "a valuing and validating of Giora's courage in rising to his feet and standing up to the assault. I insisted on some nod toward a prophetic direction; there must be efficacy. There must be hope. Giora's inquiry and his resolve had to be in some small way vindicated. So I approve of Motti's vision of leaving the theatergoer devastated, pulverized, opened up, and agitated—up to a point. The final point must point us back to purpose and redemption, not toward nihilism and defeat. So Motti and I agree, in a way, to a dialectical ending, where there is defeat and perseverance at one and the same time."

In that way, although Roth doesn't say so, the stage mirrors a dialectical moment for him, too.

At the insistence of the Jewish Community Center's CEO, Carole Zawatsky, a guideline that could be called the Fig Leaf Rule was devised: An edgy Israeli play could appear in Theater J only if it was produced in Israel. That would be the imprimatur, the political cover: If Israelis could see it, why not Americans? Or, as Zawatsky put it, there are "conversations happening in the cafés, in the theaters, in the public square in Israel, and we are bringing to the diaspora community the conversations."

Funding in Israel is always a problem, though, especially for leftist writers who often need financing by right-wing governments. In 2013, Israel's Herzliya Theater Ensemble scheduled the play, which gave Roth the green light to put a full production into Theater J's 2013–14 season. In Washington the season was announced, casting calls were issued, and then suddenly the Herzliya theater closed after thirteen years, a victim of municipal budget cuts in the Tel Aviv suburb. Instead, the play would get only a reading at one Israeli theater and a workshop at another. Under the Fig Leaf Rule, that's as much as Theater J could do as well.

But Zawatsky told Roth that because the decision to mount a full production of *The Admission* with more than five weeks of performances had already been announced, he could go ahead. She hoped the Cameri Theatre in Tel Aviv would put it into its season to provide the needed symmetry. "They didn't," she noted crisply. That left Theater J out on a limb, and she began to exact compromise.

Ari Roth likes to paint on a large canvas. He tries to give Washington audiences a full panoply of writing on the sweep of upheaval in the Middle East by mixing Arab playwrights, characters, and panelists into the Jewish milieu of the theater. The previous spring, he had sketched Theater J's annual festival, Voices from a Changing Middle East, to include both Jewish and non-Jewish voices, but that broad concept "was quickly the first thing to go." Zawatsky felt that since the wagons were going to be circled for *The Admission,* that would be enough. "This was Carole's strategic thinking in asking us not to present two moving targets at the same time," Roth said then. In other words, a small loss for a larger gain. Roth included a reading of *1948*, adapted from the Israeli author Yoram Kaniuk's memoir on his confusing plunge into combat as a seventeen-year-old refugee from Europe.

As an alternative, Roth proposed an interesting collaboration with Arena Stage, Washington's popular theater, which was to stage the world premiere of *Camp David*, based on the 1978 negotiations at the presidential retreat that produced the Israeli-Egyptian peace treaty. He thought that one-day readings at Arena of plays by Arab writers about Egypt, set before and after the Arab Spring, would enrich the portraits of the largest Arab country.

Two would be one-act adaptations by Yussef El Guindi of short stories by Salwa Bakr, an Egyptian. They had been read at Theater J in 2011, but with a slight disguise. "A couple of years ago we did a background check on her, pending a possible reading," Roth said, "and found she'd signed two petitions against Israel. So we left her name off the publicity so it wouldn't be catnip for COPMA." The second would be a work by Hassan Abdulrazzak, a London resident of Iraqi descent, who creates, in *The Prophet*, a bourgeois Egyptian couple caught up in the Arab Spring.

Professional readings can be vibrant. They are performed by actors who get into the parts and really *act*, even without much or any rehearsal, the way skilled musicians can sight-read a complicated score so it sounds nearly polished. Such readings are not just backroom presentations; they get publicity and attention.

For whatever reason, political or artistic, "those readings fell by the wayside," Roth said. Arena was "not interested in my expansiveness." So he and Arena narrowed the collaboration to a couple of panel discussions. Even those were dropped by Arena as Theater J's season headed into turmoil.

"The controversy surrounding *The Admission* didn't figure into our decision," said Khady Kamara, the chief marketing officer for Arena. "It all came back to a capacity issue. We chose to focus on our own series of conversations surrounding *Camp David*." Arena ran an ad in the *Camp David* program for *The Admission* and other parts of Theater J's Middle East festival, Kamara noted, and she insisted that "Arena Stage remains solid supporters of Theater J's efforts to engage D.C.-area audiences in dialogue . . . and look forward to future opportunities to work together again." Actually, Arena Stage had passed up an unusual opportunity for its audiences.

The handful of conservative American activists who called themselves COPMA found traction on the historical issue raised by *The Admission.* They had been infuriated by Theater J's mere reading of the play from scripts three years before. Now plans for performing it onstage with a complete set and costumes reenergized their campaign. The tiny group became Internet savvy, set up a website, and used a Listserv to pepper the Washington Jewish audience with appeals to withhold donations from the area's Jewish Federation, which helps fund the Jewish Community Center.

"So, You Thought Your Federation Donations Would Help and Not Hurt Israel?" said the lead headline on the site. "Unfortunately, You Were Wrong." The post warned, "Your Jewish charity dollars are being used to finance theatrical productions that attack and defame Israel." Another post announced, "The Tantura Massacre—a Lie Brought to You by Theater J."

The alarm resounded with some and repelled others. A prominent area newspaper, *Washington Jewish Week,* rejected a full-page ad that made Roth appear viciously anti-Semitic. "Do You Care What the Jewish Federation Does with Your Donations?" it began, then paraphrased him falsely as having said that likening Israelis to Nazis "is acceptable as long as it's contained in poetry" and that "it would be acceptable for Theater J to stage a dramatization of the *Protocols of the Elders of Zion.*" He never made either statement, but the proposed ad concluded, "The Federation violates its fiduciary responsibilities when its [*sic*] gives Jewish charity to those who defame Israel and the Jews."

Roth had actually said the opposite about the *Protocols.* He'd remarked that he'd like to produce Will Eisner's graphic novel *The Plot,* which the *Los Angeles Times Book Review* called "the ultimate illustration of how absurdly comical and cancerous *The Protocols* has been to mankind." The publisher's blurb says the book "unravels and dispels one of the most devastating hoaxes of the twentieth century." How staging the Eisner exposé of the hoax would constitute "a dramatization" of the *Protocols* was not explained by Robert Samet, who signed the ad for COPMA. He did not submit to questioning.

In any case, the ad was "frankly very destructive and also inaccurate," said Susie Gelman, an owner of the paper. "It's not a free-speech issue. People don't have a right to have the ad run. It's a business decision. The reason my husband and I purchased the paper was to create a community institution." She is a prominent benefactor, a former president of the Jewish Federation, a member of the federation's executive committee, and an inconsistent supporter of Theater J's efforts to take audiences into difficult terrain.

A toned-down alternate ad, which the *Jewish Week* agreed to publish, didn't mention Roth, listed some offending plays and discussions at Theater J, and argued that "federation funds should not support groups that demonize, delegitimize, and apply double standards in their criticism of Israel." COPMA urged donors to withhold contributions on Super Sunday, the annual day of appeals and pledges.

By selecting certain facts and omitting others, the COPMA activists spread hyperbole and dogma that troubled donors who had neither read *The Admission* nor delved into the conflicting histories of the obscure Tantura incident. Unlike its protests against the theater in earlier years, COPMA's argument over Israel's virtuous birth tapped wider support from other conservative Jewish organizations.

An Orthodox group, the National Council of Young Israel, urged the Jewish Federation to halt financing the Jewish Community Center because of the play's "neo-anti-Israeli perspective, which is contrary to the mission of the Federation . . . Such financial support runs counter to the interests of your constituency . . . Artists who denigrate the Jewish State or its citizens should not be supported by the Federation."

A wave of concern worried fund-raisers. To bureaucrats who depend on charity, political friction is like a grenade on the table. They duck for cover. In the earlier years of controversy over Theater J, the federation's chief executive officer, Steve Rakitt, seemed to be doing just that by carefully avoiding public statements. Behind the scenes, though, he guided the organization along a course of neutrality: As the collector and grantor of millions in funds, the federation said it would not stick its nose into its grantees' programming content, with that one exception of rejecting support for BDS, the sanctions movement against Israel.

Rakitt favored invisibility. He didn't like to talk for quotation. But now he replied to the Young Israel letter with an unexpectedly robust defense of Theater J and *The Admission*. The federation, he wrote, was "proud of its record on Israel and proud of its affiliation with all of our beneficiary agencies," for which it had raised hundreds of millions of dollars. The JCC, he said, "does more Israeli programming than any other agency in our community." He took note of the federation's pledge "not to fund any community programming that is affiliated with BDS" and concluded, "We do not believe that *The Admission* comes anywhere near the BDS 'red line.'" It seemed that he had actually read the play, unlike its loudest critics.

Rakitt then turned the antiboycott language against the activists, declaring, "COPMA's own call for a boycott against the Federation by encouraging donors to stop giving, is misguided . . . We believe that our community is a big tent and we need to be welcoming of all perspectives." With polite understatement, he made short work of COPMA's argument that such plays and discussions endangered Israel. The country's serious risks came from its neighbors and the international sanctions movement, he noted. While a few of the "dozens and dozens of thoughtful programs" at the JCC "may be controversial, we do not believe they threaten Israel's existence." His deft rebuttal cheered the theater's staff.

In addition, more than thirty prominent playwrights, directors, and other luminaries of the Israeli theater signed an open letter of vigorous support for Theater J, whose "artistic dialogues reflect an honest, pluralistic, multilayered representation of the state of Israel, its internal and external conflicts, its spirit and its struggle to survive."

That was an interesting way to put it: that American audiences were able to see Israel through Theater J's sophisticated lens. It's safe to say that nowhere else in the nation's capital would this be possible; commercial theaters are commercial, and free expression in an open society thrives on appeals to particular constituencies of interest.

Of course there was a conservative constituency listening to a different tune, and it seemed to be striking chords with some donors who were more interested in Israel's reputation than in an Israeli's art.

The COPMA group played to that concern. Ostensibly dedicated to historical facts, the group was casual with contemporary facts. Besides misquoting Roth, it confused Motti Lerner with another playwright, Boaz Gaon, in misattributing Gaon's work to Lerner. But the right-wingers' campaign had nothing to do with theater, the poetry of fiction, or Lerner's creativity, which is formidable. It had nothing to do with the gulfs that exist across generations or with the question of whether truth can be spoken in the plural; there may be many truths. It dealt only with Israel's virtue, and so argument was sucked into the question of whether a real massacre had occurred.

That was too bad, because the play ventures boldly into a region where people rarely tread: where the two histories mix, and where each side tries to weigh the past's burden on the present. Usually, we get one side's version or the other's, each as a flat caricature of history that masks the introspective struggles over self-identity that drive the conflict. Putting them together illuminates an ambiguous legacy. As Avigdor's son declares in the play, "Our differences will clarify the complexity."

Six months before the play was to open, rumors flew about contributions being withheld from the federation. "I don't know the names of any of the donors," Roth told me, "only that there were a few small gifts, then a gift of $3,000, and $4,000, and then, the game changer, a major donor withheld his usual $250,000 gift. That's gotten people's attention." A month later, the federation denied the report. Someone on the board also passed the word down to Roth that a particular contributor was hesitating over a major contribution for a proposed JCC capital campaign.

When I put this story to the contributor, he was surprised. "Nonsense," he said flatly. Had he ever expressed concern about the play? "None whatsoever."

Zawatsky was in a position to know, but she doesn't like to talk about donors. "To put a dollar amount on it or use the term 'donor' in some ways sort of cheapens the conversation," she says. "The conversation is about how do we talk about Israel? The dollar amount is not important." Not important? No, she insists. "I would deny that our decisions were made based on dollars" but rather on "how genuinely we represent what's happening in Israel." Instead of "donor threat," she prefers the terms "consternation and dissenting voices."

Yet she told insiders that *The Admission* fracas did exact a cost to the JCC, whose fund-raising was down $200,000 at one point, out of an $8 million budget, although the fiscal year closed only $50,000 short, Roth reported. It wasn't clear how much of that decline was provoked by the decision to stage the play in the first place and how much by displeasure over the JCC's display of "cowardice" in the face of the objections. The word was used by a prominent figure in the Jewish community.

In any event, Theater J came out whole in its own fund-raising, Roth said. So did the Jewish Federation, which saw no significant impact of the COPMA campaign, according to a board member. The would-be censors themselves were not big contributors, and only small donors cut back. But while the fears flew, the bureaucracy put its finger to the wind. Zawatsky faced a troubled board and sought concessions.

She might not have needed to do so. Robert and Arlene Kogod, for example, who are prominent patrons of the arts and generous donors, told me clearly of their devotion to free speech and open discussion. "Someone from the federation spoke to me about this," said Bob Kogod, and asked, "What should our response be?" And what did he reply? "This is a free country; it's open. My guideline is, if it's hate speech, it's not tolerable. Otherwise, it's OK."

Arlene Kogod hailed the play. "I thought it was marvelous. Just like seeing 12 Years a Slave, it doesn't bother me. It enlightens me to see the underbelly of things. I felt it told both sides, and you could come to your own conclusion. I appreciate the openness of it."

But none of that was clear months before The Admission was to open, and so the play was jeopardized. Pushed in one direction by jittery board members and in the other by her team of theater professionals and their allies, Zawatsky struggled toward a middle ground that pleased nobody, as the middle ground rarely does. Summoned to her office at 4:00 one afternoon, Roth was confronted by Zawatsky and the JCC board president, Rose Cohen, in a united request. Citing donor pressure and the Fig Leaf Rule, they asked him to cancel the show and instead do a mere reading for several nights, with actors holding scripts. Roth pushed back. "I tried to say it's really going to contaminate your tenure," he recalled. "It's going to destroy the good name of the institution—the JCC and the theater."

It was a tense period of internal argument that left Roth so distraught that he offered his resignation several times. He considered asking the actors, director, set designer, and other staff to break their contracts and move the full production to another performance space in Washington. He thought ambitiously about a long and expensive plan "to build a new theater and then compete for the same programming—not necessarily Jewish but an ecumenical thing."

He and Zawatsky make an odd couple. She respects the power of art but must also defer to the strictures of politics and fund-raising. He's the inventive subordinate who practices a creative recalcitrance. So their awkward dance around volatile issues determines what Washington theatergoers see on their stage.

Nobody comes to this kind of problem as a blank slate. Just as Roth has his upbringing to guide his long reach across difficult boundaries, Zawatsky has a momentary childhood experience with censorship. From a textbook in a loose-leaf binder, her Jewish school removed a chapter on family planning or sex ed. She doesn't remember the title or the detail of the chapter, only her mother's indignation.

"My mother went to the school and said, 'I paid for the whole book,'" Zawatsky recalls. "She was incensed that they would censor a chapter for her child. 'I'd like the whole book!'" The result? "They gave her the chapter." Because Carole tells this story without prompting, she must still hear the echo of her long-deceased mother's voice. But how clearly?

Zawatsky has made her career managing visual arts for various prominent museums. She co-founded the Maltz Museum of Jewish Heritage in Beachwood, Ohio. She speaks informatively about the way a painting is hung, the context of space and light that keeps a piece of art alive. "I believe deeply that art has the power to make us more human, to create more connections among people, to ask some of the toughest questions," she says. "The fervor that kind of bubbled up" around *The Admission* demonstrated the power but left her puzzled.

"It's a work of art," she notes. "It's one person's play. It's an expression of a group of artists who are Israeli, their expression of their experience in 2014 reflecting back to 1948. And why is that so scary? And that question remains in some ways unanswered for me. Why is the asking of that question as scary as it is?" After all, she observes, "I don't question my American patriotism, not for one second. I am one of those persons who wells up at the singing of 'The Star-Spangled Banner.'" That doesn't mean she can't look squarely at "some very ugly history" of her country. "It's the analogy," she says. "With every fiber of my being I call myself a Zionist." That doesn't mean she can't look squarely at Israel.

So the turbulence surrounding the theater has promoted introspection. "Making tough decisions is always a growth. Walking through any experience that calls on us to be reminded of our own moral compass is a growth." Hers includes the value placed on tough conversations that "can often bring us back to what we believe in that much more strongly, can help shift and shape who we are and what we become. When I saw *The Admission* and I heard a talk-back panel and I see an audience of people engaged and wrestling with the questions that come forward through that play, I say, Huh, OK, we're doing something powerful."

What she saw was the compromise—she calls it the "collaborative process"—that she and Roth finally concluded: a workshop format that would keep the play onstage but scale it down from the planned full production of five and a half weeks to a spare two and a half weeks with minimal props; a set consisting of a square table, a few chairs, and miniature models of stone Arab houses; and costumes looking as if they had come out of the actors' closets. The Fig Leaf Rule was back in force: workshopped in Israel, it could only be workshopped in Washington.

Workshops can take many forms, however, and as rehearsals progressed, the gap between a roughly hewn work in progress and a polished performance narrowed. The actors went "off book," memorizing their lines and putting aside their scripts—except for a token script perched on a music stand to stage right, meant to symbolize the workshop format.

Zawatsky seemed worried that Roth and his team were exceeding the board's restrictions. She insisted on signing off on every ingredient of the production. She demanded that the limits be codified in unprecedented "protocols" numbering fifteen pages, which she and Roth negotiated, drafted, and redrafted. The detail documented the distrust that had developed between the executive and the artistic director. "In a full production of this 14-scene play," the agreement stated, "150 props are called for. Our workshop will use 2 props per scene, with a total of no more than 28 props used in the entire play. This includes every glass representing its own prop."

Of course none of these cutbacks mollified the opponents, who wanted silence. "This is no victory," COPMA bellowed. "Would we countenance a play and panel discussion alleging that Jews masterminded the 9/11 World Trade Center Terrorist Attack?"

Nor was there delight among proponents. "It could have been worse," Motti Lerner said philosophically. The loss of trust was mentioned often by Roth, who felt the loneliness of working under people who would not stand on principle. "I think everything is hunky-dory," he said sardonically, "as long as you don't put any Palestinians onstage. We can talk about abortion; we can talk about the Tea Party, misogyny, the excesses of the Israeli right." But giving Palestinians a voice in the Jewish Community Center remained politically treacherous.

It should be cause for celebration. The wide embrace is admirable, a model of open-mindedness that draws Arabs to the theater along with Jews. Yet Roth is also attuned to the virtue of political balance, which he achieved after *The Admission* with *Golda's Balcony*, a stirring paean to the Israeli prime minister Golda Meir, played exquisitely by Tovah Feldshuh. "It was my idea," Roth said. It cost over $220,000 for a three-week run, met by higher ticket prices totaling $190,000, plus fund-raising.

"The play is actually a frank drama," he said, although not as frank as he would have liked. Years earlier he had asked the play's author, William Gibson, to insert some reference to Golda's failure to see the Palestinians as a people; she had made infamous comments to that effect. Gibson did not do so and has since died. "But there's a lot of other honest stuff" in the play, Roth noted, including her anguished contemplations about using nuclear weapons when Israel was facing defeat in the 1973 Yom Kippur War. For those who love Israel with unyielding passion, *Golda's Balcony* came as an antidote to the wrenching questions unleashed in *The Admission*. On VIP night, the audience gave Feldshuh—and the script, no doubt—a long standing ovation.

The workshop of *The Admission* really was a workshop, because Motti Lerner treated it as an occasion to rewrite and sharpen and propel his play's artistry to a higher plane. Yet the revisions proceeded in seclusion from the vitriolic debate outside. Rehearsals were conducted in quiet integrity. The darkened auditorium was a sanctuary. Nobody pressed for changes in the script, Lerner said, except to enhance the dramatic narrative and the validity of the characters. By e-mail from Israel and then in person after arriving for final rehearsals, he fielded suggestions from the director and the cast on lines and scenes; sometimes he took the ideas, sometimes not. At least once he deleted a line that one of his leads adored.

"I have this great line," said Michael Tolaydo, who played Avigdor: "'Is only the truth important to you? What about the fires it will ignite?' I mean, it's a beautiful line, because it's true . . . Sometimes things should just be left alone. Should they not be known? I don't know."

Several days later, the line was gone. Lerner thought it was too explanatory, didactic, and unnecessary in the context of Avigdor's obvious resistance to penetrating the truth.

The actors were baffled by the uproar beyond the walls, because the deeper they dug into the play, the more nuance and complexity they perceived. "I think Motti is brilliant in the way he layered every character," said Hanna Eady, a Palestinian who grew up in Israel's Galilee and played Ibrahim. "We have to find and discover the subtext, but it's so thick, and it's so rich. Every time you go through it, you just keep discovering things."

"The great thing about Motti is he makes his characters human beings," Tolaydo observed. "It's not good guys, bad guys. I don't understand why people are afraid to talk about that. That's beyond my own comprehension. Hammer it out. You know what I mean? Let's have a big discussion about it."

In an earlier draft, Lerner used a purely fictitious name for the village—Jirin—to avoid a libel suit by veterans who had sued an Israeli graduate student over a master's thesis alleging a massacre. Once historians had researched the incident, despite their disagreements over what had occurred, Lerner felt safer calling the town Tantur, close to the reality. "I changed the name because I want to make sure the audience understands I'm talking about a real event and not about a fictitious event," he said.

At the same time, he moved the story toward ambiguity, creating a Rorschach test that allows different viewers various conclusions about the reality of a massacre—or whether the killings were justified in the confused dangers of war. In so doing, he strengthened the play's grip on audiences who are now invited to find their own way through fogs of denial and self-deception. The memories of Ibrahim and Avigdor, in shifting swirls of mistiness and clarity, expose and conceal. Reality is so inexact that in post-performance discussions people displayed a spectrum of beliefs about what they had just witnessed.

One night, a man speaking from halfway back in the hall angrily denounced the play as a heavy-handed assertion of an atrocity. Another, Warren Kaplan, thought the play demonstrated the opposite, that there was no massacre. He had voiced strong concerns after Roth sent him an earlier version of the script but then wrote him an effusive e-mail after seeing the final onstage: "Seldom, if ever, in the annals of the performing arts has a successful production been so totally due to the relentless determination of a single person," Kaplan said. "Brushing aside all intimations of career suicide, you pushed steadily ahead, displaying a degree of tenacity, courage, vision, and unswerving determination that was awesome to behold. And now, vindication is well-deserved and sweet."

Actors themselves were divided about whether the audience should conclude that a massacre occurred. Tolaydo (Avigdor) relished what he saw as ambiguity. "I think it is unresolved," he said as he took a rehearsal break in a dressing room. "It depends on who you believe." Then Hanna Eady (Ibrahim) walked into the room, and Tolaydo asked him what he thought. "I think it is a massacre," Eady said, "and my character thinks it's a massacre." Yet he wished for certainty. "When I read *The Admission*, I was not very happy completely, because of the vagueness; it was not clear-cut what actually took place."

Out of respect for the uncertainty, Tolaydo told me, "There's one line in the play that troubles me, and I haven't brought it up to Motti. The old man who remembers everything talks about these villagers being lined up against a wall and machine-gunned." It's his daughter's line, actually, recounting what her father, Ibrahim, has told her. "And I think it sways the balance of the argument," Tolaydo noted.

So right after our conversation, Tolaydo took his concern to the director, Sinai Peter, asking if the play meant to insist that the massacre happened. Peter sent him to Lerner, who was standing at the side of the darkened auditorium. He is easy to talk with. A tall man in glasses, his hair cropped close to his scalp, he wears a gentle smile and an air of calm. Tolaydo told him the line made the massacre seem true—and is it true? Lerner defended the sentence, telling me later that it represented the Palestinian narrative, which needed its voice.

To Eady, the Palestinian playing a Palestinian, that made *The Admission* "at least a door that would open" to listening. "If a play or a piece of art, it doesn't matter, that is coming from an Israeli, from an Israeli side and gives us a tiny voice, even if it's a line in this play, I'm willing to take it if it's coming from them," he said during the break. "I truly believe that it has to come from the master, not from the slave."

How much listening occurred deeply enough to change minds was debatable. Zawatsky insisted on signing off on all discussion panel members; she rejected quite a few as politically unpalatable, Roth said, and pounced on a panel with "Palestinians" in its title. So it was recast. He consulted with a small group of advisers from the Anti-Defamation League and elsewhere "to help build up our centrist and right-of-center perspectives for the panels," he explained. (COPMA later attacked the lineup anyway, mentioning at least one person who hadn't even been on a panel and listing those with Arab names for automatic vilification.) Some fifty panelists were assembled through the run for discussions that ranged widely, sometimes in searching and reflective tones, sometimes in angry reiterations of well-worn arguments. Participants included rabbis and journalists, former peace negotiators and political speechwriters, scholars and authors. There were Jews and Arabs and neither. Audiences had significant insights that reflected their personal pain at what they had seen, their indignation, and their ruminations on how history is carried into the present.

But moderating a discussion after one performance, I asked the audience how many had been provoked into rethinking their views on the history or on the conflict. Only two hands were raised, both belonging to men who—it became immediately apparent when they spoke—had not reconsidered anything but were tightly fixed in their ideas, one pro-Israel, one pro-Palestinian.

They had just been treated to a couple of Arab-blaming statements by Stuart Eizenstat, a panelist and former U.S. government official. He criticized the JCC's willingness to let a small group cow it into downgrading the production and said it should never happen again. Yet his one-sided recitation of the familiar milestones of Jewish history had dragged the conversation into a well-worn rut, far from the illuminating inquiry that the play invited. Most other panelists tried their best, but Eizenstat's pedantic history had polarized the audience and trapped them in old doctrines, from which escape was practically impossible. Contemplation is a delicate endeavor, especially on this topic.

Theater J staff didn't see any COPMA activists at any performance, demonstrating a willful incuriosity that's fairly common among Americans who try to shut down speech. After railing against the play in a Sunday morning talk at a synagogue in Chevy Chase, Maryland, a physicist named Alex Safian told me that he wouldn't stay in town that evening to see it performed. He'd read an early, outdated script, and his purpose was to deny the massacre, which he did with a scientist's precise mustering of the available evidence. Nor would he stay for the next event, coming up the next hour in the same hall—a panel from Theater J that included Roth, Lerner, and Peter—saying he had to go off and give his talk again at another synagogue.

Only about forty attended the panel, half the size of the crowd that had just left the synagogue after listening to Safian. And there was little overlap between the two groups. COPMA activists didn't remain to hear what the people they were vilifying had to say, either. Some, as they left, refused to shake Motti Lerner's hand, he told me. And Eric Rozenman, the Washington director of a conservative group named CAMERA (Committee for Accuracy in Middle East Reporting in America), which sponsored Safian's lecture, said that he didn't have time to see *The Admission,* although he had time to write a long blog post denouncing *The Washington Post*'s coverage of the controversy. "Aren't you curious?" I asked. He had too much to do in the next two weeks, he replied, before he made a trip abroad.

The incurious always seem puzzling. Yet even if these folks had witnessed a performance, it's doubtful that they would have been swept along by what Peter Marks, theater critic at the *Post,* called "the wrenching production," the "wonderful, unsparing clarity with which Lerner paints all the characters," and certainly not by its success "when it finds metaphors that illuminate deeper truths, those that don't necessarily correspond to one verifiable set of facts." Indeed, Marks's rave review was ridiculed by Rozenman for giving credence to a lie.

The *Post* review and its coverage of the ongoing controversy helped to accomplish what censorship attempts invariably achieve in an open society: to make the piece of art unbearably attractive. The house was filled every night. Audience members hailed the uncluttered workshop as allowing full attention to the acting and the script without distraction. When Ari Roth appeared onstage to introduce panelists or to remind the crowds that discussions would follow—or when a panelist offered a word of praise for him—audiences burst into applause. He had grown in stature through this trial and, more significantly, had tapped into a wellspring of regard for unfettered art and debate.

Outside the hall, the campaign to shut down the play provoked an uprising of free-speech sentiment that was exhilarating in a jaded town like Washington, D.C. On opening night, anticipating a COPMA picket line that never materialized, about fifteen pro-theater demonstrators held signs: "Ari Roth Is a Mensch for All Seasons!" "Ari Roth Stimulates Conversation, Not Confrontation." "Give Me Liberty, Give Me Theater J."

A flurry of op-ed pieces and open letters rained down. Earlier, while the fate of the production was still unresolved, the big donors Susie and Michael Gelman, both past presidents of the Jewish Federation, urged Roth privately to scale back to a mere reading, which he regarded as a decided lack of support. She later attacked Roth in an e-mail to a donor. But in public they denounced COPMA's "bullying tactics," called its members "self-appointed cultural vigilantes," and praised "plays like *The Admission*" that "seek to challenge us, even provoke us, and perhaps lead us to greater empathy and understanding. That is a source of strength in our community, not something to be denied or censored."

The production was so successful that shortly after it was forced to close under the JCC's restrictive timetable, it was given new life. Two days after the play left Theater J, the Cameri Theatre in Tel Aviv scheduled it for the next season. And in Washington, thanks to $10,000 to $20,000 in seed money from Andy Shallal, the restaurateur and co-founder of the Peace Café, it reopened three weeks later for twenty-two performances in the Studio Theatre, with most of the same cast.

Instead of taking a victory lap, however, the JCC executive committee decreed that no Theater J staff could have anything to do with the extended run and that no tickets could be sold or advertising done through Theater J. Roth decided that payment should be made to the JCC from Shallal's new entity, Busboys and Poets Presents, for the props, furniture, and support material. But Roth felt vindicated to the point of tears. He e-mailed Lerner that when he learned of the Cameri decision, he hugged his wife and wept. "This is the best news in the world."

That was about as much reflection as he allowed himself. He was not looking back, not even pausing in the moment. I buttonholed him a few times in search of some big thoughts and major lessons, some cosmic observations about the smallness of censors and bureaucrats and the bigness of the American appetite for ideas, words, and difficult conversations. But he was running, running, planning, arranging, looking ahead.

The view forward did not look very bright, however. Several months later in Israel, Cameri postponed its production of *The Admission*. The decision came in the wake of a seven-week summer war in which Hamas rockets from Gaza triggered Israeli attacks on dense neighborhoods with planes, warships, artillery, and ground troops. The theater considered both finances and politics, Motti Lerner believed. Cameri's artistic director cited "purely economical" reasons, Lerner said, after suffering losses by playing to half-empty houses during the fighting. "But when asked why they postponed this production and not others, he avoided an answer," Lerner reported. "The emotions are raw. I guess the Cameri management feels that it isn't the time to present radical plays [that raise] ideas outside of the consensus. . . . The audience might resent it," and so might the minister of culture who "might refuse to help the theatre with its financial difficulties."

In Washington, a similar mixture of money and politics propelled Zawatsky and the board to eliminate Theater J's festival, Voices from a Changing Middle East, and to stage not a single play or reading, in the 2014–15 season, about Israel or its conflicts. Zawatsky even told Motti Lerner, who had just finished writing a new play, that Theater J would not do anything of his in the future, he said, a position he acutely labeled "a boycott." She then claimed he'd misquoted her. "Having just done a major work of his in the past year," she e-mailed me, "I would wait to do another play of his and give voice to other artists." She did not say how long she would "wait" but insisted that there would be no "probationary period." This sounded softer than Lerner's version, yet he stuck to his recollection. "I think I quoted her accurately," he declared. "I remember this conversation pretty well."

The success of *The Admission* turned out to be a Pyrrhic victory that sent Roth looking for some independence for the theater. But the JCC wouldn't reduce its control, vetoing even his modest proposal to create a separate entity to produce a Middle East festival elsewhere.

"We find the culture of open discourse and dissent within our Jewish Community Center to be evaporating," he wrote in a memo to Zawatsky.

"The Center, as we have heard from its Executive Committee members, seeks an environment where risk wants to be mitigated and significantly diminished. The theater wants to enter into urgent areas where risk comes with the territory; risk being the ripe 'stuff of drama,' after all."

Here was Roth's dialectic: simultaneous vindication and defeat that left him wounded but on his feet, far from pulverized but poised to step away from Theater J into some new venture where he could bring Washington audiences the clashing voices of the Middle East. In the meantime, his theater would be silent on the subject, even as the conflict there skewed dangerously into religious violence.

"Playwrights can be a reclusive bunch—Samuel Beckett, Sam Shepard, Edward Albee," wrote the actor and critic Peter Birkenhead in program notes for Roth's work *Andy and the Shadows*. "These are the writers of coiled, tense, and elusive plays about clenched, taciturn, even mute bearers of often unexamined pain. Their plays spiral inward, they tighten and narrow until they implode.

"And then there are the maximalists, the gatherers of communities and containers of multitudes. Ari Roth belongs to the tradition of Tennessee Williams, Arthur Miller, Lanford Wilson, David Rabe, and Tony Kushner, writers of wide vision: layerers, muralists, collagists and bomb-makers whose work expands, embraces, effervesces, and moves outward."

By 2014, Roth's expansive embrace cannot fit onto the narrowing stage of Theater J. It might have been otherwise. Zawatsky might have taken the remarkable achievements of *The Admission*—full houses, rave reviews, and an upsurge of community commitment to artistic freedom—as a decisive rebuttal to the small claque calling for self-censorship. Instead, she acquiesces by reducing the theater's creative space, forcing Roth toward founding his own company. She grows testy and tries to muzzle him, accusing him of "insubordination" when he tells reporters honestly about the conflict. On a cold December morning, summoned to her office, Roth is fired. The head of security hovers nearby while he cancels meetings and packs up his office.

Theodore Bikel, Tony Kushner, and other theater luminaries across the United States and Israel erupt in protests. And Ari Roth, now trying to raise funds for his new Mosaic Theater Company, embarks on a difficult course through America's rough landscape of free speech.

Afterword and Acknowledgments

Zealous attempts to remove books from classrooms have been doing hidden damage, even when they fail. Brian Read, the inspiring Michigan teacher who appears in Part One, suffered acute stress during his victorious fight to retain two challenged novels, and he then gave up his advanced placement English classes. In a wealthy suburb of Dallas, six of Highland Park High School's eighteen English teachers resigned at year's end, most of them in distress over the aftermath of a book battle they had won. As the intellectual sanctity of education is assaulted, some teachers feel violated; others flinch and engage in "soft censorship" by depriving their students of controversial readings.

The English courses Read now teaches use material less likely to be challenged, and while administrative burdens contributed to his move, the struggle to keep *Waterland* and *Beloved* is not one he wants to repeat. "I was happy to fight it, and was wonderfully supported by the community," he told me, "but these things take their toll. This was the beginning of what was to become an almost crippling state of anxiety. It was during the book challenge that I began having trouble sleeping and would find myself having panic attacks in the middle of the night. . . . I guess the feeling, despite the support, was that education had become very unsafe. It was an obvious battleground for political ideologies."

At Highland Park High School, some teachers had "panic attacks, meltdowns, or outbursts of volcanic anger," one said, and felt disrespected by a vetting process that required every newly chosen book to be justified in detail and submitted for approval by a committee comprising parents and only one teacher. The controversy began when the superintendent summarily suspended the use of seven books—during Banned Books Week, no less—including an earlier one of mine, *The Working Poor: Invisible in America*. A student's parents had objected to women's accounts of being sexually abused as children, and to one woman's searing memory of an abortion she'd had at her mother's insistence. The formal complaint, later withdrawn, also revealed a political agenda by suggesting, as alternatives, works by conservatives Ayn Rand and Ben Carson, who reject the view that even if you work hard you can be poor in America.

There are no sex scenes in my book, and no graphic depictions of rape or incest. The traumas described by adult women are included only where relevant to their poverty and parenting—that is, as reasons they cite for their inability to form healthy relationships with men, to trust others, to think well of themselves, or to be emotionally accessible. Further, while child sexual abuse appears rampant at all socioeconomic levels, women in poverty lack the finances and often the knowledge to get professional therapy, and so face disadvantages not suffered by more affluent victims. In short, the part of one chapter that addresses sexual abuse is not prurient or titillating or obscene; it is sociological and psychological, a piece of the complex mosaic of poverty in America. Yet the entire chapter, which also depicts dysfunctional parenting, is now omitted when the book is taught at Highland Park.

The section that I wrote on sexual abuse in *The Working Poor* is disturbing, no doubt. Some parents don't want their kids to know about such deviant behavior. I'll bet their kids do know, however, and if parents don't realize they know in this Internet age, that itself is disturbing. Adolescents do better talking through the troubles of this world with mature adults, whether parents or teachers, rather than just with one another. Teachers tend to understand this, because they encounter the issues every day. They may have students who themselves have been abused, who feel trapped and do not see their options.

Under a seasoned and sensitive teacher, a kid's classroom can be more comfortable than a family's kitchen to address difficult matters. Some literature—fiction and nonfiction—enables youngsters to see their own trials as part of a whole; not feeling completely alone is often a key to finding help. To tie teachers' hands by excluding certain books from their toolbox is to deny maturing young adults the assistance they need to prepare themselves for the adversities they may soon encounter. As my wife, Debby, said to me, if *The Working Poor* showed only one teenager that she could get out of an abusive situation, it would be worthwhile. Quite right—worth all the years of my work.

The Texas incident resembled the one I described in Michigan, in that a book being read in a class—in Highland Park, it was *The Art of Racing in the Rain* by Garth Stein—was abruptly removed. The others included *Siddhartha* by Hermann Hesse, *Song of Solomon* by Toni Morrison, *The Absolutely True Diary of a Part-Time Indian* by Sherman Alexie, *An Abundance of Katherines* by John Green, and *The Glass Castle* by Jeannette Walls.

After a lifelong career as an observer, I felt disoriented being a participant in just the kind of drama that begins *Freedom of Speech*. Despite receiving congratulations from friends and family for being on the right side of the conflict, I didn't really enjoy it until I got to meet some of the students who had read *The Working Poor*, some of the teachers who taught it, and parents who wanted their children challenged by difficult literature. Just over a week after suspending the books, the superintendent reversed himself and placed all seven back in the curriculum. No reviews would be conducted unless formal complaints were filed, which was done against Stein's novel and then *The Working Poor*. Both were ultimately cleared for use, and the dispute gave me more access to students than the complaining parents wanted: About one hundred students who had read the book came to an after-school Skype discussion with me, and six months later the parents' group that supported the books flew me to Dallas to give an evening talk in the school auditorium. The principal wouldn't have me visit the classes that were reading *The Working Poor*, but one teacher invited me to talk with his creative writing students and the school newspaper staff.

Being on a list with Toni Morrison and Hermann Hesse puts me in better company than I deserve. But my feelings are mixed. On one side is pride at being "banned"—a term of exaggeration in this case—by people with whom I profoundly disagree. I'm taken back to the honorable banning—in the true sense of the word—of my first book, *Russia: Broken Idols, Solemn Dreams,* by Soviet officials who confiscated copies from travelers arriving in Moscow.

On the other hand, having spent many hours interviewing conservative American parents for the opening chapters of *Freedom of Speech,* I came to know something of their anguished desires to insulate their teenage children for as long as they can. I don't think they really can, or should, but since I've always tried to get inside the minds of the people I've written about, I may be able to imagine what bothers them about *The Working Poor.* When they try to dictate what others' children may read in school, however, they trigger passionate opposition in the finest American tradition of independent thinking and devotion to intellectual freedom.

In its first season without the daring director Ari Roth, Theater J audiences were to hear no Arab voices, to see no Palestinian characters on stage. Desperate to have something apolitical from Israel, however, the theater planned on producing an adaptation of *Falling Out of Time,* based on David Grossman's novel about a father's grief over his fallen son. A more direct engagement with the Israeli-Palestinian conflict was left to Roth's Mosaic Theater Company, which scheduled a Middle East festival featuring a new Motti Lerner play, *After the War,* on the family estrangements and traumas following the 2006 Lebanon war. Other productions portrayed a Gaza physician's struggle for coexistence following Israeli shelling that killed three of his daughters, the plight of Sudanese refugees in Israel, and the conflict as seen through a playwright's introspective encounters with a dozen characters.

Roth also reached across other divides, beginning his inaugural season with a play by Jay O. Sanders on the Rwanda genocide, *Unexplored Interior (This Is Rwanda: The Beginning and End of the Earth).* Then came *The Gospel of Lovingkindness,* on a teenager who sings at the White House and is killed in Chicago. "A small edge of provocation" in Roth's offerings was to feed into his belief "that there should be healing," as he explained. He was searching hard for an audience within Washington's African-American community to pull the city's disparate populations together, to address "the whole drama of a segregated city and its coded language." Of thirty-eight actors the first year, twenty-eight were to be

African-American. He envisioned his theater as "a multicultural center with a Jewish touchpoint, with an African-American touchpoint."

The haunting question was financial. A theater typically needs 60 percent of its income from ticket sales and 40 percent from contributions, he said. "We are 65 to 67 percent contributed the first year. It's almost an unsustainable model." His $1.6 million annual budget anticipated houses only one-third full, but of course he was hoping for better. He faced no censorship except what would be imposed by the market.

Debby is my most demanding editor. She read the entire manuscript and pressed for many improvements. Michael Shipler read parts and offered excellent suggestions as well. Jonathan Segal, my editor at Knopf, made deft use of his precise pencil, and his assistant, Meghan Houser, handled administrative matters with cordial efficiency. As usual, Lydia Buechler guided the manuscript expertly through the copyediting and production process. And as always, my agent, Esther Newberg, inspired me with her relentless enthusiasm.

Most of the people to whom I am indebted appear in these pages, but some deserve additional thanks, and others who helped in the background are owed gratitude. John McKay, who was editor of the Plymouth-Canton Patch, provided names, contact information, and solid reporting on the Michigan book controversy. Gretchen Miller and Brian Read, the AP English teachers, were enormously generous with their time and access to their students. Bill Zolkowski, the high school principal, gave of his time before retiring to open Bill's Beer Garden in Ann Arbor. Matt Dame, Sharon Lollio, and her son, Tony, spent hours helping me understand their opposition to the books and their broader worries about the schools. Ginny Maziarka did the same from West Bend, Wisconsin. Debbie Piotrowski, Jeff Longe, Mike Pare, and other pro-book parents in Michigan were extremely helpful, as were librarians throughout the country, including Stephen Michael Tyree, Jason John Penterman, Annie Bush, Regina Cooper, Kristin Pekoll, and Julia Whitehead of the Kurt Vonnegut Memorial Library. At the American Library Association's Office for Intellectual Freedom, which monitors attempts throughout the country to restrict or ban books, Deborah Caldwell-Stone and Barbara Jones gave me the big picture and tipped me off to particular disputes.

It is obvious to readers that the whistleblowers Thomas Tamm, Thomas Drake, and Jesselyn Radack were remarkably open in discussing their personal and professional lives, and so were critical to the book. My thanks also to the reporters who took the time to offer glimpses of their methodology in this difficult period: James Risen, Eric Lichtblau, Jane Mayer, Scott Shane, Siobhan Gorman, and James Bamford.

Islam watchers will undoubtedly disagree with my conclusions about their work, but those who helped have my gratitude nonetheless for the efforts they spent in offering their arguments and documentation. John Guandolo allowed me to observe two of his training sessions, and he communicated by e-mail on numerous occasions. Stephen Coughlin and Denis MacEoin were especially forthcoming by e-mail. And many others could go on an anti-acknowledgment list for failing to help, but that's par for the course in the practice of journalism.

Without Ari Roth's open cooperation, there would have been no chapters on Theater J, or at least they wouldn't have had any depth. I am grateful also to Stephen Stern, Mimi Conway, Carole Zawatsky, Andy Shallal, Shirley Serotsky, Sinai Peter, Michael Tolaydo, Hanna Eady, and Pomme Koch. And, of course, to Motti Lerner, the Israeli whose art exposed some of the fault lines of American values in the landscape of creative inquiry. The play never ends.

As many readers will recognize, the title of Chapter One, "Trouble in River City," is drawn from a song in *The Music Man*. The book's subtitle comes from the famous line by Edward Bulwer-Lytton, in his 1839 play *Richelieu*: "Beneath the rule of men entirely great, the pen is mightier than the sword."

Notes

Introduction

3 **Antonin Scalia:** Jennifer Senior, "In Conversation: Antonin Scalia," *New York,* Oct. 6, 2013.

5 **As to the Executive:** Matthew Lyon, quoted in Martti Juhani Rudanko, *Case Studies in Linguistic Pragmatics: Essays on Speech Acts in Shakespeare, on the Bill of Rights and Matthew Lyon, and on Collocations and Null Objects* (Lanham, Md.: University Press of America, 2001), 74.

8 **Canada's Human Rights Commission:** Canadian Human Rights Act, R.S.C., 1985, c. H-6, § 13(1).

9 **Australia's Racial Hatred Act:** Australian Human Rights Commission, "Guide to the Racial Hatred Act," https://www.humanrights.gov.au/publications/guide-racial-hatred-act.

9 **Germany, the first country:** Public Incitement, 1985, rev. 1991, 2002, 2005, § 130(1).

The Landscape

15 **A rash of employees:** Eric Lichtblau, "V.A. Punished Critics on Staff, Doctors Assert," *New York Times,* June 16, 2014, A1.

17 **Edward R. Lane:** *Lane v. Franks,* 13-483 (2014), unanimous opinion by Sonia Sotomayor.

18 **There are many ways:** Steve Metsch, "Car Salesman Sacked over Packers Tie Doing Well in New Gig," Sun-Times Media, Sept. 23, 2011.

PART I *Books*

33 **So does a lot of great literature:** Kristina Chew, "Banned Books: Toni Morrison's *Beloved,*" Care2 Make a Difference, Oct. 1, 2011, http://www.care2.com/causes/banned-books-toni-morrisons-beloved.html#ixzz2TTGfFbod.

57 **If the conflict:** Bruce McMenomy, "Teaching 'Offensive' Literature, AP Central, College Board, http://apcentral.collegeboard.com/apc/members/features/8385.html.

PART II *Secrets*

72 **"I think there were some cables"**: Moussaoui pleaded guilty not to involvement in 9/11 but to future plans to fly a plane into the White House. He was given a life sentence.

79 **(Royce Lamberth)**: Michael Isikoff, "The Fed Who Blew the Whistle," *Newsweek,* Dec. 12, 2008.

95 **His mother described**: Beverly Rizzon, *Pearl S. Buck: The Final Chapter* (Palm Springs, Calif.: ETC, 1989), 432.

96 **With no formal training:** T. Rees Shapiro, "Harvey Dorfman, Psychologist to Top Baseball Stars, Dies at 75," *Washington Post,* March 3, 2011.

97 **His widow had given:** The school's observatory later fell into disuse, however, and was refurbished with another new telescope and computerized tracking several years ago. Andrew McKeever, "The Final Frontier," *Stratton,* http://www .strattonmagazine.com/current_issue/the-final-frontier/.

97 **The town's police chief:** Dana Lee Thompson, Officer Down Memorial Page, http://www.odmp.org/officer/13240-chief-of-police-dana-lee-thompson.

102 **In December 2004:** Office of the Inspector General, Department of Defense, "Requirements for the Trailblazer and ThinThread Systems," Dec. 15, 2004.

104 **Gorman's articles:** Siobhan Gorman, "NSA Killed System That Sifted Phone Data Legally," *Baltimore Sun,* May 18, 2006.

107 **Daniel Ellsberg:** The charges were dismissed during Ellsberg's trial by Judge William Matthew Byrne Jr. after disclosures that government officials had wiretapped Ellsberg without a warrant and had broken into his psychiatrist's office to examine confidential files and that the White House aide John Ehrlichman had met with Byrne to offer him the directorship of the FBI. "Judge William Byrne; Ended Trial over Pentagon Papers," *Washington Post,* Jan. 15, 2006.

108 **In the same year:** Later, other news organizations reported that the would-be bomber was actually a double agent. Sachtleben pleaded guilty to leaking classified information and to possessing and distributing child pornography.

109 **"Delays, technical problems":** Siobhan Gorman, "Costly NSA Initiative Has a Shaky Takeoff," *Baltimore Sun,* Feb. 11, 2007.

115 **"We don't think":** As quoted by Jane Mayer, "Lost in the Jihad," *New Yorker,* March 10, 2003, http://www.newyorker.com/archive/2003/03/10/030310fa_fact2 ?currentPage=1.

126 **"It's a joke":** James Risen at the National Press Club, May 3, 2012, http://www .youtube.com/watch?v=W6VG7PgjaYM. All other quotations from Risen are from an interview with the author, Oct. 7, 2013.

127 **(A *Washington Post* reporter):** Bradley E. Manning, Memorandum Thru Civilian Defense Counsel, Statement in Support of Providence Inquiry, Jan. 29, 2013, p. 15.

131 **Extensive monitoring of Risen:** *United States v. Jeffrey Alexander Sterling and James Risen,* No. 11-5028, 4th Cir., Brief for the United States (censored), Jan. 13, 2012.

133 **The CIA had obtained:** James Risen, *State of War* (New York: Free Press, 2006), 194–212.

134 **And Michael V. Hayden:** Margaret Sullivan, "Lessons in a Surveillance Drama Redux," *New York Times,* Nov. 9, 2013, http://www.nytimes.com/2013/11/10/public -editor/sullivan-lessons-in-a-surveillance-drama-redux.html?pagewanted=2& src=recg.

135 **Laura Poitras, a filmmaker:** Natasha Vargas-Cooper, "Enemy of the State," Advocate.com, Oct. 24, 2013, http://www.advocate.com/print-issue/current-issue /2013/10/24/enemy-state.

135 **Only eventually did Snowden:** Scott Shane, "No Morsel Too Minuscule for All-

Consuming N.S.A.," *New York Times*, Nov. 2, 2013, A1, http://www.nytimes.com /2013/11/03/world/no-morsel-too-minuscule-for-all-consuming-nsa.html?_r=0.

135 **When *The Washington Post*:** The countries that reportedly allowed the CIA to land planes and/or detain prisoners included Poland, Lithuania, Denmark, Finland, Germany, Italy, Macedonia, Portugal, Romania, Spain, Sweden, the United Kingdom, and Thailand. Human Rights Watch, "Lithuania: Reopen Investigation into Secret CIA Prisons," June 15, 2013, http://www.hrw.org/news/2013/06/25 /lithuania-reopen-investigation-secret-cia-prisons.

135 **We listen respectfully:** Bill Keller, "Is Glenn Greenwald the Future of News?," *New York Times*, Oct. 27, 2013, http://www.nytimes.com/2013/10/28/opinion/a -conversation-in-lieu-of-a-column.html?pagewanted=2&hp&_r=0.

136 **The AP sat on the story:** Adam Goldman and Matt Apuzzo, "US: CIA Thwarts New al-Qaida Underwear Bomb Plot," Associated Press, May 7, 2012, http://news .yahoo.com/us-cia-thwarts-al-qaida-underwear-bomb-plot-200836835.html.

140 **"We remember":** Mark Danner, "Frozen Scandal," *New York Review of Books*, Dec. 4, 2008.

142 **Some writers confessed:** PEN America, "Chilling Effects: NSA Surveillance Drives U.S. Writers to Self-Censor," Nov. 12, 2013. I was one of those polled. I was not among those who said that they had avoided research, writing, or speaking on certain subjects—I have not—but I did answer that I avoided some topics in e-mails or phone conversations, mainly to protect those I'm speaking with. I have not curtailed the use of social media.

145 **Since the ruling:** *Branzburg v. Hayes*, 408 U.S. 665 (1972).

145 **A hint of Powell's thinking:** Adam Liptak, "A Justice's Scribbles on Journalists' Rights," *New York Times*, Oct. 7, 2007, http://www.nytimes.com/2007/10/07 /weekinreview/07liptak.html?_r=0.

147 **"None of them know":** Abby Phillip, "Shh! Obama Gets Anti-secrecy Award," *Politico*, March 31, 2011.

147 **The only escape:** Charlie Savage, "Holder Hints Reporter May Be Spared Jail in Leak," *New York Times*, May 27, 2014.

PART III *Stereotypes*

154 **The president, however:** 18 U.S.C. § 871. Threats against president and successors to the presidency.

156 **So it was that Michael Richards:** Michael Richards Spews Racial Hate, YouTube, http://www.youtube.com/watch?v=BoLPLsQbdto.

156 **"I busted up":** Michael Richards, "It's Bubbly Time, Jerry," YouTube, http://www .youtube.com/watch?v=Wriy3ICfF9U&feature=player_embedded.

156 **No hint of such regret:** Brian Graham, "Dr. Laura Schlessinger Says 'Nigger' Repeatedly on Air to Caller," YouTube, http://www.youtube.com/watch?v=F _MGntFSAuo.

157 **Sabattus, Maine:** City-data.com, http://www.city-data.com/city/Sabattus-Maine .html.

158 **The site carries an ape-faced:** http://biseor.wordpress.com/. The site hails *Muslim Massacre* this way: "Nothing in video game history quite beats the ability to shoot apart psychotic incest beard face fucks and their hajib covered bitches as they run about screaming curses to America. You leave the ground littered in body parts and pools of blood."

159 **And so it goes:** http://www.chimpout.com/.

159 **From Stormfront:** Abe Sauer, "Primate in Chief: A Guide to Racist Obama Monkey Photoshops," *The Awl*, April 19, 2011, http://www.theawl.com/2011/04 /primate-in-chief-a-guide-to-racist-obama-monkey-photoshops.

161   **The drawing:** "GOP Club Offers 'Obama Bucks' While Democrats Rib Palin," L.A. Now, Southern California, *Los Angeles Times,* Oct. 17, 2008, http://latimesblogs .latimes.com/lanow/2008/10/obama-bucks-and.html.

161   **Don Imus:** Ben Sisario, "Don Imus Signs a 3-Year Extension for His Radio Show," *New York Times,* Dec. 11, 2012, http://mediadecoder.blogs.nytimes.com/2012/12/11 /don-imus-signs-a-3-year-extension-for-his-radio-show/.

162   **Twitter was ablaze:** Tracie Egan Morrissey, "Twitter Racists React to 'That Nigger' Getting Reelected," Twitter, Nov. 7, 2012, http://jezebel.com/5958490/twitter -racists-react-to-that-nigger-getting-reelected/.

163   **He was indignant:** Ted Szukalski, "Obama-Shines-Palin-Shoes-Unauthorised Plagiarism," http://digital-photo.com.au/gallery3/index.php/Journalism/Obama -Shines-Palin-Shoes-unauthorised-plagiarism-1#.UqYnpdJDuSo.

164   **An exception:** Denise Williams, "*NY Post* Cartoon Raises Some Eyebrows," *Huffington Post,* Feb. 18, 2009, http://www.politicsdaily.com/2009/02/18/ny-post -cartoon-raises-some-eyebrows/.

165   **"He has become":** Ta-Nehisi Coates, "Fear of a Black President," *Atlantic,* Sept. 2012, http://www.theatlantic.com/magazine/archive/2012/09/fear-of-a-black-president /309064/.

166   **Most examples of Obama's:** Kyle Becker, "Nine Most Arrogant Quotes of the Obamas," Independent Journal Review, July 2, 2013, http://www.ijreview.com /2013/07/62945-9-most-arrogant-quotes-of-the-obamas/4/.

171   **To drive home the terror:** "Rush Limbaugh Opens 2012 with More Race-Baiting Attacks," MediaMatters for America, Jan. 12, 2012, http://mediamatters.org /research/2012/01/12/rush-limbaugh-opens-2012-with-more-race-baiting/186125.

173   **The president is not "a real American":** Kyle Clark, "Rep. Mike Coffman: Obama in His Heart 'Not an American,'" 9news.com, May 16, 2012, http://www.9news .com/news/article/268305/339/Coffman-Obama-in-his-heart-not-an-American.

173   **Relying on partial quotes:** "Sean Hannity on Obama's Arrogant Speech in France," The Young Turks, YouTube, April 6, 2009, http://www.youtube.com/ watch?v=IsqX6PmlYAw.

175   **An A&E executive:** Bill Carter, "Fans Criticize Move to Suspend A&E Reality Star," *New York Times,* Dec. 20, 2013, B1.

176   **During his youth:** Drew Magary, "What the Duck?," *GQ,* Jan. 2014, http://www .gq.com/entertainment/television/201401/duck-dynasty-phil-robertson.

179   **Cohen then wrote this:** Richard Cohen, "Racism vs. Reality," *Washington Post,* July 15, 2013.

179   **But the seventy-two-year-old:** Paul Farhi, "Controversy over Richard Cohen's Comments on the de Blasio Family," *Washington Post,* Nov. 12, 2013, http://www .washingtonpost.com/lifestyle/style/controversy-over-richard-cohens -comments-on-the-de-blasio-family/2013/11/12/3c37f900-4bda-11e3-ac54 -aa84301ced81_story.html.

183   **(I reported Smith's numbers remark):** David K. Shipler, "U.S. Baptist Group Ends Israeli Visit," *New York Times,* Dec. 10, 1981.

183   *The Jewish Daily Forward* **excoriated:** Ron Kampeas, "Virginia Candidate John Whitbeck Has Anti-Semitic 'Macaca' Moment," *Jewish Daily Forward,* Sept. 18, 2013, http://forward.com/articles/184137/virginia-candidate-john-whitbeck-has- anti-semitic/.

189   **In his written introduction:** Frank Gaffney, *"An Explanatory Memorandum" from the Archives of the Muslim Brotherhood in America* (Washington, D.C.: Center for Security Policy, 2013), 6.

190   **Not only was their motion:** *U.S. v. Holy Land Foundation et al.,* Memorandum Opinion Order, 3:04-CR-0240-P, D.C., Dallas Div., N. Dist. Texas, 14. The groups also lost in the Fifth Circuit Court of Appeals.

190   **After the co-conspirator label:** "Review of F.B.I. Interactions with the Council

on American-Islamic Relations," Inspector General, U.S. Department of Justice, Sept. 2013.

191 **("I have direct sources"):** John Guandolo, interview by Robert Spencer of Jihad Watch, https://www.youtube.com/watch?v=aieUdwZoYMg.

192 **His site carries:** "The Muslim Brotherhood's 'General Strategic Goal' for North America," Discover the Networks, http://www.discoverthenetworks.org /viewSubCategory.asp?id=1235.

192 **"How did the Brotherhood":** John Guandolo, "The Muslim Brotherhood in America, Part III: 'The Settlement Process,'" *Guns & Patriots,* March 29, 2011, http://www.humanevents.com/2011/03/29/the-muslim-brotherhood-in-america -part-iiithe-settlement-process/.

192 **Douglas Farah:** Douglas Farah, "The Smoking Gun on the Muslim Brotherhood's Agenda," Counterterrorism Blog, Aug. 1, 2007, http://counterterrorismblog.org /2007/08/the_smoking_gun_on_the_muslim.php.

194 **Robert Spencer:** Robert Spencer, "Virginia Senate Candidate Tim Kaine Speaks at Dinner Honoring Top Muslim Brotherhood Official," Jihad Watch, Oct. 26, 2011, http://www.jihadwatch.org/2011/10/virginia-senate-candidate-tim-kaine-speaks -at-dinner-honoring-top-muslim-brotherhood-official.

194 **A raw, unverified FBI report:** "North American Islamic Trust: Second Annual ISNA Conference on Economic Development . . . May 28–30, 1988," presented as an FBI document by the Investigative Project on Terrorism, http://www .investigativeproject.org/documents/misc/459.pdf.

196 **"Akram was the head":** Stephen C. Coughlin, "The Killing Without Right: Islamic Concepts of Terrorism," Jorge Scientific Corporation, July 1, 2010, 77.

198 **The watchers haven't produced:** Team B, "FBI Captured Muslim Brotherhood's Strategic Plan," *Breitbart,* Oct. 27, 2010, http://www.breitbart.com/Big-Peace/2010 /10/26/FBI-Captured-Muslim-Brotherhoods-Strategic-Plan.

203 **Denis MacEoin:** Hasan al-Banna, "Toward the Light," in *Princeton Readings in Islamist Thought,* ed. Roxanne L. Euben and Muhammad Qasim Zaman (Princeton, N.J.: Princeton University Press, 2009), 58–59.

203 **"The Brotherhood will never":** Denis MacEoin, e-mail to author, Feb. 20, 2014.

203 **Qutb's writings:** Said Qutb, *Milestones,* 3, 132, http://www.izharudeen.com /uploads/4/1/2/2/4122615/milestones_www.izharudeen.com.pdf.

204 **A 2001 booklet:** Dawud Tauhidi, *The Tarbiyah Project: An Overview* (2001), 4.

204 **A longer volume:** *Tarbiyah Guide: Stage 1* (Chicago: Islamic Circle of North America), 143–44, 191, 193–94, 196, 197.

207 **At the end of his book:** John Guandolo, *Raising a Jihadi Generation: Understanding the Muslim Brotherhood Movement in America* (Vienna, Va.: Lepanto, 2013), 84–91.

209 **If any of the trainees:** Yahiya Emerick, *What Islam Is All About* (Long Island City, N.Y.: International Books and Tape Supply, 1997), 164.

216 **Soviet files indicate:** Edward Rothstein, "The Anti-Semitic Hoax That Refuses to Die," *New York Times,* April 21, 2006.

PART IV *Politics*

222 **"Before the Internet":** Zeynep Tufekci, "After the Protests," *New York Times,* March 19, 2014. She is an assistant professor at the School of Information and Library Science at the University of North Carolina.

224 **The wealthy vote:** U.S. Census Bureau, Voting and Registration, table 7, Reported Voting and Registration of Family Members, by Age and Family Income: November 2012.

224 **One researcher estimates:** Mark Robert Rank, *One Nation, Underprivileged: Why American Poverty Affects Us All* (New York: Oxford University Press, 2004), 93.

227 **By the run-up:** Kenneth P. Vogel, "Koch Brothers' Americans for Prosperity Plans $125 Million Spending Spree," *Politico,* May 9, 2014.

230 **When she joined him:** Jeremy W. Peters, "Potent Voices of Conservative Media Propelled Cantor Opponent," *New York Times,* June 11, 2014.

233 **Start with a story:** Frank Luntz, "Election Advertising Lessons from 2010" (Alexandria, Va.: Word Doctors).

236 **In the context of election:** *Citizens United v. Federal Election Commission,* 08-205 (2010).

240 **You may be convinced:** IRS, "Social Welfare Organizations," http://www.irs.gov /Charities-&-Non-Profits/Other-Non-Profits/Social-Welfare-Organizations, March 4, 2014.

245 **The ban on electioneering:** James D. Davidson, "Why Churches Cannot Endorse or Oppose Political Candidates," *Review of Religious Research* 40, no. 1 (Sept. 1998): 18. Johnson defeated Dudley T. Dougherty in the primary and Carlos G. Watson, the Republican, with 85 percent of the vote in the general election.

245 **Religious groups:** Ibid., 29.

PART V *Plays*

257 **Churchill called her piece:** Mark Brown, "Royal Court Acts Fast with Gaza Crisis Play," *Guardian,* Jan. 23, 2009, http://www.guardian.co.uk/stage/2009/jan/24 /theatre-gaza-caryl-churchill-royal-court-seven-jewish-children.

263 **Roth detested the vetting:** Ari Roth, letter to Steven A. Cook, May 30, 2014.

264 **"On behalf of the Jewish people":** Marc Fisher, "For Jewish Groups, a Stand-off Between Open Debate and Support of Israel," *Washington Post,* May 28, 2014.

269 **By the decree:** http://capone.mtsu.edu/rbombard/RB/PDFs/Excommunication.pdf.

273 **paintings removed from museums:** Such was the case in 1999 of Deputy Mayor Joseph J. Lhota of New York City, who tried to cut the Brooklyn Museum's funding after its refusal to remove a huge, semiabstract collage of the Virgin Mary, elephant dung, and images of female genitalia cut from pornographic magazines. Lhota never saw the painting, but he saw a photograph. Michael Barbaro, "For Mayoral Hopeful Who Lost Fight to Remove Art, No Regrets," *New York Times,* March 27, 2013, A1.

275 **The legacy has infused:** Ari Roth's *Andy and the Shadows* is part of a series that includes *Born Guilty,* based on a book of interviews with children of Nazis by the Austrian journalist Peter Sichrovsky.

279 **The next day:** Yad Vashem, The Righteous Among the Nations, Francesco Brondello, http://db.yadvashem.org/righteous/family.html?language=en&itemId= 4690831.

287 **Later still, Morris:** In 1998, a Haifa University graduate student, Teddy Katz, did his master's thesis on Tantura, based on extensive interviews with Jews and Arabs. He concluded that a massacre had occurred, and his dissertation was given a high grade. Then Israeli veterans of the Tantura fight sued for libel, Katz recanted because of several misquotations and other errors, and the court adopted his concession as its verdict. But several days later Katz rescinded his recantation. His revised thesis was narrowly rejected by a faculty committee, propelling historians on both sides into a furious effort to prove or disprove his contention. Morris emerged as the only reliable and objective scholar who seemed determined to drill down honestly into the facts. See Benny Morris, "The Tantura 'Massacre,'" *Jerusalem Report,* Feb. 9, 2004, 18–22.

306 **"Playwrights can be a reclusive bunch":** Peter Birkenhead, "Andy and His Shadows Over the Years," Program for *Andy and the Shadows,* April 3–May 5, 2013, Theater J, Washington DCJCC.

Index

Page numbers beginning with 313 refer to notes.

THE RIGHTS OF THE PEOPLE
How Our Search for Safety Invades our Liberties

An impassioned, incisive look at the violations of civil liberties in the United States that have accelerated over the past decade—and their direct impact on our lives. How have our rights to privacy and justice been undermined? What exactly have we lost? Pulitzer Prize–winner David K. Shipler searches for the answers to these questions by traveling the midnight streets of dangerous neighborhoods with police, listening to traumatized victims of secret surveillance, and digging into dubious terrorism prosecutions. The law comes to life in these pages, where the compelling stories of individual men and women illuminate the broad array of government's powers to intrude into personal lives. Examining the historical expansion and contraction of fundamental liberties in America, this is the account of what has been taken—and of how much we stand to regain by protesting the departures from the Bill of Rights. And, in Shipler's hands, each person's experience serves as a powerful incitement for a retrieval of these precious rights.

Political Science

A COUNTRY OF STRANGERS
Blacks and Whites in America

In this magnificent exploration of the psychological landscape where blacks and whites meet, David K. Shipler bypasses both extremists and celebrities and takes us among ordinary Americans as they encounter one another across racial lines. We learn how blacks and whites see each other, how they interpret each other's behavior, and how certain damaging images and assumptions seep into the actions of even the most unbiased. We penetrate into dimensions of stereotyping and discrimination that are usually invisible, and discover the unseen prejudices and privileges of white Americans, and what black Americans make of them.

Political Science

THE WORKING POOR
Invisible in America

As David K. Shipler makes clear in this powerful, humane study, the invisible poor are engaged in the activity most respected in American ideology—hard, honest work. But their version of the American Dream is a nightmare: low-paying, dead-end jobs; the profound failure of government to improve upon decaying housing, health care, and education; the failure of families to break the patterns of child abuse and substance abuse. Shipler exposes the interlocking problems by taking us into the sorrowful, infuriating, courageous lives of the poor. We meet drifting farmworkers in North Carolina, exploited garment workers in New Hampshire, illegal immigrants trapped in the steaming kitchens of Los Angeles restaurants, addicts who struggle into productive work from the cruel streets of the nation's capital—each life another aspect of a confounding, far-reaching urgent national crisis.

Political Science

RIGHTS AT RISK
The Limits of Liberty in Modern America

An enlightening, intensely researched examination of violations of the constitutional principles that preserve individual rights and civil liberties from courtrooms to classrooms. With telling anecdote and detail, Pulitzer Prize–winner David K. Shipler explores the territory where the Constitution meets everyday America, where legal compromises—before and since 9/11—have undermined the criminal justice system's fairness, enhanced the executive branch's power over citizens and immigrants, and impaired some of the freewheeling debate and protest essential in a constitutional democracy.

Political Science

VINTAGE BOOKS
Available wherever books are sold.
www.vintagebooks.com